TEACHER'S GUIDE
GRADE 8

READING AND WRITING
Sourcebook

Authors

Robert Pavlik
Richard G. Ramsey

Great Source Education Group

a Houghton Mifflin Company
Wilmington, Massachusetts
www.greatsource.com

Authors

Dr. Richard G. Ramsey is currently a national educational consultant for many schools throughout the country and serves as president of Ramsey's Communications. He has been a teacher and a principal for grades 1–12 for 23 years. Dr. Ramsey has also served on the Curriculum Frameworks Committee for the State of Florida. A lifelong teacher and educator and former principal, he is now a nationally known speaker on improving student achievement and motivating students.

Dr. Robert Pavlik taught high school English and reading for seven years. His university assignments in Colorado and Wisconsin have included teaching secondary/content area reading, chairing a reading/language arts department, and directing a reading/learning center. He is an author of several books and articles and serves as director of the School Design and Development Center at Marquette University.

CONSULTANT **Catherine McNary** of Proviso West High School in Illinois is a reading specialist who works with teachers of struggling readers. She has been an invaluable consultant during the development of the *Sourcebook* series. She is currently pursuing a doctorate in reading.

Readers and Reviewers

Marsha Besch
Literacy/Secondary Curr. Coordinator ISD #196
Rosemount, Minnesota

Tim McGee
Worland High School
Worland, Wyoming

Mary Grace
Marshall Middle School
Janesville, Wisconsin

Shelly L. Fabozzi
Holmes Middle School
Colorado Springs, Colorado

Jim Burke
Burlingame High School
San Francisco, California

Phyllis Y. Keiley-Tyler
Education Consultant
Seattle, Washington

Jenny Sroka
Learning Enterprise High School
Milwaukee, Wisconsin

Glenda Swirtz
Flint Southwestern Academy
Flint, Michigan

Jeff Wallack
Learning Enterprise High School
Milwaukee, Wisconsin

Jay Amberg
Glenbrook South High School
Glenview, Illinois

Sherry Nielsen
Curriculum and Instruction
Saint Cloud, Minnesota

Deborah Schroeder
Harlan Community Academy
Chicago, Illinois

Richard Stear
Central Office
Rochester, New York

Hilary Zunin
Napa High School
Napa, California

William Weber
Libertyville High School
Libertyville, Illinois

Beverly Washington
Fenger High School
Chicago, Illinois

Lyla Fox
Loy Norrix High School
Kalamazoo, Michigan

Eileen Davis
Banneker Academic High School
Washington, D.C.

Christine Heerlein
Rockwood Summit High School
Fenton, Missouri

Barbara Ellen Pitts
Detroit, Michigan

Kimberly Edgeworth
Palm Beach Lakes High School
West Palm Beach, Florida

Jeffrey Hicks
Whitford Middle School
Beaverton, Oregon

Mark Tavernier
Norfolk, Virginia

Gina La Manna
Southeast Raleigh High School
Raleigh, North Carolina

Jennifer Sharpe-Salter
Southern Nash Sr. High School
Bailey, North Carolina

Elizabeth Dyhouse
Longfellow Middle School
Flint, Michigan

Rose Chatman
Dayton Public Schools
Dayton, Ohio

Gereldine Conaway
Mumford High School
Detroit, Michigan

Barb Evans
Lorain City Schools
Lorain, Ohio

Deborah Gonzalez
Puget Sound Education School District
Burien, Washington

Rosita Graham
Winter Halter Elementary School
Detroit, Michigan

Elaine Hanson
Mounds View School District
Saint Paul, Minnesota

Barbara Heget
Milwaukee, Wisconsin

Patrick Horigan
Milwaukee, Wisconsin

Rose Hunter
Whittier Middle School
Flint, Michigan

Ray Kress
Wilson Middle School
Newark, Ohio

Evelyn McDuffie
Beaubien Middle School
Detroit, Michigan

Robin Milanovich
Jefferson High School
Edgewater, Colorado

Dr. Howard Moon
Kenosha School District
Kenosha, Wisconsin

Jeanette Nassif
Central High School
Flint, Michigan

Dr. Joe Papenfuss
Racine Unified School District
Racine, Wisconsin

Lori Pfeiffer
West Bend School District
West Bend, Wisconsin

Evelyn Price
Milwaukee, Wisconsin

Karen Rano
Educational Consultant
River Forest, Illinois

Karen Ray
Darwin Elementary School
Chicago, Illinois

Renetha Rumph
Flint Southwestern High School
Flint, Michigan

Sarike Simpson
Racine, Wisconsin

Branka Skukan
Chopin School
Chicago, Illinois

Stephanie Thurick
Minneapolis Public Schools
Minneapolis, Minnesota

Gloria Tibbets
Curriculum Institute
Flint, Michigan

Anita Wellman
Northwestern High School
Detroit, Michigan

Barb Whaley
Akron City Schools
Akron, Ohio

Ray Wolpow
Western Washington University
Bellingham, Washington

Robin Gleason
Wilson Elementary School
Wauwatosa, Wisconsin

Kay Briske
Janesville School District
Janesville, Wisconsin

Table of Contents

Table of Contents

Lesson Resources

PUPIL'S EDITION SKILLS AND STRATEGIES

The chart below identifies the strategies for each part of each pupil's edition lesson.

Selection	I. Prereading	II. Response Notes	Comprehension
1. The Turtle (story)	preview card	highlight or mark	directed reading
2. Thank You Ma'am (story)	think-pair-and-share	prediction	story frame
3. Caring for the Wounded (nonfiction)	skimming	visualize	retell
4. The President's Been Shot (nonfiction)	K-W-L chart	react and connect	reciprocal reading
5. Toby Boyce and Gideon Adams (fiction)	walk-through	question	double-entry journal
6. Shem Suggs and Judah Jenkins (fiction)	word chain	clarify	retell
7. A Moment in the Sun Field (story)	picture walk	visualize	double-entry journal
8. The One Sitting There (story)	anticipation guide	react and connect	reciprocal reading
9. Pandora (myth)	preview card	question	predict
10. Hera (myth)	think-pair-and-share	mark or highlight	graphic organizer
11. Arrival (fiction)	word web	clarify	predict
12. Arrival (continued)	anticipation guide	prediction	story frame
13. Life Doesn't Frighten Me (poem)	read-aloud	visualize	directed reading
14. Stanley Yelnats (fiction)	walk-through	react and connect	double-entry journal
15. The Revolt of Denmark Vesey (nonfiction)	picture walk	question	directed reading
16. Born into Slavery (autobiography)	think-pair-and-share	mark or highlight	directed reading
17. Nardo (fiction)	quickwrite	clarify	predict
18. Picking (fiction)	preview card	prediction	reciprocal reading
19. The Story of My Body (essay)	anticipation guide	question	directed reading
20. Child of the Americas (poem)	word web	react and connect	double-entry journal
21. The War Arrives (fiction)	picture walk	mark or highlight	predict
22. Disaster at Sea (nonfiction)	K-W-L chart	question	storyboard
23. Super-duper-cold Saturdays (fiction)	story impression	visualize	double-entry journal
24. New Kids (fiction)	think-pair-and-share	prediction	reciprocal reading

III. Prewriting			IV. Writing	Grammar/Usage	V. Assessment
a) quickwrite	b) develop your idea	c) plan	paragraph	sentences	understanding
a) recall plot	b) plan		narrative paragraph	sentence fragments	meaning
a) narrow your focus	b) develop the topic		letter	writing letters	ease
a) write a topic sentence	b) summarize details	c) write a closing sentence	summary	run-on sentences	enjoyment
a) understand a character	b) connect to characters	c) create a cluster	character sketch	capitalization	depth
a) connect with a character	b) brainstorm	c) create dialogue	dialogue	dialogue	style
a) visualize a scene	b) use descriptive words		descriptive paragraph	compound sentences	meaning
a) react to a story	b) support an opinion		review	possessives	understanding
a) recall the plot	b) continue the plot		tale	verbs	enjoyment
a) cluster	b) organize details		descriptive paragraph	subject-verb agreement	ease
a) reflect on characters	b) compare and contrast characters	c) write a topic sentence	compare and contrast paragraph	contractions	style
a) form an opinion	b) support an opinion		point of view paragraph	commas	depth
organize information			expository paragraph	capitalization	understanding
a) connect	b) gather details		journal entry	easily confused words	meaning
a) find the main idea	b) list details		summary	commas	ease
a) reflect	b) describe a topic	c) plan	descriptive paragraph	usage of *good, well, better,* and *best*	enjoyment
a) reflect on a character d) add details	b) connect	c) focus	autobiographical paragraph	capitalization	style
a) reflect	b) plan an essay		autobiographical essay	commas	depth
a) reflect	b) support an opinion		paragraph of opinion	comma splices	meaning
a) find sensory details	b) develop an idea		poem	plural nouns	understanding
a) understand characters	b) develop details	c) connect details	character sketch	adjectives	style
a) brainstorm	b) use a graphic organizer		narrative paragraph	plurals	depth
a) describe a setting	b) create a setting		descriptive paragraph	confusing words	enjoyment
a) create characters	b) plan		story beginning	easily confused words	ease

TEACHER'S GUIDE SKILLS AND STRATEGIES

The chart below identifies the strategies for each part of each teacher's edition lesson.

Selection	Vocabulary	Prereading	Comprehension
1. The Turtle (story)	a) context clues b) suffixes	a) preview b) picture walk	a) directed reading b) double-entry journal
2. Thank You Ma'am (story)	a) context clues b) idioms	a) think-pair-and-share b) quickwrite	a) story frames b) directed reading
3. Caring for the Wounded (nonfiction)	Latin roots	a) skim b) preview	retell
4. The President's Been Shot (nonfiction)	a) context clues b) homographs	a) K-W-L b) quickwrite	a) reciprocal reading b) prediction
5. Toby Boyce and Gideon Adams (fiction)	a) context clues b) synonyms	walk-through	a) double-entry journal b) reciprocal reading
6. Shem Suggs and Judah Jenkins (fiction)	etymologies	word chain	retell
7. A Moment in the Sun Field (story)	word families	a) picture walk b) quickwrite	a) double-entry journal b) retelling
8. The One Sitting There (story)	suffixes	a) anticipation guide b) picture walk	a) reciprocal reading b) double-entry journal
9. Pandora (myth)	negative prefixes	a) preview b) picture walk	a) predict b) graphic organizer
10. Hera (myth)	etymologies	a) think-pair-and-share b) quickwrite	a) graphic organizers b) directed reading
11. Arrival (fiction)	a) context clues b) prefixes	word web	a) predict b) graphic organizer
12. Arrival (continued)	antonyms	a) anticipation guide b) quickwrite	a) story frames b) directed reading
13. Life Doesn't Frighten Me (poem)	a) context clues b) prefixes	a) read-aloud b) skim	a) directed reading b) retell
14. Stanley Yelnats (fiction)	compound words	a) walk-through b) quickwrite	double-entry journal
15. The Revolt of Denmark Vesey (nonfiction)	a) context clues b) Latin roots	a) picture walk b) skim	a) directed reading b) graphic organizer
16. Born into Slavery (autobiography)	negative prefixes	a) think-pair-and-share b) read-aloud	directed reading
17. Nardo (fiction)	a) context clues b) word analysis	a) quickwrite b) word web	a) predicting b) retelling
18. Picking (fiction)	word analysis	a) preview b) quickwrite	a) reciprocal reading b) story frame
19. The Story of My Body (essay)	a) context clues b) word families	a) anticipation guide b) quickwrite	directed reading
20. Child of the Americas (poem)	a) word analogies b) homographs	a) word webs b) K-W-L	a) double-entry journal b) graphic organizer
21. The War Arrives (fiction)	a) homographs/ heteronyms	picture walk	predictions
22. Disaster at Sea (nonfiction)	a) context clues b) root words	a) K-W-L b) skim	storyboards
23. Super-duper-cold Saturdays (fiction)	a) context clues b) prefixes	story impression	double-entry journal
24. New Kids (fiction)	a) context clues b) suffixes	a) think-pair-and-share b) quickwrite	reciprocal reading

Questions	Literary Skill	Prewriting	Assessment
a) comprehension b) critical thinking	irony	topic sentences	multiple-choice test
a) comprehension b) critical thinking	foreshadowing	story frame	multiple-choice test
a) comprehension b) critical thinking	setting	topic sentences	multiple-choice test
a) comprehension b) critical thinking	chronological order	topic sentence and details	multiple-choice test
a) comprehension b) critical thinking	dynamic and static characters	cluster diagram	multiple-choice test
a) comprehension b) critical thinking	theme	brainstorm	multiple-choice test
a) comprehension b) critical thinking	mood	word bank	multiple-choice test
a) comprehension b) critical thinking	tone	opinion statement	multiple-choice test
a) comprehension b) critical thinking	plot	a) storyboard/graphic organizer b) brainstorming	multiple-choice test
a) comprehension b) critical thinking	characterization	a) cluster b) graphic organizer	multiple-choice test
a) comprehension b) critical thinking	inferences	Venn diagram	multiple-choice test
a) comprehension b) critical thinking	simile	a) opinion statement b) storyboard	multiple-choice test
a) comprehension b) critical thinking	rhythm	quickwrite	multiple-choice test
a) comprehension b) critical thinking	humor	a) choose a subject b) graphic organizer	multiple-choice test
a) comprehension b) critical thinking	flashback	group discussion	multiple-choice test
a) comprehension b) critical thinking	word choice	choose a topic	multiple-choice test
a) comprehension b) critical thinking	anecdote	character map	multiple-choice test
a) comprehension b) critical thinking	simile	anecdote	multiple-choice test
a) comprehension b) critical thinking	imagery	a) Venn diagram b) opinion support	multiple-choice test
a) comprehension b) critical thinking	repetition	graphic organizer/sensory details	multiple-choice test
a) comprehension b) critical thinking	point of view	graphic organizer	multiple-choice test
a) comprehension b) critical thinking	impressionism	a) brainstorm b) storyboard	multiple-choice test
a) comprehension b) critical thinking	flashback	brainstorm	multiple-choice test
a) comprehension b) critical thinking	local color	story map	multiple-choice test

CORRELATION TO *WRITE SOURCE 2000*

Like the *Write Source 2000* and *All Write* handbooks, the *Sourcebook* will appeal to teachers who believe that writing is a way of learning or a means of discovery and exploration. Students pursue ideas and interpretations in the *Sourcebook*. They jot notes, create organizers, plan and brainstorm compositions, and write drafts of their work. The *Sourcebook* is one way students clarify in their minds what they have read and how they respond to it. And, in the end, students learn how to write different kinds of compositions— a paragraph, a description, a letter, a character sketch, a persuasive paragraph, or a review.

In the *Sourcebook*, both the kinds of writing and the mini-lessons on grammar, usage, and mechanics afford the best opportunities to use the *Write Source 2000* and *All Write* handbooks as a reference. To make this convenient, both the writing activities and the mini-lessons are correlated below to these handbooks.

Selection Title	Writing Activity/ Write Source 2000 (pages)	Writers' Mini-Lesson/ Write Source 2000 (pages)
1. "The Turtle"	paragraph 98–106	capitalizing sentences 405.1; end with punctuation 387.1, 398.1, 400.1; complete sentences 434.2
2. "Thank You, Ma'am"	narrative paragraph 101	sentence fragments 86
3. "Caring for the Wounded"	letter 149–152, 241–250	format of a letter 149–152, 241–250
4. "The President's Been Shot"	summary 143, 213–216	run-on sentences 87
5. "Toby Boyce" and "Gideon Adams"	character sketch 123	capitalizing proper nouns and the pronoun *I* 404.1–404.5
6. "Shem Suggs" and "Judah Jenkins"	dialogue with a character 190–191, 343	quotation marks in dialogue 399.1–400.1; commas in dialogue 390.1; punctuation in dialogue 390.1, 399.1–3, 400.1
7. "A Moment in the Sun Field"	descriptive paragraph 100	compound sentences 96, 437.4
8. "The One Sitting There"	review 377, 175–181	possessive formation 403.1–4
9. "Pandora"	creative story continuation 184–185	verb tenses 448.1–6
10. "Hera"	descriptive paragraph 100	subject-verb agreement 88–89
11. "Arrival"	compare and contrast paragraph 56, 112–113, 312–313	contractions 402.1
12. "Arrival"	continued point of view paragraph 143, 190, 344	continued commas to separate items in a series 389.1; commas in dates 389.3; commas in addresses 389.3
13. "Life Doesn't Frighten Me"	expository paragraph 102	capitalizing titles 407.3; capitalizing place names 405.2
14. "Stanley Yelnats"	journal entry 48, 145–148	*it's* and *its* 426.5; *their, there,* and *they're* 431.7
15. "The Revolt of Denmark Vesey"	summary 143, 213–216	commas between coordinate adjectives 391.3
16. "Born into Slavery"	descriptive paragraph 100	*good* and *well* 425.2; *better* and *best*
17. "Nardo"	autobiographical paragraph 153–159	capitalizing titles 407.3
18. "Picking"	continued autobiographical essay 153–159	using commas to set off explanatory phrases 391.4; using commas to set off introductory phrases 391.2; using commas to set off interruptions 390.2
19. "The Story of My Body"	paragraph of opinion 115–127	comma splices 86, 391.1
20. "Child of the Americas"	poem 193–207, 342	plural nouns 408.1–409.3
21. "The War Arrives"	character sketch 123	adjective forms (comparative / superlative) 453.2-3

Selection Title	Writing Activity/ Write Source 2000 (pages)	Writers' Mini-Lesson/ Write Source 2000 (pages)
22. "Disaster at Sea"	narrative paragraph 101	plural nouns 408.1–409.3
23. "Super-duper-cold Saturdays"	descriptive paragraph 100	Usage of *affect* and *effect* 419.3 *accept* and *except* 419.2
24. "New Kids"	story beginning 188–190	*to, too,* and *two* 431.9 *than, then* 431.9

Selection Title	Writing Activity/ All Write Reference (pages)	Writers' Mini-Lesson/ All Write Reference (pages)
1. "The Turtle"	paragraph 59–61, 66–70	capitalizing sentences 330; end with punctuation 311–312; complete sentences 48
2. "Thank You, Ma'am"	narrative paragraph 63	sentence fragments 50
3. "Caring for the Wounded"	letter 119–123, 143–148	format of a letter 120–121, 146–148
4. "The President's Been Shot"	summary 104, 179–182	run-on sentences 50
5. "Toby Boyce" and "Gideon Adams"	character sketch 132–134	capitalizing proper nouns and the pronoun I 328
6. "Shem Suggs" and "Judah Jenkins"	dialogue with a character 24, 109–110, 116	quotation marks in dialogue 323–324; commas in dialogue 313–318; punctuation in dialogue 311–327
7. "A Moment in the Sun Field"	descriptive paragraph 62	compound sentences 58, 316, 372
8. "The One Sitting There"	review 40–42, 131–136	possessive formation 325, 326, 378, 381
9. "Pandora"	creative story continuation 35, 170–173	verb tenses 385–386
10. "Hera"	descriptive paragraph 62	subject-verb agreement 51–52
11. "Arrival"	compare and contrast paragraph 71–85, 326–237, 302	contractions 325
12. "Arrival" continued	point of view paragraph 59–70, 80–85, 103, 275	commas to separate items in a series 313; commas in dates 313; commas in addresses 313
13. "Life Doesn't Frighten Me"	expository paragraph 64	capitalizing titles 329
14. "Stanley Yelnats"	journal entry 107–110	Usage of *it's* and *its* 351; *their, there,* and *they're* 358
15. "The Revolt of Denmark Vesey"	summary 104, 179–182	commas between coordinate adjectives 317
16. "Born into Slavery"	descriptive paragraph 62	Usage of *good* and *well* 320 *better* and *best* 395
17. "Nardo"	autobiographical paragraph 111–118, 125–130, 272	capitalizing titles 329
18. "Picking" continued	autobiographical essay 71–75, 80–85, 111–118, 125–130, 272	commas 313–318
19. "The Story of My Body"	paragraph of opinion 76–79, 223–225	comma splices 50
20. "Child of the Americas"	poem 157–166	plural nouns 376
21. "The War Arrives"	character sketch 132–134	adjective forms (comparative / superlative) 395
22. "Disaster at Sea"	narrative paragraph 63	plural nouns 376
23. "Super-duper-cold Saturdays"	descriptive paragraph 62	Usage of *affect* and *effect* 345; *accept* and *except* 345
24. "New Kids"	story beginning 34, 99, 170–173	Usage of *to, too,* and *two* 359; *than, then* 358

OVERVIEW

The *Sourcebook* is directed to struggling readers. These students seldom receive adequate help, partly because they need so much. They need to be motivated. They need quality literature that they can actually read. They need good instruction in strategies that will help them learn how to transform a mass of words and lines into a comprehensible text. They need help with getting ready to write; with grammar, usage, and mechanics; and with writing different kinds of texts themselves—letters, journal entries, summaries, and so forth.

A Comprehensive Approach

Because of the multitude and enormity of their needs, struggling readers all too often are subjected to a barrage of different remedies. It is all too easy simply to say "This doesn't work" and turn to yet another text or strategy. The *Sourcebook* takes a holistic approach, not a piecemeal one. Through a five-part lesson plan, each *Sourcebook* lesson walks the student through the steps needed to read actively and to write well about literature.

The five-part lesson plan is:

I. **BEFORE YOU READ** (prereading)

II. **READ** (active reading and responding to literature)

III. **GATHER YOUR THOUGHTS** (prewriting)

IV. **WRITE** (writing, revising, grammar, usage, and mechanics)

V. **WRAP-UP** (reflecting and self-assessment)

Through a comprehensive, structured approach, students can see the whole process of reading and writing. By following a consistent pattern, students can internalize the steps in the process, and they can move forward and experience success along the way, on a number of different fronts at once. See also the book and lesson organization on pages 18–22.

A Strategy-intensive Approach

The *Sourcebook* also is a strategy-intensive approach. Each *Sourcebook* builds students' repertoire of reading strategies in at least three areas.

1. To build motivation and background, prereading strategies are used to get students ready to read and to help them see the prior knowledge they already bring to their reading experiences.

2. To build active readers, each *Sourcebook* begins with an overview of interactive reading strategies (called response strategies), explicitly showing students six ways to mark up texts. Then, at least one of these strategies is used in each lesson.

3. To build comprehension, each *Sourcebook* uses six to nine different comprehension strategies, such as prediction, reciprocal reading, retelling, and using graphic organizers. By embedding these strategies in the literature, the *Sourcebook* shows students exactly which strategies to use and when to use them, building the habits of good readers.

A Literature-based Approach

Above all, the *Sourcebook* takes a literature-based approach. It presents 24 selections of quality literature of various genres by a wide range of authors. Some selections focus on literature; others are cross-curricular in emphasis, taking up a subject from history or geography; and others focus on issues of importance and relevance to today's students.

An Interactive Approach

The *Sourcebook* is, in addition, an interactive tool. It is intended to be a journal for students, where they can write out their ideas about texts, plan and write out compositions, and record their progress throughout the year. Students should "own" their *Sourcebooks*, carrying them, reading in them, marking in them, and writing in them. They should become a record of their progress and accomplishments.

Lesson Planning

A **Sourcebook** lesson can be taught in approximately 10 class periods, whether that is over two, three, or even four weeks.

DAY 1 Build background and discuss unit theme. Introduce selection.

DAY 2 Read introduction. Start prereading activity.

DAY 3 Continue prereading activity. Discuss activity.

DAY 4 Introduce selection. Discuss response strategy and example. Read.

DAY 5 Finish reading and do comprehension activities in selection.

DAY 6 Start prewriting activities.

DAY 7 Continue with prewriting activities.

DAY 8 Begin writing activity.

DAY 9 Talk about mini-lesson and revise writing.

DAY 10 Reflect on selection and what was learned.

Assessment

The **Sourcebook** includes a multiple-choice test for assessment, as well as a more holistic self-assessment in the pupil's book in Part V. Either of these are useful gauges of student progress. Teachers would, of course, like to demonstrate the progress their students have made—the number of grade levels students have progressed throughout the year. In point of fact, that progress is enormously difficult to demonstrate with any degree of reliability. The best measure of student progress will most likely be a student's marked-up **Sourcebook** and the greater confidence and fluency with which students will be reading by the end of the year.

On a day-to-day basis when teaching each lesson, teachers and students should use the Readers' Checklist for assessment. Asking a different combination of 2–3 questions from the Readers' Checklist will help students become increasingly clear about why and how they are reading.

UNDERSTANDING Did you understand the reading?

Was the message or point clear?

Can you restate what the reading is about?

On a monthly basis, one of the best measures of student progress will be a student's marked-up **Sourcebook**. Teacher-student conferences can use the following questions to reflect on the quality of a student's written responses among lessons:

a. In what ways has the content of your written responses improved?
    (e.g., accuracy, clarity, amount of comprehension)

b. In what ways has the structure of your written responses improved?
    (e.g., organization, coherence, neatness, spelling, punctuation)

c. In what ways is your reading improving?

d. What new reading habits are you finding useful? Why?

WHO IS THIS BOOK FOR?

Struggling Learners

Frequently, high schools have classes specifically designed for students who consistently rank in the lower 50 percent of the class. Instead of the usual focus on literary masterworks, these classes focus on improving reading and writing skills and often are labeled with anonymous-sounding names such as English I, Applied Communication, or Fundamentals of Reading and Writing. The *Sourcebook* was designed with such courses in mind. It offers a comprehensive program of student-appropriate literature, strategy building, writing, and revising. Quite often teachers in these classes pull an exercise from one text on the shelf, a reading from another, and a blackline master activity from still another. The materials are a patchwork, with the teachers making the best of the meager offerings available.

Each *Sourcebook* has a comprehensive network of skills (see pages 6–9) that brings together the appropriate literature, reading strategies for that literature, and prewriting, writing, and revising activities. Students who work through even two or three entire selections will benefit greatly by seeing the whole picture of reading actively and writing about the text. They will also benefit from the sense of accomplishment that comes through completion of a whole task and that results in creative, original work of their own—perhaps some of the first they have accomplished.

Reading Classes

Students who clearly are reading two or more levels below grade often are put into "special reading" courses. Quite often these classes feature a great number of blackline masters on discrete skills, such as "main idea and details," "analogies," and the like. Such classes are ideal for the *Sourcebook*. Instead of covering one discrete skill, each *Sourcebook* selection offers students reading strategies that they can use on any text, and it offers them high-quality literature. All too often students in reading classes are given "high-interest" materials. The materials have regulated vocabulary and short sentences and are on topics that range from natural disasters to biographies of rock divas. The *Sourcebook* focuses on high-quality literature that is also high interest because it addresses questions and issues of significance to students.

With the *Sourcebook*, a better choice exists. The literature was chosen specifically with struggling readers in mind. It offers compelling subjects, such as the Holocaust and prejudice, and offers a worthy challenge for students.

ESL Classes

Students for whom English is a second language can also benefit from the *Sourcebook*, even though the *Sourcebook* is not an ESL program. The literature selections in the *Sourcebook* vary in difficulty level. The level for each selection is given on the first page of the *Teacher's Guide* lesson. But the subjects of the literature—immigrants, being an outsider, understanding different cultures—are ones that will naturally appeal to ESL students.

In addition, summaries of each selection appear in Spanish in the *Teacher's Guide*, along with additional help with vocabulary and comprehension. So, while not explicitly for ESL students, the program offers good support for them and may be more appropriate than some of the other materials they are currently using.

Alternative Settings

Many school systems also have whole schools or classes that are called "alternative" for students who, for a variety of reasons, are not mainstreamed. The *Sourcebook* is appropriate for these students as well, if only because of its literature selections, which focus on themes of identity, prejudice, and separateness about which many alternative students will have a natural interest.

Summary

The *Sourcebook* cannot reach every struggling student. It is not a panacea. It will be helpful with struggling readers, especially those who are reading a grade level or two below their academic grade. The challenges struggling readers face, especially those reading more than two grades below their academic grade level, ought not to be underestimated or minimized. Reading and writing deficits are hard, almost intractable problems for high school students and require a great amount of effort—on the part of the teacher and the student—to make any real improvement. The *Sourcebook* is one further tool in helping create better readers and writers.

FREQUENTLY ASKED QUESTIONS

Because the *Sourcebooks* were extensively reviewed by teachers, a number of commonly asked questions have surfaced already, and the answers to them might be helpful in using the program.

1. Why is it called a *Sourcebook*?

The word *Sourcebook* captures a number of connotations and associations that seemed just right. For one, it is published by Great Source Education Group. The word *source* also had the right connotation of "the place to go for a real, complete solution," as opposed to other products that help in only a limited area, such as "main idea" or "analogies." And, lastly, the term *Sourcebook* fits nicely alongside *Daybook*, another series also published by Great Source that targets better readers and writers who need help in fluency and critical reading, as opposed to this series, which targets struggling readers.

2. Can students write in the *Sourcebook*?

Absolutely. Only by physically marking the text will students become truly active readers. To interact with a text and truly read as an active reader, students *must* write in the *Sourcebook*. The immediacy of reading and responding right there on the page is integral to the whole idea of the *Sourcebook*. By writing in the text, students build a sense of ownership about their work that is impossible to match through worksheets handed out week after week. The *Sourcebook* also serves, in a sense, as the student's portfolio and can become one of the most tangible ways of demonstrating a student's progress throughout the year.

3. Can I photocopy these lessons?

No, you cannot. Each page of the pupil's book carries a notice that explicitly states "copying is prohibited." To copy them illegally infringes on the rights of the authors of the selections and the publishers of the book. Writers such as Paul Fleischman, John Christopher, Maya Angelou, and others have granted permission to use their work in the *Sourcebook*, but have not granted the right to copy it.

You can, however, copy the blackline masters in this *Teacher's Guide.* These pages are intended for teachers to photocopy and use in the classroom.

4. Can I skip around in the *Sourcebook*?

Teachers will naturally wish to adjust the *Sourcebook* to their curriculum. But a logical— that is, the optimum—order of the book is laid out in the table of contents. The difficulty of the literary selection, the kind and difficulty of writing assignments, the amount of scaffolding provided for a specific reading strategy—all are predicated on where they occur in the text. Easier assignments and selections, naturally, tend to cluster near the beginning of the *Sourcebook*; in the back half of the book, both the assignments and selections challenge students with more rigorous demands.

5. Where did the strategies used throughout the book come from?

Most of the reading strategies used are commonplace in elementary classrooms throughout the country. They are commonly described in the standard reading education textbooks, as well as at workshops, conferences, and in-services. What is unusual in the *Sourcebook* is the way these strategies have been applied to high school–appropriate literature.

6. Why did you label the strategies with names such as "stop and think" when they are really just directed reading or some other reading technique?

The pupil's edition of the *Sourcebook* uses student-friendly terms, such as "stop and think," "retell," or "stop and record." Throughout, an attempt was made to motivate students, not hammer them with pedagogical terms. Leaden-sounding names for reading strategies (for example, directed reading strategy or reciprocal reading) seemed counterproductive for students, even while being perfectly descriptive to teachers. The same logic explains why such student-friendly titles as "Before You Read" were used instead of "Prereading." In the *Teacher's Guide*, reference is frequently made to the more formal pedagogical term (directed reading) alongside the friendlier student term (stop and think).

7. **Has anyone told you that the *Sourcebook* doesn't follow the textbook definition of a number of strategies?**

Yes, absolutely. Teachers who reviewed the *Sourcebooks* were quick to mention that "textbook" definitions and application of strategies were not followed. One clear example is reciprocal reading. It is an intervention strategy in which a reading partner or teacher works with a student to clarify, question, predict, and summarize; but the *Sourcebook* is a text, not a walking-and-breathing reading tutor. As a result, the questioning strategy of reciprocal reading is employed in the *Sourcebook*, with full knowledge that the technique cannot be perfectly replicated using a book. Yet the force of these strategies seemed too potent simply to discard, so, like any good teacher, the *Sourcebook* authors adapted a strategy to fit their particular needs.

8. **How were the selections chosen and what is their readability?**

The decision to use "real" or "quality" literature by well-known authors was, in fact, made by teachers. They selected the authors they wanted to use with their students. They insisted that the quality and force of the literature itself—not its readability—become the primary selection criteria for the literature. Especially when a selection would become the focal point of an extended lesson, the literature had to be primary. "If my students are going to spend several days on a lesson, the literature needs to be worth spending time and attention on it," one early reviewer said.

Plus, they insisted that their struggling readers be challenged. Among teachers of struggling readers, a consistent appeal was that the literature challenge their students, yet also give them lots of support. Challenge and support were the watchwords that guided the development of the *Sourcebook* program. Choosing high-quality literature was the first consideration; secondarily, the syntactical difficulty, sentence length, and vocabulary level were also considered.

9. **How can I know if my students can read this literature?**

Teachers have a number of ways to know how well their students can read the selections. For one, they can simply try out a lesson or two.

Second, teachers can also use a 20- or 30-word vocabulary pretest as a quick indicator. For each selection, randomly select 20 words from a selection. Ask students to circle the ones they know and underline the ones they don't know. If students know only one to five or six to nine words, then the selection will probably be frustrating for them. Spend some time preteaching the key vocabulary.

10. **What if my students need even more help than what's in the book?**

This *Teacher's Guide* has been designed as the next level of support. Extra activities and blackline masters on vocabulary, comprehension, prewriting, and assessment are included here so that they can be used at the teacher's discretion. Parts of each lesson could have been scaffolded for five to ten more pages, but at a certain point more worksheets and more explanation become counterproductive. Teachers advised the authors again and again to give students worthwhile literature and activities and let the students work at them. Students' work will not be perfect, but, with the right tools, students will make progress.

ORGANIZATION

Book Organization

Each **Sourcebook** has 24 selections organized into three general categories:

1. Contemporary Issues

2. Cross-curricular Subjects

3. Literature

The purpose of this organization is to provide selections that are relevant and purposeful in students' lives. By pairing selections students can take the time to build extended background on a topic or idea (for example, identity, the Holocaust), building upon knowledge they gained in earlier selections. Each of the 12 units in the **Sourcebook** is introduced by an opener that helps teachers build background on the subject. Ways to teach and introduce each opener are included in the **Teacher's Guide**.

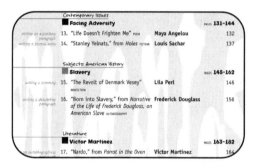

Lesson Organization

Each lesson in the **Sourcebook** has five parts:

I. Before You Read

- Each lesson begins with **I. Before You Read** to emphasize to students how important prereading is. The lesson starts with an introductory statement that draws students into the lesson, often by asking a provocative question or making a strong statement.

- The prereading step—the critical first step—builds background and helps students access prior knowledge. Among the prereading strategies (see page 6) included in Part I of this **Sourcebook** are:

- Think-Pair-and-Share

- K-W-L

- Anticipation Guide

- Preview or Walk-through

- Skimming

- Picture Walk

- Quickwrite

- Word Web

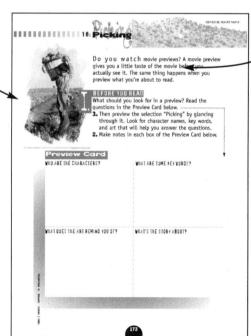

II. Read

- The reading step, called **II. Read,** begins with an invitation to read and suggestions for how to respond to the literature and mark up the text. An example is provided.

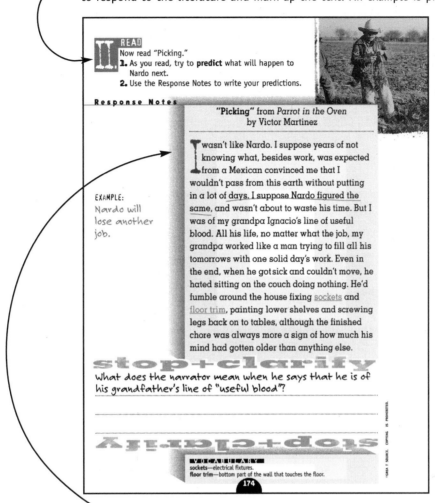

- The selection follows, with the difficult vocabulary highlighted throughout the selection and defined at the bottom of the page.

- Then, within the selection, a powerful comprehension strategy is embedded to help build in students the habits of good readers. Among the comprehension strategies included (see also page 50 in Part II of this **Sourcebook**) are these:

- Predict

- Stop and Think (directed reading)

- Stop and Clarify, Question, Predict (reciprocal reading)

- Storyboard (using graphic organizers)

- Double-entry Journal

- Retelling

- Story Frame

III. Gather Your Thoughts

- The prewriting step is called **III. Gather Your Thoughts**. It starts with the literature selection. Through two or three carefully sequenced activities, the prewriting step helps students go back into the literature in preparation for writing about it.

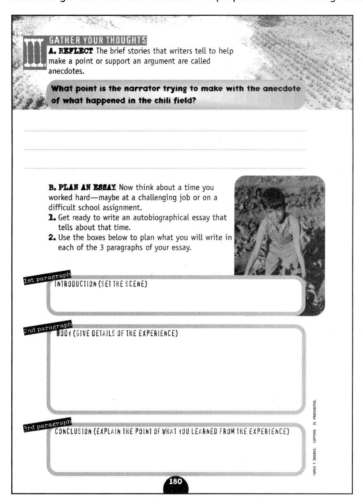

Among the more common prewriting activities are these:

- Character Map

- Main Idea and Supporting Details

- Brainstorming

- Building a Topic Sentence

- Forming an Opinion

- Supporting a Main Idea

IV. Write

- The writing step begins with step-by-step instructions for building a writing assignment. Taken together, these instructions form the writing rubric for students to use in building the assignment. Among the writing assignments students are asked to write are these:

- Paragraph with topic sentence and supporting details

- Narrative paragraph

- Expository paragraph

- Compare and contrast paragraph

- Paragraph of reflection

- Autobiographical paragraph

- Journal entry

- Story

- Character sketch

  See page 7 for a full list.

VICTOR MARTINEZ

WRITE

Now write an **autobiographical essay** about a time you worked hard.

1. Use the notes on the previous page to help you organize your writing into 3 paragraphs.

2. Use the Writers' Checklist to help you revise.

Continue your writing on the next page.

181

Continue your writing from the previous page.

WRITERS' CHECKLIST

COMMAS

❏ **Did you use commas to set off explanatory phrases?** EXAMPLE: My dad's car, a green Honda, backfired.

❏ **Did you use commas to set off introductory phrases?** EXAMPLE: During June, my sister graduated from high school.

❏ **Did you use commas to set off interruptions?** EXAMPLE: It was, of course, the most exciting basketball game I've seen.

- Each **IV. Write** also includes a **Writers' Checklist**. Each one is a brief mini-lesson on a relevant aspect of grammar, usage, or mechanics. The intent of the **Writers' Checklist** is to ask of the students appropriate questions after they write, instilling the habit of going back to revise, edit, and proof their work. The **Writers' Checklist** also affords teachers the opportunity to teach relevant grammar, usage, and mechanics skills at a teachable moment.

V. Wrap-up

- The last step of each lesson is to reflect. Students are asked a question about their reading and writing experience from the **Readers' Checklist**. This "looking back" is intended to help students see what they learned in the lesson. They are intentionally asked more than simply, "Did you understand?"

- For good readers, reading is much, much more than "Did you get it?" Good readers read for pleasure, for information, for the pure enjoyment of reading artfully written material, for personal curiosity, for a desire to learn more, and countless other reasons. So that students will begin to see that reading is worthwhile to them, they need to believe the payoff is more than "Did you get it?" on a five-question multiple-choice test.

- The **Sourcebook** attempts with **V. Wrap-up** to help students ask the questions good readers ask of themselves when they read. It attempts to broaden the reasons for reading by asking students to consider six reasons for reading:

- Meaning

- Enjoyment

- Understanding

- Style

- Ease

- Depth

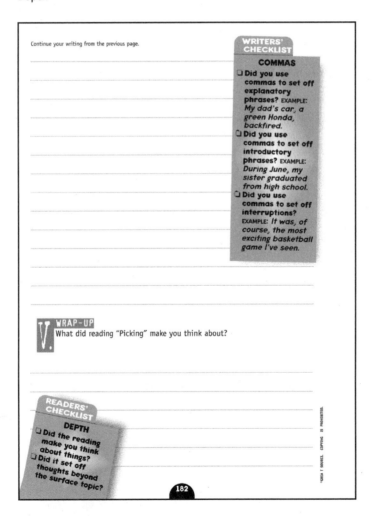

Organization

TEACHER'S LESSON PLANS

Each lesson plan for the teacher of the *Sourcebook* has eight pages:

PAGE 1 Overview and Background

- The chart at the beginning of each lesson plan gives an "at-a-glance" view of the skills and strategies, plus the difficulty level of the reading and five key vocabulary words.

- Background on the author and selection and a graphic are included.

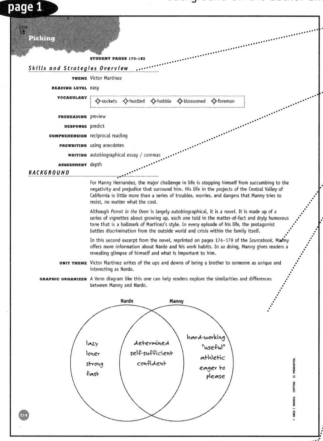

overview chart

additional background

tie-in to theme

model graphic organizer

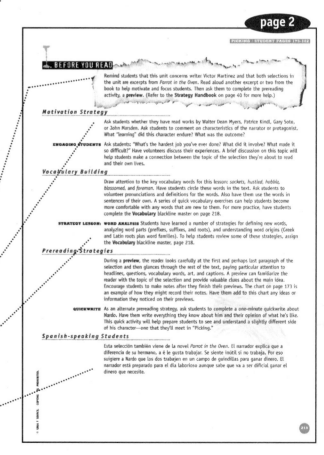

how to teach the pupil's
page "at-a-glance"

additional strategies

cross-reference to blackline
master

selection summary in Spanish

PAGE 2 Before You Read

- The first page of the teacher's plan begins with a motivation strategy and a suggestion for vocabulary building. Additional prereading strategies are suggested, along with a summary of the selection in Spanish.

Each lesson plan in the *Sourcebook Teacher's Guide* follows the pupil's lesson step-by-step.

PAGE 3 **Read**

- The response strategy gives students one way to interact with the text as they read.

- Additional comprehension strategies are suggested, along with a *Comprehension* blackline master found later in the lesson.

- The discussion questions cover both literal and interpretative levels of thinking.

- A literary skill is suggested for each selection, allowing teachers to build literary appreciation as they provide basic support with reading comprehension.

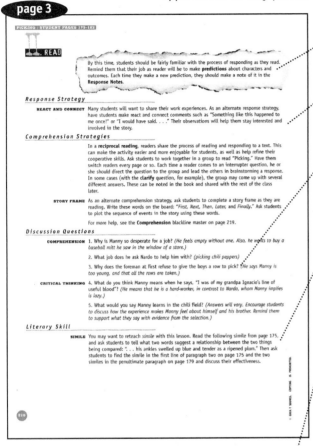

how to teach the pupil's page "at-a-glance"

interactive reading (or response) strategy

additional help with comprehension

discussion questions and literary skill

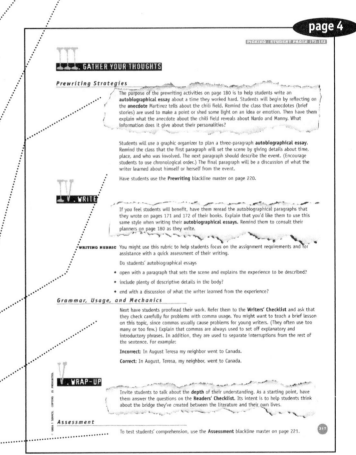

how to teach the pupil's page "at-a-glance"

additional prewriting strategies

mini-lesson on grammar, usage, and mechanics

two forms of assessment—Readers' Checklist and test

PAGE 4 **Gather Your Thoughts, Write, Wrap-up**

- The page begins with additional help with prewriting and references another blackline master that offers additional support.

- Next, the students write and are directed to the **Writers' Checklist** in the pupil's book, which gives the grammar, usage, and mechanics mini-lesson.

- The writing rubric gives teachers a way to evaluate students' writing.

- The lesson ends with reference to the **Readers' Checklist** in the pupil's book, encourages students to reflect on what they have read, and cross-references the **Assessment** blackline master.

Each lesson plan in the *Sourcebook Teacher's Guide* has four blackline masters for additional levels of support for key skill areas.

PAGE 5 Vocabulary

- Each **Vocabulary** blackline master helps students learn the meanings of five words from the literature selection and focuses on an important vocabulary strategy, such as understanding prefixes, root words, and word families.

page 5

PICKING / STUDENT PAGES 172-182

Name _____

VOCABULARY
Words from the Selection

DIRECTIONS Read these sentences. Write the words from the box that best fit each of the following descriptions.

◇ sockets   ◇ hobble   ◇ hustled   ◇ blossomed   ◇ foreman

1. These are electrical fixtures. _____
2. This is slang for "sold." _____
3. This is what it's called when you walk awkwardly. _____
4. This is a person in charge of a work crew. _____
5. This word means "to become developed." _____

Strategy Lesson: Word Analysis

DIRECTIONS Write the word from the list below that correctly answers each question.

◇ spunky   ◇ scalding   ◇ enthusiastically   ◇ scrawny   ◇ suspicious

6. Which word is a synonym for *excitedly*? _____
7. Which word has a suffix meaning "state or quality of"? _____
8. Which word means both "spirited" and "lively"? _____
9. Which word is an antonym for *fat*? _____
10. Which word means "burning"? _____

© GREAT SOURCE. PERMISSION IS GRANTED TO COPY THIS PAGE.

218

meanings from five words from the selection are taught

important vocabulary strategy introduced and practiced

additional support for understanding every selection

different strategy from the one used in the pupil's book

page 6

PICKING / STUDENT PAGES 172-182

Name _____

COMPREHENSION
Story Frame

DIRECTIONS Fill in this story frame about "Picking." Add lines if you need to.

The story takes place _____

_____ is a character in the story who _____

_____ is another character in the story who _____

. A problem occurs when _____

. After that, _____

And _____

The problem is solved when _____

The story ends with _____

© GREAT SOURCE. PERMISSION IS GRANTED TO COPY THIS PAGE.

219

PAGE 6 Comprehension

- Each **Comprehension** blackline master affords teachers still another way to build students' understanding of the selection, using a different strategy from the one found in the *Sourcebook*.

PAGE 7 Prewriting

- Occasionally students will need even more scaffolding than appears in the pupil's lesson as they prepare for the writing assignment.

- The "extra step" in preparing to write is the focus of the **Prewriting** blackline master.

PAGE 8 Assessment

- Each lesson in the *Sourcebook* ends with the opportunity for students to reflect on their reading with the **Readers' Checklist**. This self-assessment is an informal inventory of what they learned from the reading.

- The **Assessment** blackline master gives a multiple-choice test on the selection and suggests a short-essay question for a more formal assessment.

---

page 7

PICKING / STUDENT PAGES 173-182

Name _____

PREWRITING
Writing an Autobiographical Essay

DIRECTIONS Use this organizer to plan the details of your essay.
  1. Answer each question as thoroughly as you can.
  2. Then include the information from the organizer in your essay.

Introduction

| PARAGRAPH 1 | Who was there | Where we were | When the event occurred |

Body

| PARAGRAPH 2 | What happened first | What happened next | What happened after that |

Conclusion

| PARAGRAPH 3 | What I learned about myself | What I learned about others | How I felt once the whole thing was over |

additional support for the writing assignment

graphic organizers help prepare students to write

---

page 8

PICKING / STUDENT PAGE

Name _____

ASSESSMENT
Multiple-Choice Test

DIRECTIONS On the blanks provided, write the letter of the item that best answers each question or completes each statement.

_____ 1. Who in his family is Manny most like?
   A. his brother Nardo   C. his grandfather
   B. his father   D. his mother

_____ 2. How would Manny describe his grandfather?
   A. He was a hard worker.   C. He could never find a job.
   B. He was lazy.   D. all of the above

_____ 3. What does Manny do with his cousins Rio and Pete?
   A. They hang out on the street.   C. They lift weights.
   B. They play baseball.   D. They sell fruit.

_____ 4. Why does Manny want to go to work?
   A. His father requires him to do so.   C. He needs to pay tuition.
   B. He wants to buy things.   D. He has debts to pay off.

_____ 5. Why does Manny ask Nardo to work with him?
   A. He wants to get closer to his brother.   C. He needs a ride.
   B. His father asks him to.   D. all of the above

_____ 6. How does Manny's father feel about the boys picking chili peppers?
   A. He is thrilled.   C. He is skeptical.
   B. He is nervous.   D. He is angry.

_____ 7. The man at the field says "no" at first to the boys because . . .
   A. Manny looks too young.   C. all the rows had been taken.
   B. it was too late to start. D. all of the above

_____ 8. What kind of work were the brothers finally given?
   A. They picked from a scrawny row.   C. They dug ditches.
   B. They filled the soda machine.   D. They were given no work.

_____ 9. How long did the brothers work?
   A. 1 hour   C. 3 hours
   B. 2 hours   D. 30 minutes

_____ 10. What is the author's purpose in writing "Picking"?
   A. to entertain   C. to persuade
   B. to tell the steps in a process   D. none of the above

Short-Essay Test

How do you think Manny feels about his brother?

formal, ten-question multiple-choice test

essay question for interpretive assessment

Teaching Struggling Readers

BY DR. RICHARD G. RAMSEY

What It Means to Teach

I enjoy being an educator. . . . We have the best job in the world, because we touch the future every day. We are in the business of making dreams come true for children. . . . And every day that I get up I'm excited about just going to work because now I know I have an opportunity to touch another life. . . . We have so many kids right now in our country coming to us from all walks of life, walking through our school doors every single day. When they walk through those doors, they're looking for one thing: they have open eyes, open minds, and open hearts seeking your validation. . . . The last thing children need to have done to them when they walk into your classroom is to be discouraged. They need hope, they need to be inspired by you every single day. . . .

The names of those who practice our profession read like a hall of fame for humanity: Booker T. Washington, Buddha, Confucius, Ralph Waldo Emerson, Leo Buscaglia, and many, many others. . . . Through and through the course of being a teacher, I've been called upon to be an actor, a nurse, a doctor, a coach, a finder of lost articles, a money lender, a taxicab driver, and also a keeper of the faith. I'm a paradox and I speak loudest when I listen the most to my students. I, as a teacher, am the most fortunate person who labors. A doctor is allowed to bring life into the world in one magic moment, but I, as a teacher, I am allowed to see that life is reborn each and every day with new questions, ideas, and friendship. I'm a warrior doing battle every single day against peer pressure, negativity, fear, conformity, and prejudice. . . .

Elements of Teaching

ATTITUDE But there are three things I always say that a teacher has to have to be able to survive: The first thing you have to have is the proper attitude. . . . I say attitudes are contagious, is yours worth catching? . . . Our attitude plays a big role when we're dealing with children and I tell myself to come to school smiling every day, be happy. . . . Children are looking for you to be that positive example for them. . . . Every day we have two choices. . . . You can complain about your job every day and let children fail or you can begin to love what you do every single day and make sure that every child has the opportunity to be successful. . . .

Life is a challenge. We are challenged with diverse populations that we're not accustomed to working with. Life is a gift. Teach our children that you only go around one time and it's not a practice run. Respect the gift of life. Life is an adventure. . . . Life is also a saga . . . and teach our kids that there will be a better tomorrow if they just hold on and don't quit. Life is also a tragedy; unfortunately we are going to lose kids to homicide, drug abuse, and all kinds of dreadful diseases. And I say, hold on to those that we have because they are our future. Life is also a duty; you have a duty as a teacher to teach every child the way you would want somebody to teach yours, and if you do that, you've done your duty for that day. Life is also a game; be the best player so you can help children. Life is an opportunity; take advantage of it and make sure that the children understand that opportunities in life only come one time. Life is also a struggle; fight it with every ounce of energy that you have to do the best with children. Life is also a goal; set goals for yourself, set goals for the children. But more importantly, make sure that you work with them so they can achieve the goals they've set. Finally, life is a puzzle; but if all of us today take back what we have and work together as a team, we can solve that puzzle and make sure that children are successful in life. To teach is to heal, to teach is to love, to teach is to care, to teach is to set high expectations. You are a teacher. There are many kids waiting for you and looking in your eyes every day and saying, "I need your help, I need your motivation." But remember, you don't motivate with fear, you may get compliance, but you certainly won't get commitment.

CARE Good teaching, as I tell my teachers all the time, does not come from behind the desk, it comes from behind the heart. . . . And kids know whether you care about them, and kids can be successful because excellence can be obtained if you just care more than other people think is wise, risk more than others think is safe, dream more than others think is practical, and expect out of your students more than others think is possible. An unspoken belief can teach young minds what they should be. You as a teacher can make that difference. . . . Remember, good teachers explain, superior teachers demonstrate. The great teachers, they inspire their students every single day. And if a kid can be inspired by you, he's going to want to come to your class every day, he's going to give you his best or her best every single day. . . .

COMMITMENT I'm going to tell a little story to you called, "Three Letters of Teddy."

"Teddy's letter came today and now that I've read it, I will place it in my cedar chest with the other things that are important in my life. I, as a teacher, had not seen Teddy Starlin since he was a student in my fifth-grade class fifteen years ago. It was early in my career and I had only been teaching for two years. From the first day he stepped into my class, I disliked him. Teachers are not supposed to dislike any child, but I did and I showed my dislike to this young boy."

Any teacher would tell you it's more of a pleasure to teach a bright child. It's definitely more rewarding to one's ego with any teacher, with their credentials, a challenge working with a bright child and keeping them challenged and learning while they spend a major effort for those students who need help. Any teacher can do this, most teachers do, but she said she didn't, not that year. In fact, she concentrated on her best students and let the others follow along the best they could. Ashamed as she is to admit it, she took pleasure in using her red pen. And every time she came to Teddy's paper, the cross marks, and they were many, were always a little larger and a little redder than necessary. While she didn't actually ridicule the boy, her attitude, ladies and gentlemen, was obvious and quite apparent to the whole class for he quickly became the class goat, the outcast, the unlovable and the unloved child in that classroom. He didn't know why she didn't like him, nor did she know why she had such an intent dislike for this boy. All he wanted was somebody just to care about him, and she made no effort on his behalf. . . .

She knew that Teddy would never catch up in time to be promoted to the sixth-grade level. She said he would be a repeater. And to justify herself, she went to his folder from time to time. He had very low grades for the first four years but not failures. How he had made it, she said, she didn't know. But she closed her mind to all of the personal remarks in Teddy's folder. It said: first grade—Teddy shows promise by working attitude but has poor home situation. Second grade—Teddy could do better but his mother is terminally ill and he receives no help at home. Third grade—Teddy's a pleasant boy, helpful but too serious, slow learner. His mother, she passed away at the end of the year. Fourth grade—very slow but well behaved. His father shows no interest at all. She said, well, they passed him four times but he would certainly repeat the fifth grade, she said, it would do him good.

And then the last day before the holidays arrived, the little tree on the reading table supported paper and popcorn chains and many gifts were underneath the tree awaiting a big moment. Teachers always get several gifts at Christmas, she said, but hers that year were more elaborate than ever. Every child had brought her a gift and each unwrapping brought squeals of delight and the proud giver received profusive thank yous. His gift wasn't the last one she picked up; in fact, it was in the middle of the pile. Its wrapping was a brown paper bag and he had colored Christmas trees and red bells all over it and it was stuck together with masking tape. And it read "For Ms. Thompson, from Teddy, I love you." The group was completely silent, and for the first time she felt very embarrassed because all of the students stood there watching her unwrap that gift. And as she removed the last bit of masking tape, two items fell to her desk, a gaudy rhinestone bracelet with several stones missing and a small bottle of dime store cologne half empty. She heard the snickers and the whispers from the students and she wasn't even sure that she could hold her head up and look at Teddy, but she said, "Isn't this lovely." And she asked Teddy to come up to help her fasten the clasp. He smiled as he fixed the clasp on her arm and then there were finally a few hesitant oohs and ahs from the students. But as she dabbed the cologne behind her ears, all the little girls got up to get a dab behind theirs. She continued to open the gifts until she reached the bottom of the pile. They ate their refreshments and the bell rang. The children filed out and shouted, "See you next year, Merry Christmas," but Teddy, he waited at his desk. When they all had left, he walked toward her clutching his books and his gift to his chest with tears streaming down his face and he said to her, you smell just like my mom, her bracelet looks real pretty on you, too. I'm glad you like it. He left quickly. She got up and locked the door, sat at her desk, and wept resolvedly to make Teddy what she had deprived him of, to be a teacher who cared.

She stayed every afternoon with Teddy until the last day of school. Slowly but surely, he caught up with the rest of the class. Gradually, there was a definite upward curve in his grades. He didn't have to repeat the fifth grade; in fact, his average was among the highest in the class. Even though he was moving next year with his father, she wasn't worried because Teddy had reached a level that would serve him anywhere, because her teaching training had taught her that success deals success. She didn't hear from Teddy until seven years later when his first letter appeared in the mailbox. It said, "Dear Ms. Thompson, I want you to be the first to know that I'll be graduating second in my class next month, very truly yours, Teddy Starlin." She sent him a congratulatory card, wondering what he would do after graduation. Four years later she received another letter. It said, "Dear Ms. Thompson, I want you to be the first to know that I was just informed that I will be graduating first in my class. The university hasn't been easy; however, I liked it." She sent him silver monogrammed cufflinks and a card, so proud of him that she could burst. The final note came from him. It said, "Dear Ms. Thompson, I want you to be the first to know that as of today I am Theodore J. Starlin, M.D., how about that?" He said, "I'm going to be married in July, to be exact, and I want to ask you if you would come and do me a big favor, I would like you to come to my wedding and sit where my mom would have been if she was alive. I have no family now because my dad died last year. Ms. Thompson, you are all I have left, please come to my wedding, very truly yours, Teddy Starlin." She said, "I'm not sure what kind of gift one sends to a doctor on completion of medical school and state board; maybe I'll just wait and take a wedding gift," but she said, "my note cannot wait." It said, "Dear Ted, congratulations, you made it, you did it yourself. In spite of those like me and not because of us, this day has come for you. God bless you and I'll be at your wedding with bells on."

You have a lot of students like that in your classroom right now; all they need is a push. These kids are coming to us and they're looking for that special person to be there for them. . . .

RESPONSIBILITY We have a responsibility to touch the lives of children. But the question is: "Are we walking away from the children who need us, or are we coming to them and picking them up when they fall down? Children are not responsible for their parents, they are not responsible for where they live, they're only trying to make it with the conditions that they have. . . . Don't quit on children. Let them know they can be somebody. . . .

NOTE The article above is a transcript adapted from a lecture.

BY DR. ROBERT PAVLIK

REFLECTIONS • What was one of your most valuable learning experiences that involved reading and writing?

• What made the learning experience so valuable? So memorable?

Defining Expert Readers and Writers

Experts in various professions have extensive content knowledge and efficient skills:

> . . . experts have acquired extensive knowledge that affects what they notice and how they organize, represent, and interpret information in their environments. This, in turn, affects their abilities to remember, reason, and solve problems. (Bransford, Brown, and Cocking, 1999)

Novices, in contrast, lacking extensive content knowledge and efficient skills, tend to make confusing interpretations, record and retrieve information laboriously, and solve problems inaccurately.

The overall goal of the *Sourcebook* is to build expert readers and writers, learners who develop extensive content knowledge and efficient skills for using reading and writing to meet their needs within and beyond school. Expert readers and writers also develop their own "voices" for interacting within and among families, fellow learners, and community members. Far too many middle school students, especially those at the lower end of the academic spectrum, lack extensive content knowledge or efficient skills. As a result, they can become confused, confusing, inefficient, and ineffective when attempting to use reading and writing to meet their needs. In addition, far too many high school students do not develop their own "voices."

REFLECTIONS • For which school subjects were you a novice or an expert reader? A novice or expert writer? How did you know?

• How would you describe your "voice" in middle school? today?

• Which of your recent/current students would you describe as novice or expert readers? As novice or expert writers? How do you know?

• How would you describe the "voices" of your students?

Using Culturally Diverse Literature

Rapidly changing national demographics require us to reconsider what fiction and nonfiction literature we include in our curricula. In essence, to what extent do we study the literature from and about people who helped shape the United States, and to what extent do we study the literature from and about people who shape the United States today and are shaping the future of the United States?

The *Sourcebook* provides fiction and nonfiction selections that represent current demographics of middle school students. Approximately 60 percent of the selections represent traditional ideas and values, while the remaining 40 percent represent the ideas and values of several other cultures. This range of culturally diverse literature provides optional selections for meeting students' needs to

• understand themselves.

• understand the worldviews and culture of the United States.

• understand others.

• understand the worldviews and cultures of other countries.

For students, this range of culturally diverse literature provides meaningful, authentic opportunities to read and write and to learn new and familiar vocabulary in a variety of contexts. In addition, the breadth and depth of the selections can inspire further student reading, student-teacher discussions, and student-student discussions.

REFLECTIONS
- How culturally diverse was the fiction you studied as a middle school student? The nonfiction?

- How valuable was the literature you studied in middle school for the four needs cited above?

- What are the demographics of your students?

- What cultures and "voices" must your literature selections address?

Using an Interactive Instructional Approach

Current approaches for improving the reading and writing of middle school students range . . .

- from telling students to "practice, practice, practice" their reading and writing. In essence, teachers tell students to read a lot to become better readers and write a lot to become better writers.

- to identifying a student's level of skill mastery for reading and writing and, then, organizing students into groups for appropriate reading and writing skills instruction.

- to inviting students to discover their own strategies through teacher-guided discussions.

- to creating stimulating environments and meaningful projects around significant themes that motivate students to build and refine their uses of reading, writing, speaking, listening, and viewing.

All of these approaches to instruction have proven effective in recent decades, especially with populations of similar students. However, increasing numbers of middle school students represent diverse cultures, perform well below their potential, speak English only in school, and attend school irregularly.

Vygotsky's thinking (1978) inspires and informs much of our approach to instruction. We believe that today's middle school students can become expert readers and writers despite the challenges confronting them. To do so, students need

- meaningful, authentic fiction and nonfiction.

- an approach to instruction that respects how they are trying to learn within their fragmented, often chaotic lives.

- teachers and materials that direct and guide them to form, state, and test strategies for reading with peers and adults.

Therefore, our overall instructional approach involves modeling what expert readers and writers do as they negotiate with fiction and nonfiction and, then, inviting students to adapt what they learn from the modeling to their own reading and writing strategies. In the process, students can build and refine their thinking with others in order to apply the strategies on their own as needed.

For example, the **Sourcebook** opens with a feature entitled **"Responding to Literature"** that directs and invites students to

- see examples of written responses to ideas in a short selection from an expert reader-writer.

- engage a strategy sheet for making similar responses.

- make similar responses to a short selection on their own.

We apply this overall instructional approach throughout the **Sourcebook**.

REFLECTIONS
- What instructional approaches did your teachers apply to improve your reading and writing?

- Which approaches did you as a middle school student find valuable? Not valuable?

- As a teacher, what instructional approaches have you found effective and why? Ineffective and why?

Teaching Meaning-making Strategies

Research studies on expert readers and writers reveal two important insights:

- Expert readers and writers will use a variety of strategies automatically when they encounter new and difficult tasks—strategies that novice readers and writers would not use.

- A number of reading and writing strategies have been developed and can be taught (Paris, Wasik, and Turner, 1991; Dahl and Farnan, 1998).

Within our five-part lesson framework for each piece of fiction and nonfiction, students apply several meaning-making strategies to become expert readers and writers.

Part I. Before You Read

Struggling novice readers tend to avoid most types of reading in and outside of school. Even some expert readers often choose to spend only a few minutes each day reading in and outside of school, on either assigned or independent reading. The reasons why middle school students choose not to read range from having poor reading skills to responding to peer pressure and even gender expectations.

The *Sourcebook* addresses these avoidance behaviors by presenting two prereading strategies per selection and guiding students to apply the strategies successfully. We assign specific strategies for each selection to get students doing something before they read, e.g., asking their opinions, engaging with a sample from the selection to read, or responding to a quick survey about their expectations. Our prereading strategies applied among the selections include these:

- Walking through a selection

- Using an anticipation guide

- Using K-W-L

- Using word webs

- Using a read-aloud

- Using a think-pair-and-share

- Previewing

- Skimming and scanning

Initially, engaging students in the prereading strategies motivates them to "get into" any selection. Eventually, students apply these prereading strategies to build background, activate prior knowledge, or raise questions that become part of the purpose for reading. With consistent practice, coaching, and guided reflection over the use of prereading strategies, students can build and refine their own lifetime prereading strategies.

Part II. Read

Novice readers usually do not choose to read with pencil in hand and mark up the text. Their reasons range from fearing to write in the text to not having a personal system of symbols for their responses, to fearing to make their "thinking tracks" public, to not having accurate language for describing the author's content and structure in annotations. Expert readers typically mark up a text, though not always. They will often mark up texts in which they find new or difficult information. They will rarely mark up texts in which they find familiar, easy-to-access or easy-to-remember information.

The *Sourcebook* addresses these varying comfort levels by presenting one or more interactive reading strategies per selection and guiding students to apply the strategies successfully. Our goal is to get students actually to write in their texts. The interactive reading strategies include these:

- Marking and highlighting
- Questioning
- Clarifying
- Visualizing
- Predicting
- Reading and connecting

The major purposes of these interactive reading strategies are to help students learn how and when to mark up texts and how to focus on specific content or structures of texts. Later, as their abilities develop for describing, labeling, commenting on, and reorganizing the information they read, students may find that these strategies slow down rather than accelerate their reading—a behavior indicating that they are becoming more expert readers.

Struggling novice readers often find themselves reading with no understanding or, even worse, reading with their eyes closed and imagining they are making sense of a piece of fiction or nonfiction. Expert readers develop new levels of understanding each time they read whole texts or parts of texts. They have learned where to pause and reread and how to apply any of several strategies to help understand what they read.

The comprehension strategies applied in the *Sourcebook* include these:

- Directed reading
- Predicting
- Using graphic organizers
- Using reciprocal reading questions
- Retelling
- Making double-entry journals

We assign one of these tried-and-true strategies to the appropriate types of fiction and nonfiction. Our goal is to model how expert readers come to understand a text. Ultimately, after students experiment with a variety of comprehension strategies, they will modify the strategies for their purposes until the strategies are no longer recognizable as they are developed in the *Sourcebook*—another indication of an expert reader in the making.

Part III. Gather Your Thoughts

Struggling novice writers usually do not choose to engage in any prewriting activities when they have a choice. Expert writers, while they vary widely in the breadth and depth of their prewriting strategies, view prewriting activities as the time when personally significant learning takes place. Prewriting activities provide the time and the means for engaging in critical and creative thinking.

Part III of the *Sourcebook* presents one or more prewriting strategies per selection. Students receive step-by-step guidance for applying each strategy successfully. The prereading strategies we apply among the selections include these:

- Discussing in pairs and small groups

- Clustering details

- Drawing a place

- Brainstorming

- Quickwriting

- Using anecdotes

- Comparing and contrasting

- Using a graphic organizer

- Using storyboards

Most of these prewriting activities involve two or more persons. Most thinking is social, according to Vygotsky; group interactions following various learning experiences, including reading and before writing, provide students with valuable opportunities to develop, refine, and internalize their purposes and plans for writing.

Part IV. Write

Struggling novice writers often think of completing a writing assignment as involving a two-step, one-time process—just sit down and write. They often postpone completing writing assignments, thinking that once they sit down and write, they can complete the assignment in one work session. Expert writers think of completing a writing assignment as involving several steps, e.g., narrowing the topic, planning, gathering data, drafting, revising one or more times, sharing and publishing; personalizing ways to complete each of the steps; and involving more than one work session.

The *Sourcebook* invites students to engage in several small writing tasks. Note the types of writing listed in the Table of Contents to the left of each selection title. The writing tasks become increasingly larger so that students come to view the writing process as a series of recursive, interlocking steps. When students present and reflect on their best writing samples, they come to understand how the writing process varies among types of writing and among students—another indication of an expert writer.

Part V. Wrap-up

Being able to answer such reflection questions as these indicates how well readers and writers understand the fiction and nonfiction selections they study:

1. **UNDERSTANDING** Did I understand? How do I know?

Is the message or point clear?

Can I restate what it was about?

2. **EASE** Was it easy to read?

Was I able to read it smoothly and without difficulty?

3. **MEANING** Did I learn something or take away something from it?

Did it affect me or make an impression?

4. **STYLE** Did I find it well written?

Was the writing well crafted, the sentences well constructed, the words well chosen?

Does it show me how to be a better writer?

5. **DEPTH** Did it make me think about things?

Did it set off thoughts beyond the surface topic?

What are the immediate implications for me? Others?

What are the long-term implications for me? Others?

6. ENJOYMENT Did I like it?

Was the experience pleasurable?

Would I want to reread it or recommend it to someone?

Answering such questions as these honestly and consistently for a wide variety of texts and purposes indicates that a learner is becoming an expert reader.

REFLECTIONS • What strategies do you find personally valuable

for prereading?

for reading?

for gathering your thoughts?

for writing?

for reflecting on your reading and writing?

• What are your roles when using the **Sourcebook** to build expert readers and writers? How might your roles change during this school year?

• How can you create the most significant learning experiences when your students use reading and writing?

REFERENCES Bransford, J. D., A. L. Brown, and R. R. Cocking, eds. *How People Learn: Brain, Mind, Experience and School.* Washington, D.C.: National Academy Press, 1999.

Cawelti, G., ed. *Handbook of Research on Improving Student Achievement.* 2nd ed. Arlington, Va.: Educational Research Service, 1999.

Graves, M., and B. Graves. *Scaffolding Reading Experiences: Designs for Student Success.* Norwood, Mass.: Christopher-Gordon Publishers, 1994.

BY CATHERINE McNARY

The Situation in High School

In middle school, strategic reading is an essential learning tool. Two primary learning mediums are used to disseminate information—classroom lecture and textbook reading. The middle school student is expected to have sufficient vocabulary, background knowledge, metacognitive strategies, and motivation to translate textbook print into usable, applicable information.

For some students, the expectations are realistic. For many, they are not. (The 1998 NAEP assessment stated that 31 percent of fourth graders, 33 percent of eighth-graders, and 40 percent of twelfth-graders attained a proficient level of reading [Donahue, Voelkl, Campbell, & Mazzeo, 1999].) What happens with the 67 percent of students in eighth grade and the 60 percent of students in twelfth grade who are not proficient readers? What strategies and teaching methods have been proven to provide this group with the best possible instruction in reading so that they, like their more able peers, may keep pace with the high school curriculum?

In the literature, five traits have been identified that provide readers with the cognitive tools to learn from text: general cognitive capacity, reader strategies and metacognition, inferential and reasoning abilities, background knowledge, and basic reading skills (Van Den Broek & Kremer, 2000). Most middle school students, even those reading two years below grade level, have adequate basic skills, and general cognitive capacity is beyond the purview of the middle school. However, the remaining abilities are integral to an instructional program at the middle school level and include these:

- Reader strategies and metacognition
- Inferential and reasoning ability
- Background knowledge.

Best Practices to Use with High-Risk Students

Dr. Norman Stahl has suggested ten recommendations for programs from research for teaching high-risk college students (Stahl, Simpson, and Hayes, 1994). Dr. Stahl's list can be consolidated into four components that are relevant to middle school reading programs and that match the five traits for success outlined by Taylor and others.

Best practices for a middle school reading program should reflect instruction in these four components:

1. develop background knowledge

2. model metacognitive strategies and promote their independent usage

3. incorporate writing into the curriculum

4. develop vocabulary

Develop Background Knowledge

The importance of developing background knowledge has been emphasized by several researchers (Alvermann and Moore, 1996). Because reading is thought to be a construction of meaning in which the reader not only absorbs information from the text but also combines that information with his or her own prior knowledge, background is essential. The reader cannot interact with the text without prior understanding of the content. He or she would have no groundwork upon which to build.

Teachers use several strategies to build background before reading. These include field trips, films, guest speakers, discussions, short articles, library research and projects, anticipation guides, K-W-L, brainstorming, quickwrites, DRTA, simulations, questionnaires, structured overviews, and advance organizers.

The *Sourcebook* is organized with a prereading activity at the beginning of each selection. These prereading activities include quickwrites, K-W-L, anticipation guides, previews, and other sound activities. Not only do these lessons serve as models for prereading strategies, they also provide strategic practice for students.

Other important prereading practices that go hand-in-hand with background building are setting purpose and previewing. Just as a reader must have background information to interact with text, a reader must also have a clear understanding of why he or she is reading a selection. Purpose can be set by teacher direction. Instead of suggesting, "Read Chapter Five for a quiz on Tuesday," the teacher should probably say, "Read Chapter Five to find three reasons why or how a problem was solved. Concentrate on the sequence of the solution." This small change gives a concrete purpose to the reading and helps students to focus on the main idea.

Previewing is another strategy that directs a student to discover the main idea of the text. Previewing activities include looking at titles, subheadings, chapter questions, photos, and captions. The information gathered acts as a director for how the student approaches the information.

These strategies are not new to teachers. The challenge is the number of times students must practice the strategy before it is internalized, until it can be done independently. The *Sourcebook* provides numerous opportunities for practicing each strategy. Repeated practice helps the student make the strategy automatic. The *Sourcebook* also provides the student with a written record of his or her strategy development. This record allows the student to monitor his or her own progress.

Model Metacognitive Strategies

It is clear from the literature that strategic readers comprehend print more efficiently (Paris, Wasik, and Turner, 1996) than those readers without strategies. Typically, the less-able reader has no plan for attacking print—he or she just reads every word, each with the same emphasis. He or she skips problematic words or passages or rereads them in exactly the same manner—with no strategies for monitoring the effectiveness of his or her comprehension. The goals of strategic reading instruction are to model a variety of strategies to students (both teacher- and student- generated), to give students sufficient guided and independent practice to incorporate the strategies into his or her own portfolio, and to observe the student using these strategies in his or her own independent reading. This instruction will then allow students to monitor the effectiveness of their own reading—and adjust if the reading has not been sufficient.

For many middle school readers, self-monitoring of comprehension is a new concept. Explicit instruction and practice are necessary for these students to develop self-monitoring techniques. Several strategies are available. While a student reads, he or she should mark up the text, underlining and highlighting information. In addition, note-taking of text during reading is also suggested. Students should be taught to write down the questions that come up while reading; write down issues that need clarification or that they wish to discuss; draw pictures of characters they need to visualize; note any parts or quotes within the selection that provoke a reaction; and graph any process or sequence that seems important. The *Sourcebook* is excellent for modeling and providing students with the opportunity to practice student-generated during-reading strategies.

In the space called "**Response Notes**," students record questions, clarifications, pictures, and graphic representations. Highlighting and underlining are also modeled. In addition, students can write in their books. Reading teachers are often at a disadvantage in teaching self-monitoring because students do not own the books and cannot write in the books they are reading. Consequently, these strategies are ignored or modified beyond recognition. With the *Sourcebook,* these activities can be practiced as they are meant to be—in the book. This is an opportunity for both teacher monitoring and self-monitoring of strategy acquisition.

Many of the during-reading strategies are teacher-generated. These include K-W-L, DRTA, and study guides. Two of the teacher-generated strategies the *Sourcebook* encourages during reading are **stop and think** questions and the **double-entry journal. Stop and think** (directed reading) activities function like a within-text study guide. Text is broken, at a strategic place, with a question box. Students are expected to stop and answer the question and then continue reading.

The location of the **stop and think**, within text, is of great value. This proximity helps to keep students connected to text to evaluate both their response and the place in text that referenced it. The repeated usage of **stop and think** in the *Sourcebook* permits students the practice to make the connection from text to response, as well as to establish a habit of questioning to check for understanding while reading.

The **double-entry journal** also appears within text. The student is required to stop reading and respond to a quote. This strategy not only emphasizes the importance of closely attending to text but also brings the student's experience and prior knowledge into the reading process. The strategy is quite useful in helping students learn how to interpret text, especially when they later write about it.

Many activities are used to assess knowledge of a selection after reading. These include dramatizations, debates, tests, and group and individual projects. These culminating activities reflect the use of many strategies but are not a single strategy themselves. Any unit in the *Sourcebook* lends itself to the development of a culminating activity. For example, after reading "Disaster at Sea," a culminating activity might be for groups in the class to choose an aspect about World War II on which to present. After-reading strategies that reflect the reader's process of organizing and applying his thoughts about the selection can be exemplified by content mapping, summarizing, discussion, and guided writing.

The *Sourcebook* uses the strategies of content mapping and summarizing, as well as journaling and webbing, to encourage student reflection. The content mapping, which is text structure sensitive, is a particularly good way for students to "gather their thoughts" after reading. In this manner, graphic organizers are modeled and made available for practice.

One of the most powerful strategies for showing an understanding of main idea and subsequent detail is the ability to summarize. Summarization is not an easy task. Several activities that include mapping main idea and detail, both graphically and in prose, accompany summary writing activities in the *Sourcebook*. Graphic and prose organizers are explained in a step-by-step fashion. Repeated practice, paired with these several instructional models, is a valuable practice.

Incorporate Writing into the Curriculum

In reviewing the literature on writing, one statement summarizes the current thinking:

> We believe strongly that in our society, at this point in history, reading and writing, to be understood and appreciated fully, should be viewed together, learned together, and used together. (Tierney and Shanahan, 1996)

Writing and reading complement each other. Each can be used as a strategy to strengthen the other. **Quickwrites** at the beginning of a selection can bring up background and focus purpose for reading. During reading, note-taking and questioning can increase metacognitive awareness and enhance comprehension. After reading, summarizing, journaling, and paragraph and theme writing can extend thought and enhance higher-order thinking.

The *Sourcebook* is an excellent resource for presenting reading and writing in tandem. Writing is integrated into before-, during-, and after- reading instruction. Journal responses, paragraph and theme writing, summarization, quickwrites, and the graphic organizers are integrated seamlessly with the reading, creating a complete, fully integrated lesson.

Develop Vocabulary

Several researchers have shown that direct instruction in vocabulary does enhance comprehension (Beck and McKeown, 1996). It is known that effective vocabulary instruction connects prior knowledge to new words (Lenski, Wham, and Johns, 1999) and provides instructional strategies that promote the active processing of words (Beck and McKeown, 1996). Examples of strategies that do this are: list-group-label, concept mapping, semantic feature analysis, synonym clustering, semantic mapping, and word sorts. Each of these strategies is involved in mapping word relationships. For example, a synonym cluster begins with a word and attaches three synonyms to that word. Attached to those three synonyms are three more synonyms, and so on.

All the above strategies can be used independently with a word journal or a word box, in pairs or small groups with a word box or a word journal, or as a whole-class activity with a word box or a word wall. It is most effective if new vocabulary is highly visible and used.

The *Sourcebook* best enhances vocabulary instruction by making the student aware of the need for growth in vocabulary. Each selection has difficult vocabulary words highlighted in the text and defined at the bottom of the page. In addition, the *Teacher's Guide* includes practice on selected words from the lesson and introduces students to a vocabulary strategy.

Conclusion

The teaching of reading is not an easy endeavor. Pressures by other teachers, students, and administrators are apparent daily. Not only is the reading teacher faced with the classroom challenges of students with diverse and serious issues but also with unrealistic expectations and goals from other teachers and administrators.

Because students in the classroom are diverse in their educational needs, the secondary reading teacher is constantly juggling curriculum and time to focus on the individual needs of his or her students. Each reading teacher is his or her own research assistant, constantly reviewing the literature for best practices and strategies, through that to motivate and engage the reluctant reader. He or she is forever combing the teacher store for materials that are relevant, strategic, and appropriate.

The *Sourcebooks* are a fine resource. Not only do they model strategies at the cutting edge of research, they are also made up of good-quality, highly motivating literature, both narrative and expository. Selections from authors such as Landston Hughes, Maya Angelou, John Christopher, and Victor Martinez reflect the populations of our classes and their multicultural nature.

Here is a quick guide to the main prereading, comprehension, and reflecting strategies used in the *Sourcebooks*. In order to help students internalize these strategies, the number and use of them were limited so that students could encounter them repeatedly throughout the book.

Overview

PREREADING STRATEGIES
Picture Walk

What It Is

A picture walk is a prereading activity in which students look at the images from a selection to get a sense of what the selection will be about. Other strategies may be more powerful, but a picture walk is a necessary strategy for all students to have in their repertoire. Once they become more skilled readers, they will most likely use it in conjunction with other prereading strategies—for example, skimming.

How to Introduce It

Have students page through the selection and look at the images.

Ask them questions such as the ones below to help them reflect on the images.

- How do the images make you feel?

- Based on the images, what do you think the selection will be about? Why?

Read the selection.

Encourage students to generate other questions of their own.

After reading, invite students to return to the images to discuss the accuracy of their predictions.

Example

The photo of . . .	tells me . . .
The photo of . . .	tells me . . .

Why It Works

Picture walks get students, especially visual learners, actively involved in the prereading process. Questions about the images spark students' interest, activate prior knowledge, and encourage prediction.

Comments and Cautions

As an extension to the activity, invite students to add a new image, either before reading (to illustrate their prediction) or after.

Picture walks work well with both fiction and nonfiction material. You can also use a modified version for selections involving graphic sources, such as maps and diagrams.

What It Is

K-W-L is a pre- and post-reading strategy designed to facilitate students' interest in and activate their prior knowledge of a topic before reading nonfiction material. The letters *K, W,* and *L* stand for "What I **K**now," What I **W**ant to Know," and "What I **L**earned."

Look at the example of a K-W-L chart from Lesson 4, "The President's Been Shot."

Example

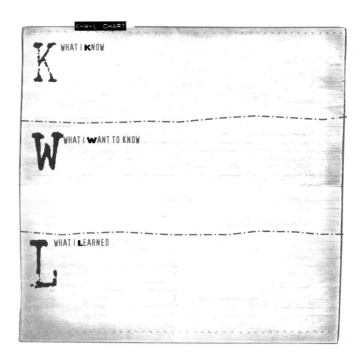

How to Introduce It

For students unfamiliar with the strategy, you might try to introduce K-W-L as a whole-class activity. Once students are familiar with the strategy, they can complete the charts on their own.

Ask students what they know about the topic. List their answers in the *K* column.

Discuss what students hope to learn about the topic from reading the selection. Write their questions in the *W* column.

Read the selection.

Return to the chart and list what students learned in the *L* column.

Why It Works

Brainstorming (the *K* part) activates prior knowledge. What sets K-W-L apart from other prereading strategies is that K-W-L also encourages students to ask questions (the *W* component), thereby setting meaningful purposes for their reading. Returning to the chart (the *L* component) brings closure to the activity and demonstrates the purposefulness of the task.

Comments and Cautions

Don't worry about the accuracy of the answers under the *K* column; this is a brainstorming activity; students can correct any errors later during the *L* part of the activity.

After brainstorming, have students categorize their lists into three or four general groups.

You might add a fourth column, "What I Still Need to Learn," for questions that aren't answered in the text or that arise after reading the material.

Anticipation Guide

What It Is

An anticipation guide is a series of statements to which students respond, first individually and then as a group, before reading a selection. For example, in Lesson 12, students are asked to circle the number that best represents their opinion about each statement.

Example

ANTICIPATION GUIDE

There is life on other planets.

1	2	3	4	5	6	7	8	9	10

strongly disagree   strongly agree

At some point in my life, I will encounter a being from another planet.

1	2	3	4	5	6	7	8	9	10

strongly disagree   strongly agree

I would like to visit another planet.

1	2	3	4	5	6	7	8	9	10

strongly disagree   strongly agree

I would like to find out more about galaxies beyond our own.

1	2	3	4	5	6	7	8	9	10

strongly disagree   strongly agree

Science-fiction stories always have some basis in fact.

1	2	3	4	5	6	7	8	9	10

strongly disagree   strongly agree

How to Introduce It

Have students read the statements. (When making your own guides, keep the number of statements to fewer than 10. More than that makes it difficult to discuss in detail.)

Discuss the students' responses. This is the point of an anticipation guide—to discuss. Build the prior knowledge of one student by adding to it the prior knowledge of other students, which can be done through discussion. The discussion of anticipation guide statements can also be a powerful motivator, because once students have answered the statements, they have a stake in seeing if they are "right."

Encourage students to make predictions about what the selection will be about based on the statements.

Then read the selection.

After reading the selection, have students return to their guides and reevaluate their responses based on what they learned from the selection.

Why It Works

Anticipation guides are useful tools for eliciting predictions before reading both fiction and nonfiction. By encouraging students to think critically about a series of statements, anticipation guides raise expectations and create anticipation about the selection.

Comments and Cautions

This is a motivational activity. Try not to allow the class discussion to become divisive or judgmental; the teacher's role is that of a facilitator, encouraging students to examine and reexamine their responses. The bigger stake students have in an opinion, the more they will be motivated to read about the issue.

The focus of the guides should not be whether students' responses are "correct" or not but rather the discussion that ensues after completing the guides individually.

Anticipation guides can help students learn to express their opinions about major topics, as in lesson 12.

You can turn the entire anticipation guide process into a whole-group activity by having students respond with either "thumbs up" or "thumbs down."

Preview or Walk-through

What It Is

Previewing is a prereading strategy in which students read the title and first paragraph or two of a selection and then reflect on a few key questions. It asks the students to "sample" the selection before they begin reading and functions very much like the preview to a movie. Occasionally it is simply referred to as a *walk-through* and is a less formal variation of skimming and scanning.

How to Introduce It

Previewing can be done as an individual or group activity. You might introduce it to the group and in later lessons encourage students to work on their own.

Read aloud, or have students read to themselves, the first paragraph or two of a selection.

Have students respond to four or five questions about the selection. Their responses will be predictions based on their initial sampling of the piece. Questions might include these:

- What is the selection about?
- When does it take place?
- Who is in it?
- How will the selection end?

Read the rest of the selection.

Return to the questions and discuss the accuracy of students' predictions. Were they surprised at how the selection turned out based on their initial preview? Why or why not?

Example

PREVIEW CARD	WHAT ARE SOME KEY NAMES AND PLACES?	WHAT REPEATED WORDS DID YOU FIND?
	WHAT ARE SOME KEY EVENTS?	WHAT UNFAMILIAR VOCABULARY WORDS DID YOU SEE?

Why It Works

Previews work because they provide a frame of reference in which to understand new material. Previews build context, particularly when students read about unfamiliar topics. Discussing the questions and predicting before reading help students set purposes for reading and create interest in the subject matter.

Comments and Cautions

Previews work best with more difficult reading selections, especially texts with difficult vocabulary. Previewing helps students to understand a context for a selection—what's the subject? Where's the story located? Who's involved?

Once students are familiar with previews, you might ask them to generate their own list of questions and have a partner respond to them.

Quickwrite

What It Is

A quickwrite is just what the name implies, a short, one- to ten-minute activity in which students write down their thoughts about a topic. Quickwriting is impromptu writing, without concern for spelling and grammatical conventions. It is intended to help students articulate some of the prior knowledge they have on a subject.

How to Introduce It

Provide students with a topic on which to focus.

Invite students to write about whatever comes to mind regarding the topic.

Encourage students to share their quickwrites in a small group. Discuss their similarities and differences.

Ask students to predict what they think the selection will be about based on their quickwrites.

Read the selection.

Discuss the connections between students' quickwrites and the selection.

Example

BEFORE YOU READ

Think of why you act the way you do.
1. Then do a quickwrite for 1 minute. Tell about something you did recently and why you did it.
2. Write everything you can think of.

1-minute Quickwrite

Why It Works

Quickwriting works as a prereading strategy on a number of levels. For one, the very process of writing without regard to writing conventions frees up students to write from a deeper level of understanding. Quickwriting encourages students to make connections between their own lives and the reading material, activates prior knowledge, and sparks interest. Quickwriting can also help correct misconceptions about a topic.

Comments and Cautions

As an extension to the activity, have students quickwrite again after reading the selection and compare their two quickwrites to see what they've learned from reading the material.

Skimming

What It Is

Skimming is a prereading strategy in which students look over the entire selection to get a sense of what it will be about. It is one of the best prereading strategies and best known. Much of the time, however, students never learn how to skim effectively and what to look for.

How to Introduce It

Skimming is a useful tool, both for prereading and content area reading, but one that many students have difficulty mastering. Therefore, introduce skimming as a whole-group activity; teacher modeling might work best for the initial activity. Skimming involves these activities:

- Examining the table of contents
- Reading the first and last paragraph
- Checking the selection's length and reading difficulty
- Reading any captions
- Looking over illustrations
- Noting section headings, diagrams, and other graphic sources

Example

SKIMMING

Who was Clara Barton?

When did she live?

What did she do?

Why was her work so important?

To help students master the technique of skimming, provide them with a series of questions to answer about the selection, as in the example above. Questions such as these provide a clear purpose for skimming and help students focus their attention on the key parts of the selection.

Why It Works

Skimming is an excellent tool for setting purposes and activating prior knowledge before reading nonfiction material. Like a picture walk, skimming draws students into a selection.

Comments and Cautions

Skimming works best when students have a clear purpose for going through a selection. Direct students, for example, to underline one to two words in each line of the first and last paragraph, or to circle names or words that appear a number of times.

Teach a clear method for skimming and try not to assume students will know what it means.

Think-Pair-and-Share

What It Is

Think-pair-and-share is a prereading strategy that encourages group discussion and prediction about what students will read. Students work in pairs to discuss sentences selected from the text.

How to Introduce It

Break students into groups of two or three. Present three to six sentences from the selection. Ask group members to read the sentences and discuss what they mean and in what order they appear in the text.

Encourage groups to make predictions and generate questions about the reading.

Then read the selection.

Have groups discuss the selection and the accuracy of their think-pair-and-share sentences. How many were able to correctly predict the order in which they appeared? How many could predict what the selection was about?

Example

Think-Pair-and-Share

_____ "Here I am trying to get home to cook me a bite to eat, and you snatch my pocketbook!"

_____ The woman said, "You ought to be my son. I would teach you right from wrong."

_____ Then she said, "Now ain't you ashamed of yourself?"

_____ It was about eleven o'clock at night, dark, and she was walking alone, when a boy ran up behind her and tried to snatch her purse.

_____ "I want a pair of blue suede shoes," said the boy.

Why It Works

Think-pair-and-share can be a powerful tool for getting students motivated to read. Small-group work such as this gives students the chance to discover that they don't always have to come up with all the answers themselves; sometimes two or three heads *are* better than one. Working in groups also provides reluctant readers with the understanding that all readers bring different skills and schema to the reading task. The activity also begins the critical process of "constructing meaning" of the text.

Comments and Cautions

Enlist students in building the think-pair-and-share activity. Have each group member write one sentence from the text on a file card. Then ask groups to exchange file cards—one group pieces together the sentences of another group.

The active, social nature of this activity stimulates students, which can be highly motivational and beneficial if properly channeled into purposeful activity.

Word Web

What It Is

A word web is a prereading activity in which students brainstorm and make connections to a key concept from the reading material.

Example

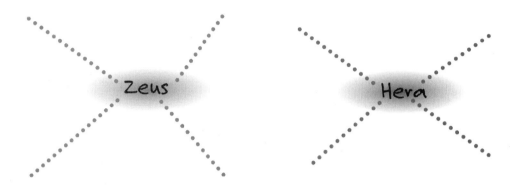

How to Introduce It

Word webs can be done independently or as a whole-group activity. You might want to do the initial word webs with the whole group and assign later word webs for independent learning.

Write a key concept in a circle. For example, in Lesson 10, "Hera," students are to describe Hera or Zeus.

Have students brainstorm words related to the concept on spokes coming out of the circle.

Discuss with students how the key word is connected to the reading material.

Read the selection.

Return to the word web and add any new ideas brought about by reading the selection.

Why It Works

Word webs are excellent tools for developing students' conceptual knowledge. They tap into students' prior knowledge and help students make connections between what they know and what they will learn.

Comments and Cautions

Even though this is a brainstorming activity, do challenge incorrect assumptions about the concept, particularly when using the word web with a whole group. You want to be sure that students go into the reading assignment with an accurate impression of the concept.

If students get "stuck," encourage them to write down words, phrases, examples, or images they associate with the concept.

RESPONSE STRATEGIES

The response strategies are introduced at the beginning of each *Sourcebook* (pages 8–10). They are the heart of the interactive reading students are asked to do throughout the book. In Part II of each lesson, one or two response strategies are suggested to help teach students how to mark up a text and become active readers.

Struggling readers do not naturally know how to interact with a text, so these strategies are designed to help them get started. Examples are also provided in each lesson to model the strategy. The intent is to build the habit of reading with a pen in hand and marking up the text until it becomes a natural way to read.

Response Strategies

1. Mark or highlight

2. Question

3. Clarify

4. Visualize

5. Predict

6. React and connect

Example

The purpose of these response strategies in each lesson is to

1. help students learn how to mark up a text

2. help students focus on specific aspects of a text and find the information they need

3. build lifelong habits for students by repeating good reading practices

COMPREHENSION STRATEGIES
Directed Reading

What It Is

Directed reading is a structured activity designed to guide students through a reading selection. Directed reading is composed of a series of steps, including readiness, directed silent reading, comprehension check and discuss, oral rereading, and follow-up activities. In the *Sourcebook*, students gain readiness in Part I, read silently in Part II, and then encounter questions that check their comprehension throughout the selection. Teachers are encouraged to have students go back through selections with this strategy and read the selection a second time. Repeated reading of a selection often increases reading fluency, which in itself often increases comprehension.

How to Introduce It

First, help students get ready to read by activating their prior knowledge, creating interest, and setting purposes. The prereading strategies described in Part I of the lesson offer suggestions for activities that promote reading readiness.

Next, have students read the selection silently. Guide them as they read by providing stopping points, such as the stop and think sections in the *Sourcebook*. Encourage them to focus on the purpose for reading that they established in Part I.

Example

STOP aND THiNK

What have you learned so far about Denmark Vesey?

After students have read the selection, take a moment to engage them in a discussion about what they read.

During or directly after the discussion, have students orally reread the selection to answer any remaining questions or clear up any confusion about the reading material.

During the discussion and oral rereading stages, you can get a sense of what kind of difficulties students are having with the material. Use follow-up activities to work on these areas of weakness and to extend students' understanding of the material, or use the additional comprehension activities included in each *Teacher's Guide* lesson. Follow-up activities range from direct skill instruction designed for individual or small-group work to response activities, such as those found in the *Sourcebook*.

Why It Works

Directed reading enhances students' ability to think critically and reflectively about the reading material. It helps them ask the questions good readers ask themselves as they read. The structured format ensures that students of all reading levels will be asking the right kinds of questions needed to comprehend the text.

Comments and Cautions

As with any comprehension strategy, directed reading needs to be modified to fit the needs of individual students.

Directed reading can be overly prescriptive, and overuse can contribute to passive reading, if it is relied on exclusively. Including activities that require student speculation and higher-level thinking will foster more active reading.

Prediction

What It Is

Prediction is both a comprehension strategy and a prereading strategy, but in the *Sourcebooks* it is formally used mostly as a comprehension strategy. Nearly all of the prereading strategies used in the *Sourcebooks* involve some level of prediction, but prediction is categorized as a comprehension strategy. When students predict during reading, they rely on information they have already read in the selection.

How to Introduce It

Break the selection into three or four parts.

Have students read to the first stopping point and then ask them to predict what they think will happen. Predictive questions include these:

- What will happen to the character?
- How do you think the problem will be resolved?
- How do you think the selection will end?

Example

STOP AND PREDICT

What do you think the family will do?

....

....

....

As students read on, encourage them to reflect on their predictions and modify them as further information is provided.

After reading, discuss the accuracy of students' predictions, not to determine if the predictions were "correct" but to provide closure to the activity and validate students' responses. Reflecting on the predictions will also help students see the information they might have used from the selection to predict but did not.

Why It Works

Because of the students' assertions about "what will happen," predicting gives students a stake in what they read. Their opinion is on the line, and this helps students set purposes for reading.

Comments and Cautions

Look for natural stopping points in texts; obvious spots to stop and predict what will happen next usually occur before episodes, or events, that occur in the story.

Prediction is best used with fiction, although it can also be applied to nonfiction with readers skilled at making predictions.

Graphic Organizer

What It Is

A graphic organizer is a visual representation of the key information for a reading selection. Graphic organizers can be as simple as a two-column chart or as complicated as a multi-dimensional diagram. They come in many sizes and shapes, such as plot charts, cause-effect charts, and character maps.

How to Introduce It

Begin by explaining the purpose of the graphic and the kind of information students should put into each of its parts.

Invite students to fill in the graphic organizer as they read, and then review it and make any modifications after completing the selection. For example, on page 207 in "Alaskan Bears," students use the graphic organizer to keep track of the details about grizzly bears in Alaska. As they read, they write the name of an animal in each column and describe how it adapts to the desert.

Examples

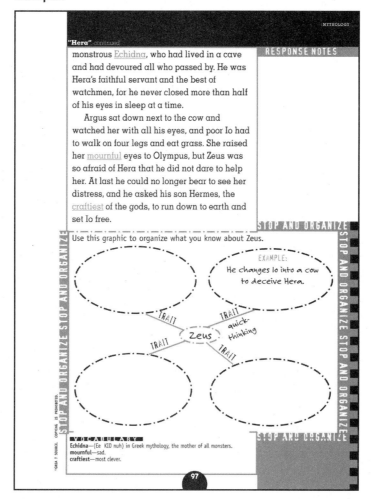

Examples

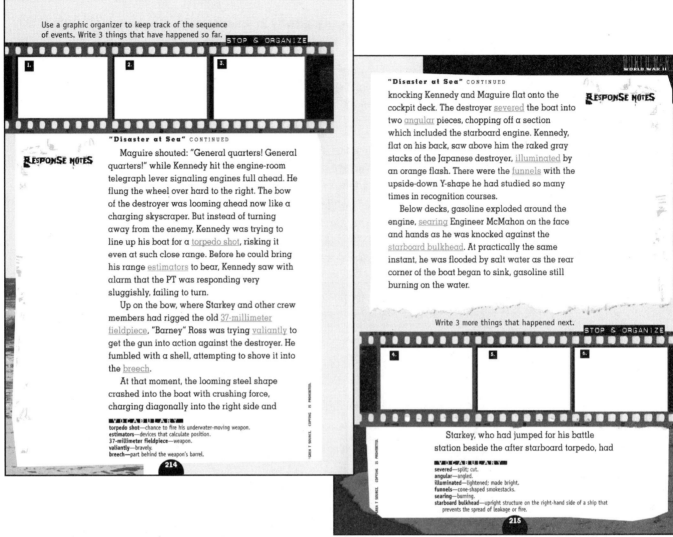

Why It Works

A graphic organizer is a useful tool for helping students to structure what they understand from their reading. It also helps students make connections between ideas, especially in flow charts or cause-effect charts.

Comments and Cautions

Some of the more common graphic organizers are these:

- Venn diagram for showing comparison and contrast

- Cause-and-effect chart for demonstrating causal relationships

- Sequence map for keeping track of a series of events

- Problem-solution map for identifying the problem and its solution(s)

- Word web for representing information about a particular concept

Graphic organizers are excellent tools for all students but are especially helpful for visual learners.

Reciprocal Reading

What It Is

Reciprocal reading is a small-group activity in which students take turns reading aloud to each other or with a tutor. It is such a powerful reading strategy that it has been modified for use in the *Sourcebooks*. The power of the questions generated does not diminish when reciprocal reading is taken out of the group work or tutor/pupil setting and transferred to a pupil-and-text relationship. The strategy is characterized by asking students to ask questions, clarify, predict, and summarize.

How to Introduce It

Take a moment to introduce the strategy to the whole class. Explain that this strategy involves working with a partner or reading tutor and asking four kinds of questions: clarifying ones, predicting ones, exploratory ones, and summarizing ones.

Invite one student to read the title and opening paragraphs aloud. At the first question point, ask for a volunteer to answer the question. Work through the entire selection with students as a group. Then, ask students to reread the selection again in pairs, taking turns asking and then answering the questions.

Example

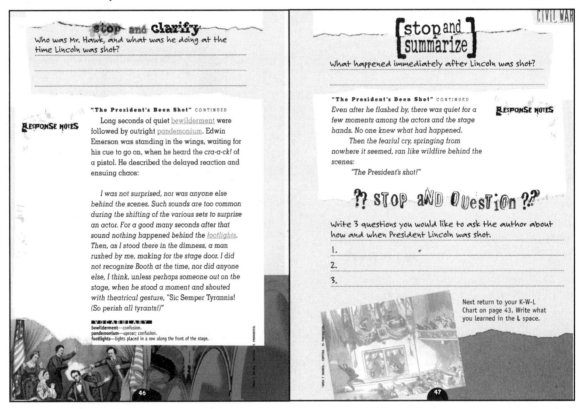

Why It Works

Reciprocal reading can be an excellent tool for both reinforcing listening skills (an often-overlooked skill) and improving reading fluency. It structures the work of students working with a reading partner and naturally helps them ask useful questions—the kinds good readers automatically ask—about a text.

Comments and Cautions

To ensure that the activity doesn't turn into a word-attack session, go over unfamiliar vocabulary before reading.

For reciprocal reading to be successful, it is important to introduce the idea to the whole class before turning students loose with a reading partner. Taking the time to walk through the process will prove beneficial later on when students are asked to work with their reading partners because they will have a structured routine to fall back on.

Double-Entry Journal

What It Is

A double-entry journal is an adaptation of the more familiar response journal. Typically, the left column includes quotes or facts from a selection, while the right column offers students the opportunity to respond to the quotation or idea. It is a very good strategy to build students' ability to comprehend and interpret a text.

How to Introduce It

Begin by having students list quotations from the selection that interest them, or you can pull out some quotations yourself, as is done in the *Sourcebook*. The benefits of selecting the quotations for students are that the focus is then on interpreting passages of the text and that the task is simplified, making it easier for students to succeed.

Invite students to reflect on the meaning of each quotation and write their thoughts in the right column.

Example

Write your thoughts about the quote given. Then add a quotation from the story that you think is interesting and respond to it.

DOUBLE-ENTRY JOURNAL

QUOTES	MY THOUGHTS
1. "The Warden owns the shade."	1.
2.	2.

Why It Works

Double-entry journals encourage students to become more engaged in what they are reading by focusing on just one part of the text at a time. With this kind of journal, students naturally make connections between the literature and their own lives. Double-entry journals expand on students' understanding of the material and build an initial interpretive response. By beginning the interpretation of literature, students will find writing about a text easier if they focus on the quotations they (or you) selected and their interpretations of them.

Comments and Cautions

Even if you structure the activity by selecting quotations, invite students to add those that have particular meaning to themselves as well.

Encourage students to use double-entry journals in other reading situations, including content-area reading.

Retelling

What It Is

Retelling is a comprehension strategy and assessment tool in which students retell a selection. It works best with chronological selections as a means of checking whether students followed the sequence of events.

How to Introduce It

Before reading the selection, let students know that they will be asked to retell or summarize their reading in their own words.

Either at the end of the selection or at certain stopping points within the selection (as done in the *Sourcebook*), have students retell what they have read as if they are telling it to a friend who has never heard it before.

Have students compare their retellings to examine each other's interpretations of the reading material.

Why It Works

Because retelling allows students to respond in their own words to what they've read, it increases both the quality and quantity of what is comprehended. Retelling also helps students make the text more personally meaningful and provides a deeper understanding of the reading material.

Comments and Cautions

You might have students tape-record the retellings and let students listen and assess their own work.

For fictional selections, try having students retell the story from another character's point of view to provide a different perspective to the tale.

A student's retelling offers a window into the student's thinking and is, therefore, a valuable assessment tool as well.

Story Frame

What It Is

A story frame is a visual representation of one or more of the key elements of a story: character, setting, plot, and theme. It helps students graphically construct the main elements of a story.

How to Introduce It

First, explain the idea of a story frame and its elements: plot, setting, characters, and themes. Be sure students understand that story frames can organize events, too. Just as there are many kinds of stories, students need to understand that there are many kinds of story frames.

Example

THE STORY TAKES PLACE IN

_____ IS A CHARACTER IN THE STORY WHO

_____ IS ANOTHER CHARACTER WHO

A PROBLEM OCCURS WHEN

AFTER THAT

THE PROBLEM IS SOLVED WHEN

THE STORY ENDS WITH

After completing the frame, have students use it as the basis for discussion about the selection or to help in their written responses.

Comments and Cautions

Story frames come in all shapes and sizes. Modify the frame to fit the needs of the students and the focus of the material. For instance, in "Thank You, Ma'am," the story frame focuses on plot, characters, and setting; others focus on character development throughout a story. Other frames might focus on theme or other story elements.

For students who need more guidance filling in their frames, provide them with question prompts, such as "What happened first?" "What happened next?" "Who did it happen to?" Let students know this is a strategy they are free to experiment with and use in whatever way they find is most helpful.

REFLECTIVE READING STRATEGIES

The reflective reading strategies occur in **Part V** of each lesson. They help students take away more from what they read. All too often students are asked, "Did you get it?" Reading seems like a code they have been asked to decipher but cannot. They feel stupid and think they have failed.

How can we turn around struggling readers if the only payoff for reading is "getting it"? Good readers read for a variety of reasons: to entertain themselves, to expand their understanding of a subject or develop their thinking in an area, or simply because they have to read. Yet good readers naturally take away more from what they read. For example:

- We read novels by Nobel Prize winners because of their writing **style**.

- We read sports pages because they are **enjoyable**.

- We read philosophy or religious meditations to add more **depth** to how we think about things.

- We read about such topics as Lamaze childbearing techniques or natural foods because they are personally **meaningful** to us.

- We read cartoons and *People* magazine because they are **easy** to browse through.

- We read directions about setting up a computer because we **have to**; we need to have that particular understanding.

We read, in other words, for a variety of reasons. As teachers, we need to help struggling readers see that—and not just that they did not "get it" on the multiple-choice test. So, **Part V** of each lesson in the *Sourcebook* is a "reflective" assessment, a looking back, so students can see what they *gained* from the lesson, not what they failed to understand.

Example

The purposes of the **Readers' Checklist** in each lesson are to:

1. model for students the questions good readers ask of themselves after reading.

2. expand the reasons for which students want to read.

3. build lifelong habits for students by repeating best reading practices.

Reflective Assessment

1. **Understanding**

   Did you understand the reading?

   Was the message or point clear?

   Can you restate what the reading is about?

2. **Ease**

   Was the passage easy to read?

   Were you able to read it smoothly and without difficulty?

3. **Meaning**

   Did you learn something from the reading?

   Did it affect you or make an impression?

4. **Style**

   Did you find the passage well written?

   Are the sentences well constructed and the words well chosen?

   Does the style show you how to be a better writer?

5. **Depth**

   Did the reading make you think about things?

   Did it set off thoughts beyond the surface topic?

6. **Enjoyment**

   Did you like the reading?

   Was the reading experience pleasurable?

   Would you want to reread the piece or recommend it to someone?

   Invite students regularly to provide examples and reasons for their answers to these questions.

Unit Background   GROWING UP (pages 11–32)

Two short stories, "The Turtle" and "Thank You, Ma'am," are included in this unit, the first by Jim Bishop and the second by Langston Hughes.

Jim Bishop (1907–1987) was born in Jersey City, New Jersey, and was a journalist, columnist, and editor. After working for the *New York Daily News* and the *Daily Mirror,* he became an associate editor for *Collier's* magazine and then executive editor for the *Catholic Digest.* He also wrote novels and nonfiction, including *The Day Lincoln Was Shot* (1955), *The Day Kennedy Was Shot* (1968), and *The Days of Martin Luther King, Jr.* (1970).

Langston Hughes (1902–1967) was born in Joplin, Missouri; graduated from high school in Cleveland; and attended Columbia University for a year. His first poetry collection, *The Weary Blues,* was published in 1925, and he became a bright star in the Harlem Renaissance, along with the painters and musicians who made Harlem famous. Hughes was a strong champion of human rights, and he celebrated the ordinary working people who struggled against poverty and racism in his poetry, essays, and fiction. "Thank You, Ma'am" was first published in 1959.

Teaching the Introduction

Photos on page 11 show two teenagers, a turtle, and some old-fashioned children's toys.

1. Read the unit introduction on page 11 with students, and ask them whether they are anxious to grow up. What one thing would they like to be able to do that they can't do now?

2. Ask students to make some inferences about the stories they are about to read based on the images on page 11.

Opening Activity

Ask students to illustrate an alternate opening page for this unit on growing up, using any medium they wish. Students who want to work together could assemble a collage. Others might take one or more photographs or draw or paint some aspect of growing up. Cartoonists might like to depict an amusing or exasperating aspect of growing up.

Skills and Strategies Overview

THEME Growing Up

READING LEVEL easy

VOCABULARY ◇wail ◇irritable ◇inexorably ◇casket ◇chisel

PREREADING preview

RESPONSE mark or highlight

COMPREHENSION directed reading

PREWRITING main idea and details

WRITING paragraph / sentences

ASSESSMENT understanding

BACKGROUND

Jim Bishop (1907–1987) was a newspaper columnist who wrote more than a thousand columns in his lifetime. Interestingly, Bishop was merely a mediocre student in grade school who consistently earned failing grades in English. He dropped out of school in the tenth grade and eventually gravitated toward newspaper work. When he told his father that he'd like to write for a living, his father stared at his son—who had flunked grade-school English—and said, "You're crazy." Nevertheless, he helped the boy get a job with the *New York Daily News*.

At the *News*, Bishop worked his way up from the copy desk to lead columnist. Eventually, he earned the reputation as the "voice of America" and developed a citywide audience. In 1966 he compiled a collection of his favorite columns and published them in a book called *Jim Bishop: Reporter*. "The Turtle" is included in that anthology.

UNIT THEME Jim Bishop explores the feelings a child has for his first pet.

GRAPHIC ORGANIZER A chart like this one can help students respond inferentially to a text.

WRITER'S PURPOSE
- to entertain

PEOPLE AND PLACES THE WRITER MENTIONS
- Dennis, his mother, his father, Oscar—at home

WRITER'S FEELINGS ABOUT DENNIS
- affectionate
- amused by

THEMES THE WRITER EXPLORES
- growing up
- childhood
- loss

WRITER'S MOOD
- solemn in the beginning; surprising at the end

WRITER'S STYLE
- matter-of-fact; short, simple sentences, easy vocabulary
- childlike

1. BEFORE YOU READ

Read through the introduction to the lesson with students. The purpose of these two paragraphs is to introduce the theme and motivate students. Then ask them to complete the prereading activity, a **preview**. (Refer to the **Strategy Handbook** on page 40 for more help.)

Motivation Strategy

ENGAGING STUDENTS In "The Turtle," Jim Bishop tells about a young boy's first experiences with a pet. Ask students to think about pets they've known and loved. What made these animals special? A brief discussion on this topic will help students connect to Bishop's story and theme.

Vocabulary Building

Help students use **context clues** to figure out the meanings of difficult words as they read, especially the key vocabulary words for this lesson: *wail, irritable, inexorably, casket,* and *chisel.* Have students circle these words in the text. Although the footnotes define these words, model using context and then checking your ideas against the footnote: "I don't know the meaning of the word *wail.* I see, though, that it follows a description of Dennis crying. Could *wail* mean 'crying hard' or 'sobbing'? I can check the footnote to see if my guess is correct." For additional practice with these words, see the **Vocabulary** blackline master on page 66.

STRATEGY LESSON: SUFFIXES If you feel students need some additional vocabulary work, you might teach a short lesson on suffixes. Write this sentence on the board: "The government has decided to legalize the sale of fireworks." Point out that *legalize* has the common suffix *-ize* (meaning "make" or "cause to be"). Because we know the meaning of the root and suffix, we can infer that *legalize* means "make legal."

For additional practice on this strategy, see the **Vocabulary** blackline master on page 66.

Prereading Strategies

A **preview** is a sort of mini-introduction to the topic and theme of a reading. During a preview, students read the first paragraph closely and then quickly glance through the rest of the text. They watch for words, phrases, and ideas that pop out and art that catches their attention. Although it is not mandatory that they record what they notice on a preview, most readers find it helpful to jot down a few impressions before they actually begin reading. As always, the act of writing can help focus their attention and encourage them to read more carefully. In addition, a preview card like the one on page 12 can give them a specific purpose for reading—to see if the quick predictions they made about the text are in fact correct.

PICTURE WALK As an alternate or additional prereading strategy, ask students to do a picture walk of the selection. This prereading strategy is similar to a preview, although in their picture walks, readers pay attention only to the art and any captions. After they've finished a careful picture walk of "The Turtle," have students talk about the pictures. Based on what they've seen, what do students predict the selection will be about? When they've finished reading, they might return to the pictures and explain what connections they see between the art and the story.

Spanish-speaking Students

En esta selección, un niño, Dennis, aprende de la muerte cuando su tortuga parece morirse. Los padres de Dennis intentan consolar a Dennis, pero está demasiado triste. El padre finalmente logra aliviar el esprítu de Dennis cuando le sugiere que tenga un funeral formal para la tortuga.

II. READ

Before students begin their close readings of the selection, ask them to read silently the directions at the top of page 13. Be sure that students understand how important it is for them to **highlight** or **mark** the text as they are reading. They should underline, circle, or highlight things that they find interesting, important, confusing, or surprising. They should also make notes in the margins about anything they want to be sure to remember.

Response Strategy

VISUALIZE Jim Bishop's writing style is so simple and accessible that students should have no trouble visualizing the people and events he describes. Ask students to keep track of these mental pictures by having them make quick sketches in the **Response Notes**. Their sketches might come in handy later if they have trouble remembering a part of the plot or an aspect of character.

Comprehension Strategies

Directed reading is a way of helping reluctant or low-level readers better comprehend what they are reading. In a directed reading, the teacher guides a silent reading of the selection and monitors the progress of students who seem to be having trouble. Before they begin, tell the class that they'll be stopping at three different points along the way in order to answer questions about the selection. When the whole class has finished, you may want to review students' answers to the questions or you may opt for a more general discussion of Bishop's story.

DOUBLE-ENTRY JOURNAL As an alternate comprehension strategy, you might have students respond to one or two quotations from the selection. Write the quotes on the board and then have them say what the quotes make them think about. A double-entry journal is an excellent way to help students make a connection between what they are reading and their own lives.

For more help, see the **Comprehension** blackline master on page 67.

Discussion Questions

COMPREHENSION 1. Who is Oscar? *(Dennis's pet turtle)*

2. Why does Dennis begin crying when he comes home from school? *(He finds Oscar floating on his back in the bowl.)*

3. What does Dennis's father promise that helps Dennis stop crying? *(a funeral for the turtle)*

CRITICAL THINKING 4. How do Dennis's feelings about the turtle change from the beginning of the piece to the end? *(Ask students to refer to their books as they answer this question. Encourage them to quote lines or passages that support their interpretations.)*

5. Why is the ending of "The Turtle" such a surprise? *(Have students explain the ending and why it caught them off guard. Did any of your readers correctly predict what would happen?)*

Literary Skill

IRONY "The Turtle" presents a perfect opportunity to introduce irony to students. *Irony* is a contrast between what appears to be and what really is. In *situational irony,* there is a great difference between what one expects to happen and what actually happens. For practice, ask students to explain how Dennis's suggestion, "Let's kill him," is an example of irony.

III. GATHER YOUR THOUGHTS

The goal of the prewriting activities on pages 17 and 18 is to prepare students to do some writing of their own. First, students will **quickwrite** about an animal that is now or once was important to them. Have them take a moment or two to think of the animal that they'd like to write about, and then encourage them to write freely, without stopping, for a minute or more about this animal.

Next, students will complete two **graphic organizers** that help them plan the **main idea and supporting details** of their paragraphs. Remind the class that the main idea is what the author wants you to remember most about the writing. The details a writer uses support the main idea.

Prewriting Strategies

TOPIC SENTENCES You might want to help students write a topic sentence for their paragraph. Explain that a topic sentence states the subject of the paragraph in addition to a feeling or an attitude about the subject. Have students use this simple formula when writing topic sentences:

(A specific topic) + (a specific feeling) = a good topic sentence.

Have students use the **Prewriting** blackline master on page 68.

IV. WRITE

Read aloud the directions on page 19 to be sure that students understand the assignment. Remind them that their **paragraphs** should begin with their main idea or topic sentence. The body of the paragraph should support the first sentence. Encourage students to be as detailed as possible in describing their animal. Tell them that you would like readers to be able to "see" and "hear" and even "feel" the animal.

WRITING RUBRIC Use this writing rubric to help students focus on the assignment requirements and for assistance with a quick assessment of their writing.

Do students' paragraphs

- begin with a topic or main idea sentence that names the animal and how they feel about it?

- contain details that support the topic sentence?

Grammar, Usage, and Mechanics

After students have written a first draft, have them exchange papers with a partner. Partners should check that the paragraph opens with a clear topic sentence and contains adequate supporting details. When they are ready to proofread their work, refer students to the **Writers' Checklist** and teach a mini-lesson on writing sentences. Remind the class that every sentence they write must begin with a capital letter, end with a punctuation mark, and express a complete thought. For example:

Incomplete thought: Oscar was swimming on his back in the

Complete thought: Oscar was swimming on his back in the bowl.

V. WRAP-UP

Take a moment at the end of the lesson for students to reflect on their **understanding** using the **Readers' Checklist**. The questions on this checklist are the ones that good readers ask themselves either consciously or unconsciously at the end of every reading.

Assessment

To test students' comprehension, use the **Assessment** blackline master on page 69.

Name _____

VOCABULARY

Words from the Selection

DIRECTIONS Using context and your knowledge of the story, say what you think each vocabulary word means.

1. "His shoulders shook and his breath caught and a **wail** came from his lips."

I think *wail* means _____

2. "She phoned her husband at his office. He was **irritable.** He had a business to conduct."

I think *irritable* means _____

3. "The father kept talking quietly, insistently, and **inexorably.**"

I think *inexorably* means _____

4. "'This is Oscar's **casket.** He will be the only turtle in the world buried in solid silver.'"

I think *casket* means _____

5. "'And I will get a big rock and **chisel** Oscar's name on it so that centuries from now, everybody will know that Oscar is buried there.'"

I think *chisel* means _____

Strategy Lesson: Suffixes

Suffixes come at the end of a word. A suffix can give you clues about the meaning of a word and how it should be used in a sentence. For example, if you add the suffix *-ity* to the noun *abnormal*, you get the noun *abnormality*, which means "a condition of not being normal."

DIRECTIONS Add one of the suffixes in the box to each of the words below. You many need to change the spelling by dropping one or more of the last letters in the root. Then use each new word in a sentence of your own.

> *-ity* = state of, quality of, or condition of
> *-ize* = make or cause to be

6. visual + ____ = _____

7. sincere + ____ = _____

8. public + ____ = _____

9. native + ____ = _____

10. mobil + ____ = _____

Name _____

COMPREHENSION
Graphic Organizer

DIRECTIONS Use this organizer to show what you know about Dennis. Feel free to look up details in your book if you need to.

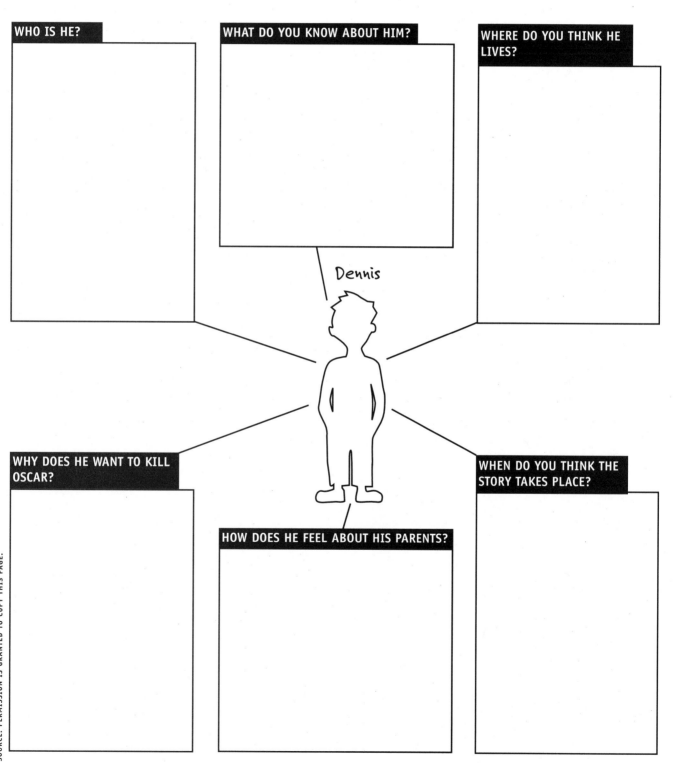

WHO IS HE?

WHAT DO YOU KNOW ABOUT HIM?

WHERE DO YOU THINK HE LIVES?

Dennis

WHY DOES HE WANT TO KILL OSCAR?

HOW DOES HE FEEL ABOUT HIS PARENTS?

WHEN DO YOU THINK THE STORY TAKES PLACE?

Name _____

PREWRITING
Writing a Topic Sentence and Details

Every paragraph you write must have a topic sentence. A topic sentence tells the subject of the paragraph and how you feel about the subject. You can use this formula to help you write a topic sentence.

(A specific topic) + (a specific feeling) = a good topic sentence.

DIRECTIONS Follow these steps to write a topic sentence and supporting details.

STEP 1. Write a topic sentence about your animal.

(_____) + (_____) = _____ .

   (animal)   (how I feel about it)   (my topic sentence)

STEP 2. Next plan details that support your topic sentence. They will give readers important information about your topic.

detail #1: _____

_____

detail #2: _____

_____

detail #3: _____

_____

STEP 3. Write a concluding sentence that is a restatement of your topic sentence.

My concluding sentence: _____

_____

_____

_____

Name _____

ASSESSMENT

Multiple-Choice Test

DIRECTIONS On the blanks provided, write the letter of the item that best answers each question or completes each statement.

_____ 1. What is Dennis's favorite toy?
   A. Erector sets
   B. an orange scooter
   C. a baseball mitt
   D. a twenty-five-cent turtle

_____ 2. How old is Dennis?
   A. six
   B. eight
   C. ten
   D. twelve

_____ 3. What does Dennis do first when he comes home from school?
   A. He checks on his turtle.
   B. He plays baseball with friends.
   C. He watches TV.
   D. He does his homework.

_____ 4. What does Dennis think when he first sees Oscar floating on his back?
   A. The turtle is stuck.
   B. Oscar has learned a new trick.
   C. The turtle is dead.
   D. Oscar is feeling hot.

_____ 5. How does Dennis feel when he sees Oscar floating on his back?
   A. sad
   B. happy
   C. puzzled
   D. tired

_____ 6. What does his mother do to try to stop Dennis from crying?
   A. She yells at him to stop.
   B. She promises him a new turtle.
   C. She makes his favorite meal.
   D. none of the above

_____ 7. To whom does his mom turn for help with Dennis?
   A. a doctor
   B. a veterinarian
   C. Dennis's father
   D. Dennis's best friend

_____ 8. What does Dennis's dad say to explain the mystery of death?
   A. Death comes when your body gets tired.
   B. Death comes when God wants to be with us.
   C. Death is a natural part of living.
   D. none of the above

_____ 9. Dennis slowly stops crying because . . .
   A. he is promised another turtle.
   B. his parents say they love him.
   C. he is promised a funeral for the turtle.
   D. all of the above

_____ 10. Where is Oscar at the end of the story?
   A. flushed down the toilet
   B. buried in a silver case
   C. in Dennis's pocket
   D. swimming in his tank

Short-essay Test

How do Dennis's feelings about Oscar change from the beginning of the story to the end?

Thank You, Ma'am

Skills and Strategies Overview

THEME	Growing Up
READING LEVEL	easy
VOCABULARY	◇permit ◇frail ◇snatch ◇frowned ◇presentable
PREREADING	think-pair-and-share
RESPONSE	prediction
COMPREHENSION	story frame
PREWRITING	sequencing events
WRITING	narrative paragraph / sentence fragments
ASSESSMENT	meaning

BACKGROUND

Langston Hughes was one of the most gifted American poets and storytellers of the twentieth century. Against all odds, Hughes realized a goal he set for himself when he was in high school: he wanted to be a famous writer who would "write stories about Negroes, so true that people in faraway lands would read them—even after I was dead."

In the beginning, African Americans and whites alike were surprised by Hughes's gritty, highly realistic writing style. Many people thought he spent too much time describing things that were "ugly" or "harsh." Eventually, however, they came to understand the message that pervades almost all of his work—that there can be beauty even in the midst of struggle. "Thank You, Ma'am" reflects Hughes's determination to show both the strength and the weaknesses present in all people. The character of Mrs. Luella Bates Washington Jones may have been based on Hughes's own grandmother, who had a strong moral compass that she was determined to pass along to her grandson.

UNIT THEME In "Thank You, Ma'am," a boy on the streets learns a lesson from a woman who had her own share of troubles when she was growing up.

GRAPHIC ORGANIZER Students might use an organizer like this one to compare the two major characters.

Mrs. Jones	Story summary	Roger
determined strong-willed honest compassionate kind-hearted	A young boy named Roger tries to snatch a purse from a woman on the street. Instead of calling the police, the woman takes him home and teaches him a lesson about honesty and truth.	misguided confused unsure polite appreciative?

BIBLIOGRAPHY Students might enjoy these books by Langston Hughes: *The Ways of White Folks* (1934, short stories) and *The Langston Hughes Reader* (1958, collection).

I. BEFORE YOU READ

Read through the introduction to the lesson (page 21) with students. Remind them of the theme of the unit (Growing Up) and then have them complete the prereading activity, a **think-pair-and-share**. (Refer to the **Strategy Handbook** on page 40 for more help.)

Motivation Strategy

In "Thank You, Ma'am," Langston Hughes describes a woman who acts as a "moral compass" for a young boy. Ask students to think of someone they know who has taught them right from wrong. What has this person done or said that has had an effect on students? When they actually begin reading, students can think about the person they've named and compare him or her to Mrs. Jones.

ENGAGING STUDENTS Ask students to think of a time they got into trouble. What happened? How did things turn out? What was their family's reaction to the event? How did the experience change the student's feelings about himself or herself? A brief discussion about this topic will help students forge a prereading connection between themselves and the theme of the selection.

Vocabulary Building

Discuss with students the key vocabulary words for this story: *permit, frail, snatch, frowned,* and *presentable*. Have students circle these words in the text, and then encourage them to define the words in context before checking the footnoted definition. Later, you might ask a volunteer to point out the **context clues** he or she used to define the five words. Students will benefit from as much context work as you can give them. For this reason, you may want to assign the **Vocabulary** blackline master on page 74.

STRATEGY LESSON: IDIOMS As you know, an idiom is an expression that cannot be understood from the literal meanings of its words. For this reason, idioms are often puzzling to those who speak English as a second language. To help, explain that it's often possible to visualize what the idiom says or describes. For example, if you form a mental picture of the idiomatic expression "on your toes," you realize that it must mean "ready for action; alert."

For additional practice with this strategy, see the **Vocabulary** blackline master on page 74.

Prereading Strategies

On page 21, students are asked to complete a **think-pair-and-share** activity that provides a thematic warm-up to Hughes's story. During a think-pair-and-share, students work together to solve different types of "puzzles" that relate to the selection. In this case, they'll read a series of quotations from the story and then try to guess the proper ordering of the quotes. The purpose of this activity is to help students begin thinking about the selection. Also, the quotations have been chosen to pique interest in the reading. You might use this activity as a motivator for those students who are reluctant to begin or who feel intimidated by the length of the story.

QUICKWRITE Another excellent prereading strategy is the quickwrite. Read aloud the first paragraph or two of "Thank You, Ma'am." Ask students to do a one-minute quickwrite about a topic from a list you write on the board. Items on your list might include: *growing up, learning right from wrong, my worst childhood memory*, and *an adult who is special to me*.

Spanish-speaking Students

"Gracias, Señora" es un cuento conmovedor del valor de ayudar a otra gente. Un joven pobre intenta robar a una mujer en la calle, pero ella impide su empeño. En vez de llevarle al policía, sin embargo, insiste en que vaya con ella a su casa. Allí, la mujer le da comida y dinero, y confiesa que también había hecho malas cosas en su vida. El joven escucha el consejo, y busca las mejores palabras para expresar su gratitud.

READ

Before they begin, tell the class to make a series of during-reading **predictions** about the story. Point out the sample prediction in the margin on page 22, and explain that their predictions can be as simple and quick as this one. As you know, making predictions can keep readers interested in a story. More often than not, their predictions will motivate them to continue reading. They'll naturally want to find out which of their predictions turn out to be true.

Response Strategy

QUESTION   As an alternate response strategy, have students keep track of the questions that occur to them as they are reading. Ask students to jot down questions as they come up, no matter how silly or unimportant they seem. Students will find that some of these questions will be answered as they go along. Other questions, however, won't be so easy to answer and will require some inferential thinking. Work as a class to discuss answers to these questions.

Comprehension Strategies

Students will need to fill in a set of **story frames** as they are reading "Thank You, Ma'am." Story frames can help readers understand the sequence of events in a story. As such, they help readers get a handle on plot. Rather than simply asking students to "tell what happens," a story frame gives a framework for response. In addition, it can prod readers into thinking carefully about elements of setting, character, and even theme. Encourage students to reread their story frame notes once they've finished the selection. They may want to make some small revisions to their thoughts and ideas before they complete the big frame on page 29.

DIRECTED READING   As an alternate comprehension strategy, try doing a directed reading of the selection. In a directed reading, the teacher or group leader directs a silent reading of the text. Readers pause every once in a while to answer **stop and think** questions designed to elicit factual and inferential responses. A directed reading will help you see what (if anything) is causing problems for readers. Using students' comments as a guide, you might speed up or slow down the pace of future readings or spend more time clarifying the facts and details of this selection.

For more help, see the **Comprehension** blackline master on page 75.

Discussion Questions

COMPREHENSION   1. How do Roger and Mrs. Jones meet? *(He tries to snatch her purse.)*

2. Why does she take Roger home with her? *(She says she wants to wash his face.)*

3. What does Mrs. Jones reveal about her own childhood? *(She did things she was ashamed of too.)*

CRITICAL THINKING   4. What lesson does Mrs. Jones teach the boy? *(Answers will vary. Students might suggest that she teaches him to be honest or humble or thankful.)*

5. What is the significance of the title? *(Remind the class that the words "thank you, ma'am" are never spoken by Roger. Why do they think Hughes used this phrase as his title?)*

Literary Skill

FORESHADOWING   You might want to introduce the literary term *foreshadowing*, the technique of providing hints or clues about the future action in a story or play. Students are asked to make predictions as they read "Thank You, Ma'am"; therefore they will be alert to indications from the first three paragraphs on that Mrs. Jones will deal firmly with Roger.

III. GATHER YOUR THOUGHTS

The prewriting activities on page 30 are meant to prepare students to write a **narrative paragraph** about an important event in their lives. Students will begin by reflecting on the plot of "Thank You, Ma'am." They will list the four most important things that happen in the story, consulting their story frames as necessary. The purpose of this activity is to help students understand the **sequence of events** in a narrative.

Next, students will make notes about a time someone taught them right from wrong. The planner on page 30 asks them to list the most important parts of the event. It also gives them a model for the sequence of their narrative paragraphs.

Prewriting Strategies

STORY FRAME As an alternate prewriting strategy, ask students to complete a story frame about the event they plan to describe in their paragraphs. Write out a story frame similar to the one on page 29 and then photocopy one for each student. Have students refer to this story frame and story planner when writing their paragraphs.

Have students use the **Prewriting and Writing** blackline master on page 76.

IV. WRITE

If you feel students will benefit, review the characteristics of a **narrative paragraph.** Remind the class that a narrative paragraph tells a story. It should have a clear progression—a beginning, a middle, and an end.

After students have written a first draft, have them exchange papers. Their editing partners should read the paragraph and evaluate it in terms of organization and sequence. Student editors might consult the following writing rubric when evaluating their partner's writing:

WRITING RUBRIC Do students' narrative paragraphs

- tell about a time someone taught the writer right from wrong?

- have a clear progression—a beginning, a middle, and an end?

- include adequate details describing the event?

Grammar, Usage, and Mechanics

When students are ready to proofread, refer them to the **Writers' Checklist.** At this point, you might want to teach a lesson on sentence fragments. Remind the class that every sentence must express a complete thought. For practice, ask students to say which of these sentences is a fragment:

Fragment: The woman that I met on the street yesterday afternoon.

Complete: Mrs. Jones took me inside.

Fragment: Langston Hughes, who wrote short stories, essays, and poetry.

V. WRAP-UP

Take a moment at the end of this unit for students to reflect on the literature and the theme of growing up. Point out the **Readers' Checklist** on page 32. Ask students to discuss what Hughes's story **meant** to them personally.

Assessment

To test students' comprehension, use the **Assessment** blackline master on page 77.

Name _____

VOCABULARY

Words from the Selection

DIRECTIONS Using context clues, fill in each blank with the most appropriate word from the list.

> ✦permit   ✦frail   ✦snatch   ✦frowned   ✦presentable

1. My parents will not _____ me to go to the mall, nor will they allow me to have friends over tonight.

2. My mother told me I have to look _____, so I put on a tie and washed my face.

3. I decided to _____ a cookie from the jar when my father wasn't looking.

4. The _____ woman was too weak to get out of bed.

5. My teacher _____ at me, so I knew he was angry.

Strategy Lesson: Idioms

An idiom is an expression that cannot be understood from the literal meanings of the words. Instead, these colorful expressions must be "translated." For example, "Lunch was on the house" means that lunch was free.

DIRECTIONS Read the underlined idioms in the sentences below. From the list at the right, choose what you think each idiom means and write the "translation" on the blank.

A. remain where he was

6. Mrs. Jones really <u>gave him a piece of her mind</u>.

B. scolded him

_____

C. be careful

7. She thought Roger <u>didn't have a leg to stand on</u>.

D. meet trouble bravely

_____

E. had no defense

8. Roger had to <u>face the music</u>.

_____

9. She told him to <u>stay put</u> while she prepared dinner.

_____

10. He felt that with Mrs. Jones he had to <u>walk on eggs</u>.

_____

Name _____

COMPREHENSION
Graphic Organizer

DIRECTIONS Use this herringbone organizer to record what you know about "Thank You, Ma'am." Then write the main idea of the story.

Who?
1.
2.

(Did) what?
1.
2.

When?
1.
2.

Where?
1.
2.

How?
1.
2.

Why?
1.
2.

Main idea of "Thank You, Ma'am": _____
_____
_____
_____

Name _____

PREWRITING AND WRITING
Writing a Narrative Paragraph

A narrative paragraph tells a story. It should have a beginning, a middle, and an end.

DIRECTIONS Follow these steps to write a narrative paragraph.

STEP 1. WRITE A TOPIC SENTENCE. Complete this sentence in several different ways.

When I was _____ years old, I _____

_____

_____

STEP 2. ORGANIZE DETAILS. Now think of sensory details that can help your reader see, hear, smell, taste, and feel the event you are describing. Use this chart to make notes.

I saw . . .	
I felt . . .	
I smelled . . .	
I tasted . . .	
I heard . . .	

STEP 3. WRITE A CONCLUSION. Write a concluding sentence that restates the topic sentence and tells what you learned from your experience.

My concluding sentence: _____

_____

_____

Name _____

ASSESSMENT

Multiple-Choice Test

DIRECTIONS On the blanks provided, write the letter of the item that best answers each question or completes each statement.

_____ 1. How do Roger and Mrs. Jones meet?
   A. They bump into each other.
   B. His mother introduces them.
   C. Friends introduce them.
   D. He tries to snatch her purse.

_____ 2. Why is Roger unsuccessful in stealing the purse?
   A. It turned out not to be a purse.
   B. The purse was too heavy and he dropped it.
   C. He lost his balance and fell.
   D. none of the above

_____ 3. What does Mrs. Jones do when she sees Roger lying on the ground?
   A. She kicks him.
   B. She threatens to call the police.
   C. She tells him to go home.
   D. She shouts for help.

_____ 4. Why does Mrs. Jones decide to take Roger to her house?
   A. She wants to call the police.
   B. She wants to call his school.
   C. She wants to let him sleep.
   D. She wants to wash his face.

_____ 5. Where does Mrs. Jones let go of Roger?
   A. She lets go of him on the street.
   B. She lets go of him inside her room.
   C. She doesn't let go of him.
   D. She never touched him.

_____ 6. Roger confesses he wanted to steal the purse so he could buy . . .
   A. blue suede shoes.
   B. a baseball mitt.
   C. a gift for his mother.
   D. cigarettes.

_____ 7. What does Roger find out he has in common with Mrs. Jones?
   A. She was homeless growing up.
   B. She was an orphan.
   C. She too wanted things when she was young.
   D. all of the above

_____ 8. What does Mrs. Jones do for a living?
   A. She drives a bus.
   B. She is an accountant.
   C. She is a teacher.
   D. She works in a beauty shop.

_____ 9. What does Mrs. Jones give Roger before he leaves?
   A. ten dollars
   B. her phone number
   C. a bag of food
   D. an invitation to come back

_____ 10. What does Roger say to Mrs. Jones as he leaves?
   A. "Thank you, ma'am."
   B. "I don't need your gift."
   C. "I'm very sorry, ma'am."
   D. He doesn't say anything.

Short-essay Test

Does Roger appreciate what Mrs. Jones did for him? Use details from the story to support your answer.

Civil War

Unit Background   **CIVIL WAR** (pages 33–50)

An excerpt from a memoir by Clara Barton and an excerpt from *The Day Lincoln Was Shot* by Richard Bak make up this unit.

Clara Barton (1821–1912) was a teacher for 18 years in Massachusetts and New Jersey before she moved to Washington, D.C., and became a clerk in the U.S. Patent Office. At the start of the Civil War, she organized the obtainment and distribution of supplies to help wounded soldiers. While in Europe, she became associated with the International Red Cross, which inspired her to establish the American Red Cross in 1881. She served as president of the organization until 1904.

Richard Bak (born 1954) is also the author of several biographies of sports figures, including Casey Stengel, Lou Gehrig, Joe Louis, and Ty Cobb. He is a graduate of Eastern Michigan University and lives in Michigan.

Because "The President's Been Shot" deals only with the act of assassination, you may want to tell students a little more about John Wilkes Booth (1838–1865). Booth was an actor, as were his father, Junius Brutus Booth, who had immigrated to the United States from England, and two of his brothers, Junius, Jr., and Edwin. Although the Civil War was virtually over when John Wilkes assembled a group of Confederate sympathizers around him, his intention was to kidnap Lincoln. There is some dispute about whether he acted on his own or as an agent of the Confederate government, but when this plan fell through, Booth instead planned to assassinate Lincoln while the president was attending the theater. Since Booth was familiar with Ford's Theater, having acted there, the logistics of the plan were fairly simple for him. It is also possible that the setting and the theatricality of his leap to the stage appealed to his sense of drama. Booth was shot to death outside a burning barn in Maryland and several of his co-conspirators were later hanged.

Teaching the Introduction

Photos on page 33 show Lincoln, Booth, and a Civil War hospital as well as a map of the Union and Confederate states. Clara Barton is pictured on page 39.

Abraham Lincoln

John Wilkes Booth

A Civil War hospital

The Civil War (1861–1865) was one of the bloodiest wars in American history. It bitterly divided the country, pitting brother against brother and North against South. The Northern states fought to end slavery, while the Southern states battled to preserve slavery. Although the North triumphed in the end, victory came at a high price.

33

1. Read the unit introduction with students, and tell them that the war did indeed pit family members against each other. Several of Lincoln's in-laws, relatives of his wife, Mary Todd Lincoln, fought on the Confederate side. Ask students to find Washington, D.C., and Richmond on the map on page 33. Tell them that Richmond was the capital of the Confederacy at the start of the war.

2. Ask students to tell what they know of the Civil War, Booth, or Lincoln from study in other classes.

3. It may be hard for students to imagine the state of medical knowledge at the time of the Civil War. Tell them that thousands died of disease and wounds that would be cured or repaired today. There were no antibiotics, hygiene was rudimentary, primitive anesthetics were possible only in some places but not often in field hospitals, and surgery on internal injuries was virtually impossible. To prevent gangrene, amputation was the usual treatment for serious injuries to limbs. Caring for the wounded required almost as much bravery as fighting on the battlefield.

Opening Activity

Remind students that 11 states seceded from the Union, and tell them that one of Lincoln's major objectives was to preserve the Union. Ask students to discuss why they think it was so important to keep the states united. What would have happened had the country been permanently divided into North and South?

Caring for the Wounded

STUDENT PAGES 34–42

Skills and Strategies Overview

THEME	Civil War
READING LEVEL	average
VOCABULARY	◇cautious ◇anguish ◇abdomen ◇dismal ◇relieve
PREREADING	skim
RESPONSE	visualize
COMPREHENSION	retell
PREWRITING	narrowing a topic
WRITING	letter/greeting and closing of a letter
ASSESSMENT	ease

BACKGROUND

Clara Barton (1821–1912) organized the American Red Cross in 1881. After the outbreak of the Civil War in 1861, Barton carried supplies to soldiers and nursed wounded men on the battlefields. Her work attracted national attention and earned her the name "angel of the battlefield." When the war ended, Barton formed a coalition to search for missing men. Barton and fellow volunteers succeeded in marking more than 12,000 graves in the Andersonville National Cemetery in Georgia.

Although her work during the Civil War left her exhausted and weak, Barton continued her ministerings on the battlefield. She cared for the wounded during the Franco-Prussian War (1870–1871) and took charge of relief work in the aftermath of the Johnstown, Pennsylvania, flood (1889) and an 1893 hurricane in the South. She wrote two books: *History of the Red Cross* (1882) and *The Red Cross in Peace and War* (1899).

UNIT THEME Clara Barton describes a battlefront experience during the American Civil War.

GRAPHIC ORGANIZER This sequence organizer can help students analyze a specific episode from a text.

Episode Analysis: "Caring for the Wounded"

HOW IT BEGAN
At three o'clock in the morning, Barton is asked to help with a mortally wounded soldier.

WHAT HAPPENED
Barton goes to the soldier and allows him to think she is his sister. She stays with him through the night.

HOW IT ENDED
Soldier awakens and Barton explains that she has come to help. He tells her how thankful he is. . . .

WHAT I LEARNED FROM IT
— facts about Barton
— her message of compassion
— the brutality of war

BEFORE YOU READ

Read through the introduction to the lesson (page 34) with students. If you like, start things off by leading a general discussion about the Civil War. Then turn students' attention to the prereading activity, a **skim**. (Refer to the **Strategy Handbook** on page 40 for more help.)

Motivation Strategy

You might begin by asking students to review what they know about Clara Barton. Who was she and for what was she famous? Ask a volunteer to make a few notes on the board. Students might refer to these notes as they're reading "Caring for the Wounded."

ENGAGING STUDENTS Explain that "Caring for the Wounded" is a personal memoir about the Civil War. Ask students to complete this statement: "I think war is _____." A brief discussion about this topic will help the class begin thinking about the unit's theme.

Vocabulary Building

Point out key vocabulary words for this lesson: *cautious, anguish, abdomen, dismal,* and *relieve.* Ask students to circle these words in the text. These words appear in an exercise on the **Vocabulary** blackline master on page 84. Encourage students to learn the pronunciations and definitions for these words so that they can begin incorporating the words into their own vocabularies.

STRATEGY LESSON: LATIN ROOTS Long or complex words sometimes can be broken down into smaller units that can give clues about their meaning. Since many words in English come from Latin sources, it's important for students to know a little about Latin word families. For example, explain these Latin roots and ask students to build word families for them: *dict* (speak, say), *brev* (short), and *aud* (hear).

For additional practice on this strategy, see the **Vocabulary** blackline master on page 84.

Prereading Strategies

During a **skim**, students glance through the selection quickly, looking for words and phrases that can reveal information about the topic. Skimming gives readers an idea of what they can expect during their close reading and can alert them to words or ideas that might cause them difficulty. If you like, work through the skimming questions on page 34 as a group. This can help students see that everyone skims differently. Not everyone will catch every detail.

PREVIEW As an alternate prereading strategy, ask students to preview the selection. This also will help familiarize them with the subject and writing style of "Caring for the Wounded." Have them look at art, headlines, vocabulary words, and interrupter questions. Then ask: "What is the topic of this selection? Who is the narrator? What do you think the most challenging part(s) of the selection will be?"

Spanish-speaking Students

"Cuidando a los lastimados" describe el valor y la fuerza interna de los médicos y enfermeras durante la Guerra Civil. Se enfoca en una mujer en particular, Clara Barton. Además de dedicarse a salvar las vidas de otros, ella se dedicaba a mejorar los espíritus de los lastimados por darles apoyo emocional.

READ

Before students begin their close readings, be sure they understand the response strategy of **visualizing**. Explain that when they read, they should try to pay attention to the "mental movies" that occur naturally. Each time they "see" something new or interesting, they should make a sketch of it in the **Response Notes**. These sketches can come in handy later, when it's time to summarize or retell parts of the selection.

Response Strategy

QUESTION As an alternate response strategy, ask students to make a note of questions that occur to them as they are reading. Each time they have a question about the author, action, or characters, they should jot it down in the **Response Notes**. Later, they can return to their questions and see which they can answer. This strategy helps students think more critically about a text and can assist in building inferential responses.

Comprehension Strategies

As they read, students will stop occasionally in order to **retell** the events described. Retelling a story or an article can help readers make connections that they might not have noticed the first time. When they retell, students should be brief but thorough. They should focus only on the major events and ignore minor details.

For more help, see the **Comprehension** blackline master on page 85.

Discussion Questions

COMPREHENSION 1. Who was Clara Barton? *(She was a nurse during the Civil War.)*

2. Why does the wounded soldier call for his sister, Mary? *(He is delirious from his injuries and is badly frightened. He wants Mary to comfort him.)*

3. Why does he think that Barton is Mary? *(She allows him to assume that she is his sister because it brings him comfort.)*

4. What does the soldier ask Barton to do with the letter from his mother? *(He wants Barton to write her name alongside his mother's name. He wants both names by him when he dies.)*

CRITICAL THINKING 5. What three words would you use to describe Clara Barton? *(Answers will vary. Ask students to support what they say with evidence from the selection.)*

6. What is your opinion of Barton's decision to let the wounded soldier believe that she is Mary? *(Have students explain their feelings about her "lie of omission." Do they consider it justified in light of the soldier's agony?)*

Literary Skill

SETTING *Setting* is the time and place in which the events of a narrative happen. Although students know that the setting of "Caring for the Wounded" is a Civil War battlefield, ask them to find clues to the historical period ("flickering candle"), time ("three o'clock in the morning"), and physical location (wood, hills). Then ask what students can infer about medical care from the description of the battlefield setting.

GATHER YOUR THOUGHTS

The prewriting activities on page 40 will help prepare students to write a letter about an experience they had on the previous day. The first activity shows students how to **narrow the focus** of their writing. They will take a large topic, such as "Yesterday's Activities," and break it apart into a more manageable size.

On the second half of the page, students will **develop** their writing **topic** by answering a series of who, what, where, when, and why questions. Remind the class that much of the writing they do will involve answers to these 5-W questions (plus a sixth question about "how"). This holds true when they write for other classes, such as history and social studies.

Prewriting Strategies

TOPIC SENTENCES After students limit their topics, you may want to help them write an opening sentence for their letters. Explain that the first sentence of a paragraph is called the topic sentence. A topic sentence states the subject of the paragraph in addition to how the writer feels about the subject. This simple formula can help students write their topic sentences:

(A specific topic) + (a specific feeling) = a good topic sentence.

Have students use the **Prewriting** blackline master on page 86.

WRITE

Ask the class to read the directions at the top of page 41, and then have a volunteer summarize the assignment requirements. Remind students that when they write their **letter,** they'll need to use sensory details that help readers see, hear, feel, smell, and even taste the experience they describe.

WRITING RUBRIC Use this writing rubric to help students focus on the assignment requirements and for assistance with a quick assessment of their writing.

Do students' letters

* begin with a topic sentence that identifies the experience to be described?

* include a discussion of how the writer feels about the experience?

* provide personal facts or details to support that opinion?

Grammar, Usage, and Mechanics

After students have completed a first draft, refer them to the box on the right-hand side of page 41 and the **Writers' Checklist** on page 42. Remind the class to capitalize each word in the greeting but only the first word in the closing. Both the greeting and the closing are followed by a comma. In addition, students will need to remember the proper form for the letter's date. It appears at the top right-hand corner, with a comma separating the day from the year.

WRAP-UP

Take a moment at the end of the lesson for students to evaluate "Caring for the Wounded." Encourage students to use the **Readers' Checklist** as a starting point. When they've finished their silent reflections, ask the class to comment on whether they found the reading **easy** or difficult. If they found it challenging, ask them to explain why.

Assessment

To test students' comprehension, use the **Assessment** blackline master on page 87.

Name _____

VOCABULARY

Words from the Selection

DIRECTIONS To build vocabulary, answer these questions about five words from the selection.

1. If a soldier is being <u>cautious</u>, is she being careful or careless?

    _____

2. If a patient is in <u>anguish</u>, is he in pain or feeling better?

    _____

3. If your <u>abdomen</u> hurts, do you have a headache or a stomach ache?

    _____

4. If the weather is <u>dismal</u>, is it gloomy or bright? _____

5. If someone comes to <u>relieve</u> you, is she there to watch or help out?

    _____

Strategy Lesson: Latin Roots

DIRECTIONS Study this Latin root and its meaning. Then choose the word from the box that correctly fits in each sentence and write it on the blank.

aud- = hear

◆audible   ◆auditorium   ◆audience   ◆audition   ◆audiovisual

6. The school uses _____ equipment such as radios, VCRs, and television sets.

7. The students gathered in the _____ to hear the guest speaker.

8. The _____ behaved well during the presentation about the Civil War.

9. Without a microphone, the speaker would have been barely _____.

10. I wanted to try out for the school play, so I signed up for an _____.

Name _____

COMPREHENSION
Graphic Organizer

DIRECTIONS Use this storyboard to retell Clara Barton's experience with the wounded soldier. Put one event in each box. Then draw a quick sketch of the event.

1.	2.	3.

4.	5.	6.

Name _____

PREWRITING
Writing Sensory Details

When you write, try to make your details as meaningful and interesting as possible. If your details are boring, your writing will be boring. Sensory details can make your writing interesting. Sensory details are details that come to you through the senses *(smell, touch, taste, hearing,* and *sight)*. These kinds of details give the reader a "you are there" feeling.

EXAMPLE: *I could smell the spicy sausage on the grill and feel the warmth of the sun on my back.*

DIRECTIONS Imagine you are Clara Barton. What did you smell, taste, hear, see, and touch when you were caring for the wounded soldier?

I smelled _____

_____

I saw _____   I heard _____

_____   _____

_____   _____

_____   _____

I am Clara Barton. That
night on the battlefield . . .

_____

I looked _____   I tasted _____

_____   _____

_____   _____

_____   _____

This is how I felt when the night was over: _____

_____

_____

Name _____

ASSESSMENT

Multiple-Choice Test

DIRECTIONS On the blanks provided, write the letter of the best answer for each question.

_____ 1. Who asks Barton to come with him and see a soldier?
    A. another soldier   C. a general
    B. a surgeon   D. a farmer

_____ 2. In what part of his body has the soldier been wounded?
    A. in the abdomen   C. in the back
    B. in the leg   D. in the head

_____ 3. For whom does the wounded soldier call?
    A. Clara Barton   C. his sister
    B. his mother   D. his daughter

_____ 4. Why does the wounded soldier call for his loved one?
    A. He wants to say he is sorry.   C. He has a question to ask.
    B. He wants to reveal a secret.   D. He doesn't want to die alone.

_____ 5. What does Barton do when she sees the wounded soldier?
    A. She calls him Brother.   C. She calls him Husband.
    B. She calls him Son.   D. none of the above

_____ 6. How does the wounded soldier react to Barton's presence?
    A. He becomes happy.   C. He becomes confused.
    B. He becomes angry.   D. He becomes afraid.

_____ 7. What tells Barton that she did the right thing by pretending to be the soldier's sister?
    A. He falls quickly to sleep.   C. He immediately gets up.
    B. He cries tears of joy.   D. He asks for her forgiveness.

_____ 8. What does Barton do when the wounded soldier falls asleep?
    A. She goes back to her house.   C. She stays with him all night.
    B. She helps other soldiers.   D. She tries to find his family.

_____ 9. How does the wounded soldier react to Barton's "trick"?
    A. He is angry.   C. He is sad.
    B. He is grateful.   D. none of the above

_____ 10. What is in the wounded soldier's pocket?
    A. his mother's last letter   C. his address
    B. coins   D. a picture

Short-essay Test

Why do you think the wounded soldier wants Barton's name with him when he dies?

The President's Been Shot

Skills and Strategies Overview

THEME	Civil War
READING LEVEL	easy
VOCABULARY	✦fortify ✦frenzied ✦mortise ✦knobby ✦pandemonium
PREREADING	K-W-L
RESPONSE	react and connect
COMPREHENSION	reciprocal reading
PREWRITING	topic sentence and supporting details
WRITING	summary / run-on sentences
ASSESSMENT	enjoyment

BACKGROUND

John Wilkes Booth (1838–1865) assassinated President Lincoln at Ford's Theater in Washington, D.C., on April 14, 1865. Booth sympathized with the South during the Civil War, believed that Lincoln was responsible for the war, and was furious about Lincoln's stance on slavery. In the months leading up to the assassination, Booth organized a group whose aim was to kidnap Lincoln and ransom him in exchange for imprisoned Confederate soldiers. When the Confederate army surrendered on April 9, however, Booth changed his mind about the kidnapping plan and told the group that its agenda was now one of murder. Booth and his cohorts hoped to kill Lincoln first and then murder Vice-President Andrew Johnson, General Ulysses S. Grant, and Secretary of State William H. Seward.

After firing at Lincoln, Booth jumped to the theater stage shouting *Sic Semper Tyrannis!* (So perish all tyrants!), the Virginia state motto. With this short speech, the assassin made his sympathies perfectly clear. Booth broke his leg in the jump but escaped on horseback to Virginia. Federal troops trapped him in a barn. Booth refused to surrender and was shot.

UNIT THEME On April 14, 1865, President Abraham Lincoln became another casualty of the Civil War, the bloodiest war in U.S. history. Richard Bak reveals the events leading up to his murder.

GRAPHIC ORGANIZER A plot line can be used to show the progress of a narrative. This plot line shows the events surrounding the assassination of President Lincoln.

Booth rushes into Lincoln's box and fires a bullet into the President's head.

CLIMAX

He jams the outer door and pulls a pistol out from under his coat.

Booth jumps from the box onto the stage and shouts "Sic Semper Tyrannis!"

RISING ACTION

FALLING ACTION

Booth bores a peephole so that he can see Lincoln in the box.

Booth escapes on horseback to Virginia.

Booth gathers supplies and arrives at Ford's Theater early in the day.

Federal troops capture and kill Booth in a barn near Port Royal, Virginia.

EXPOSITION

RESOLUTION

BEFORE YOU READ

Remind students of the theme of this unit: Civil War. Then read aloud the opening of the lesson. When students are ready to begin, ask them to turn to the prereading activity, a **K-W-L**. (Refer to the **Strategy Handbook** on page 40 for more help.)

Motivation Strategy

ENGAGING STUDENTS Divide the chalkboard into two sections with the headings "Myths" and "Facts." Ask the class to say what they know about Lincoln's assassination. Have them sort what they know into the two categories. After they've finished the reading, they can return to the lists they made and move items from one side to the other as needed.

Vocabulary Building

Help students use **context clues** as they read to figure out the meanings of difficult words, especially the key vocabulary for this lesson: *fortify, frenzied, mortise, knobby,* and *pandemonium.* Ask students to circle these words in the text. Although the footnotes define these words, you may want to model using context and then checking your ideas against the footnote: "I don't know the word *mortise.* I see, though, that it appears after a sentence describing a hole Booth cut in the plaster so that he could observe Lincoln. Could *mortise* mean 'hole'? I can check the footnote to see if my guess is correct." For additional practice with these words, see page 92.

STRATEGY LESSON: HOMOGRAPHS As an additional vocabulary strategy, you might want to teach a lesson on homographs. Homographs can cause difficulty for low-level readers or students who speak English as a second language. Show students this list of homographs, all of which are in "The President's Been Shot." Ask them to think of two different definitions for each word: *bored, box,* and *lines.*

For additional practice on this strategy, see the **Vocabulary** blackline master on page 92.

Prereading Strategies

A **K-W-L** can be helpful to those students who have trouble settling down to read and write. In addition to assisting with organization, the K-W-L gives students the chance to activate prior knowledge about a subject. After recording what they already know, they can think carefully about gaps in their knowledge. This way, *they* (as opposed to *you)* decide what they need to learn.

QUICKWRITE As an alternate prereading strategy, ask students to do a quickwrite that is related to the theme of the unit. If you like, assign a topic from the list below and ask students to write for one minute about this topic without stopping. Encourage students to include sensory details (details that appeal to the five senses) in their writing. Later, they may want to use some of their images in their summaries. Possible topics for a quickwrite include:

- a famous Civil War battle

- heroes of the Civil War

- John Wilkes Booth

- the assassination of Abraham Lincoln

Spanish-speaking Students

En esta selección Richard Bak explica los momentos inmediatamente antes y después del asesinato de Abraham Lincoln. El presidente estuvo con su mujer en un teatro viendo una comedia cuando John Wilkes Booth lo mató. No se sabe exactamente las últimas palabras del presidente, pero sí se sabe que el teatro erupтó en pandemónium al oír el disparo fatal.

II. READ

> As students begin to read, point out the sample response in the **Response Notes** on page 44 and then explain the purpose of **react** and **connect**. Remind the class that when they make personal connections to a story or an article, the piece becomes easier to understand and more interesting to read. Each time a thought or an idea occurs to them, they should make a note of it in the margins of their book. Later, they can refer to these notes as they write their summaries.

Response Strategy

QUESTION As an alternate response strategy, ask students to keep a running list of questions in the **Response Notes**. When they've finished Bak's piece, have volunteers read their questions aloud. Work as a class to find answers.

Comprehension Strategies

Students will do a **reciprocal reading** of "The President's Been Shot." During a reciprocal reading, students read the selection aloud in pairs or small groups, switching readers after every page. As students read, they'll be asked to answer questions that help them predict outcomes, clarify the action of the narrative, summarize the events, and raise additional questions about the topic. Encourage students to stop as often as they like during their oral readings to make comments or ask questions of each other.

PREDICTION Another comprehension strategy that will work well with "The President's Been Shot" is predicting. Making predictions as they read can help students stay interested and alert. At the bottom of each page, students can stop and decide what they think will happen next. Even the most general prediction questions, such as "What will Booth do now?," can prompt meaningful responses. When they've finished reading, students can review their predictions to see which came true.

For more help, see the **Comprehension** blackline master on page 93.

Discussion Questions

COMPREHENSION 1. Who was John Wilkes Booth? *(He was President Abraham Lincoln's assassin.)*

2. Where was Lincoln murdered? *(at a theater while attending a play)*

3. How did Booth escape from the box and the theater after shooting Lincoln? *(He jumped down to the stage and ran out the back door. He had a getaway horse waiting for him.)*

CRITICAL THINKING 4. Why might Booth have chosen this time and place to kill Lincoln? *(Lincoln would not be in motion, his attention would be focused on the stage, and his back would be to the door.)*

5. Why do you think there are two versions of Lincoln's last words? *(Students might suggest that Mary Lincoln was confused or upset or that she later wanted Lincoln's last words to be memorable.)*

Literary Skill

CHRONOLOGICAL ORDER Bak uses *chronological order* to tell the story of Lincoln's assassination. You might take this opportunity to teach a brief lesson on time order and the use of transitions in a narrative. Remind students that when writers use chronological order, they usually use time order transitional words and phrases to help the narrative read smoothly. Words and phrases such as *first, last, later, after that, the next day, a week later,* and so on cue readers as to where they are in the story. You might want to keep a list of transitional words and phrases posted on the board. Students can refer to the list as they write their paragraphs, articles, and essays.

III. GATHER YOUR THOUGHTS

Prewriting Strategies

The prewriting activities on page 48 will help students reflect carefully on the information in Bak's article. Students' purpose is to sort through what they have learned so that they can write a detailed, accurate **summary** of "The President's Been Shot." Students will begin by writing a **topic sentence** and **details**. Remind the class that the supporting details they choose should tell the who, what, where, when, why, and how of the topic.

When they have finished writing their topic sentence and details, students will write a closing sentence that restates the topic sentence and leaves the reader with something interesting or important to think about.

Have students use the **Prewriting** blackline master on page 94.

IV. WRITE

Set aside plenty of time for students to write their **summaries.** Since Bak's article is highly detailed, you might want to allow some additional time for them to complete the writing assignment. Remind them to consult their topic sentence / supporting details organizer as they write.

WRITING RUBRIC Use this writing rubric to help students focus on the assignment requirements and for assistance with a quick assessment of their writing.

Do students' summaries

- clearly state Bak's main idea?

- explain how he supports his main idea?

- include a discussion of the most important details from the text?

Grammar, Usage, and Mechanics

When students have finished their rough drafts, have them review the information on the **Writers' Checklist.** Consider teaching a mini-lesson on run-on sentences. Explain that a run-on sentence is actually two sentences joined without adequate punctuation or a connecting word. Writers can fix a run-on either by breaking it into two separate sentences or by adding a comma and/or a conjunction such as *and, or, but, so,* or *yet.* For example:

Incorrect: I thought Booth would make a mistake he didn't.

Correct: I thought Booth would make a mistake, but he didn't.

Correct: I thought Booth would make a mistake. He didn't.

V. WRAP-UP

Take a moment at the end of the lesson for students to reflect, using the **Readers' Checklist.** This checklist asks students to judge their **enjoyment** of "The President's Been Shot" and models for them the type of questions good readers ask themselves when they've finished a reading.

Assessment

To test students' comprehension, use the **Assessment** blackline master on page 95.

Name _____

VOCABULARY

Words from the Selection

DIRECTIONS To build vocabulary, answer these questions about five words from the selection.

1. If an advertisement says a vitamin will <u>fortify</u> your body, does it mean that it will strengthen or weaken you? _____

2. If people run out of a theater in a <u>frenzied</u> manner, are they calm or crazed?
   _____

3. If there is a <u>mortise</u> in the wall, is there a patch or a hole?
   _____

4. Are a boy's <u>knobby</u> knees bony or muscular? _____

5. If there is <u>pandemonium</u> in the lobby, is there confusion or silence?
   _____

Strategy Lesson: Homographs

A *homograph* is a word that has the same spelling as another word but a different origin and meaning. For example, *date* (day, month, and year) and *date* (sweet dark fruit) are homographs.

DIRECTIONS Circle the correct meaning for the underlined homograph in each sentence.

6. Booth was not a <u>fan</u> of President Lincoln. (device to stir up the air, admirer)

7. No one was able to <u>foil</u> Booth's plan to assassinate Lincoln. (prevent from carrying out, metal sheet)

8. We tried to <u>pry</u> the gun out of his hands before it was too late. (look with curiosity, lift with force)

9. Booth <u>bored</u> through the door so that he could see Lincoln. (made a hole, made weary)

10. Booth left the theater several times while the <u>play</u> was in progress. (have fun, dramatic performance)

Name _____

COMPREHENSION
Graphic Organizer

DIRECTIONS Use this time line to show the sequence of events Richard Bak describes in "The President's Been Shot." Feel free to use your book if you need to.

First . . .

↓

Next . . .

↓

Then . . .

↓

After that . . .

↓

Finally . . .

Name _____

PREWRITING

Writing a Summary

To write a good summary, you must select the most important ideas and combine them into clear, easy-to-understand sentences.

DIRECTIONS Follow these steps to write a summary for "The President's Been Shot."

STEP 1. READ. Read the article carefully. Highlight key words and phrases.

STEP 2. LIST. Make a list of the most important events and quotes in the article.

Important events and quotes:

- _____
- _____
- _____
- _____

STEP 3. CHOOSE. Select the most important event or quote from your list and make this the main idea of your summary. Write a topic sentence that states the main idea.

Richard Bak's main idea in "The President's Been Shot" is:

_____

_____

STEP 4. FIND DETAILS. Gather important details from the article. Names, dates, times, and places are examples of important details.

Bak's important details:

1.	6.
2.	7.
3.	8.
4.	9.
5.	10.

STEP 5. WRITE. Now write your summary.

⇒ Begin with the topic sentence.

⇒ Then summarize Bak's most important details.

⇒ End with a concluding sentence that ties everything together.

Name _____

ASSESSMENT

Multiple-Choice Test

DIRECTIONS On the blanks provided, write the letter of the best answer for each question.

_____ 1. Where was Lincoln assassinated?
   A. at a hospital
   B. at the White House
   C. at an elderly man's home
   D. at a theater

_____ 2. Why did Booth leave the theater several times during the play?
   A. to look for his ride
   B. to check his gun
   C. to have a drink
   D. to watch for police

_____ 3. What role did Edmund Spangler play in the assassination?
   A. He gave Booth a pistol and knife.
   B. He held Booth's getaway horse.
   C. He helped Booth find the presidential box.
   D. He distracted Mrs. Lincoln.

_____ 4. How did Booth prepare for the assassination?
   A. He drilled a peephole.
   B. He jammed the door.
   C. He brought along a gun and knife.
   D. all of the above

_____ 5. According to Mrs. Lincoln, where did Lincoln say he wanted to visit?
   A. London
   B. France
   C. Jerusalem
   D. Athens

_____ 6. What did actor Harry Hawk remember about Mrs. Lincoln?
   A. She was smiling.
   B. She had something in her hand.
   C. She seemed nervous.
   D. She was sleeping.

_____ 7. What did Edwin Emerson hear while standing in the wings?
   A. He heard a horse running away.
   B. He heard the crack of a pistol.
   C. He heard a prop fall.
   D. He heard a cymbal crash.

_____ 8. Why weren't people behind the stage surprised to hear the loud sound?
   A. They couldn't hear it.
   B. It sounded like the moving of sets.
   C. It sounded like clapping.
   D. none of the above

_____ 9. Why didn't anyone stop Booth from running to the stage door?
   A. They were looking the other way.
   B. Booth paid them to let him go.
   C. They didn't recognize him as an assassin.
   D. They were afraid.

_____ 10. How did people in the theater find out about the shooting?
   A. The news spread by word of mouth.
   B. They read about it in the newspaper.
   C. They were told by the police.
   D. none of the above

Short-essay Test

Why do you think Booth shouted, *"Sic Semper Tyrannis!"* (So perish all tyrants!), after he shot Lincoln?

Paul Fleischman

Unit Background   **PAUL FLEISCHMAN** (pages 51–68)

Four excerpts from the fictional *Bull Run* by Paul Fleischman are included in this chapter.

Paul Fleischman was born in 1952 and grew up in Santa Monica, California. He attended the University of California at Berkeley from 1970 to 1972 and received a B.A. from the University of New Mexico in 1977. He has written many books for young readers. Some of his most recent titles include *A Fate Totally Worse Than Death* (1995), *Dateline: Troy* (1996), *Whirligig* (1998), *Mind's Eye* (1999), and *Cannibal in the Mirror* (2000).

Some details about the Bull Run battles are included in this guide with the introduction to the second excerpt on page 106. Toby Boyce is a southern character, and Gideon Adams, Shem Suggs, and Judah Jenkins are northern characters.

Teaching the Introduction

Two young Civil War soldiers and the book cover of *Bull Run* are shown on page 51.

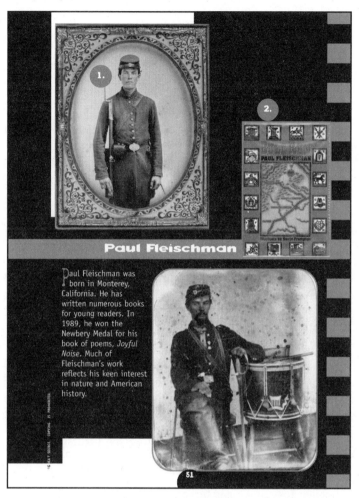

Paul Fleischman

Paul Fleischman was born in Monterey, California. He has written numerous books for young readers. In 1989, he won the Newbery Medal for his book of poems, *Joyful Noise*. Much of Fleischman's work reflects his keen interest in nature and American history.

51

1. Students interested in the Civil War might like to research various uniforms worn by Confederate and Union soldiers and report to the class.

2. A wealth of detail exists about the Bull Run battles; interested students might research one or both battles. Alternatively, students who have visited or live near Bull Run or Manassas or another Civil War battlefield might report to the class.

Opening Activity

At the end of *Bull Run,* Fleischman provides a list of southern and northern characters and the page numbers on which they appear and reappear as an aid to those who might like to perform *Bull Run* as readers' theater. If this is an option for your class, obtain the book, and start preparing readers. Characters, all fictional except for General Irvin McDowell, are both male and female, though there are more males.

Toby Boyce and Gideon Adams

STUDENT PAGES 52–60

Skills and Strategies Overview

THEME	Paul Fleischman
READING LEVEL	easy
VOCABULARY	◆Yankee ◆miracle ◆furrowed ◆regiment ◆daze
PREREADING	walk-through
RESPONSE	question
COMPREHENSION	double-entry journal
PREWRITING	cluster diagram
WRITING	character sketch / capitalization
ASSESSMENT	depth

BACKGROUND

The Civil War (1861–1865) took more American lives than any other war in history. Unlike any war before or after, the Civil War was so divisive that in some families, brother fought against brother and father fought against son. The chief issue at stake during the Civil War was slavery. The southern states were determined to preserve slavery and thus retain their agricultural way of life. The northern states wanted to end slavery and continue moving toward a more industrial way of life.

When the Civil War started, neither the North nor the South had a plan in place to call up troops for fighting. The two sides tried to enlist as many volunteers as they could and sometimes paid an enlistment fee (or bounty) to every man who agreed to join. Because enthusiasm for the cause ran high at the beginning of the war, recruitment offices on both sides were flooded with volunteers. Even those who were not eligible to enlist begged to be taken.

UNIT THEME In this excerpt from the novel *Bull Run,* Paul Fleischman explores the eagerness some men and boys felt about enlisting during the Civil War.

GRAPHIC ORGANIZER Although Toby Boyce and Gideon Adams represent different sides of the conflict, they are very similar. A Venn diagram can be used to compare the two characters.

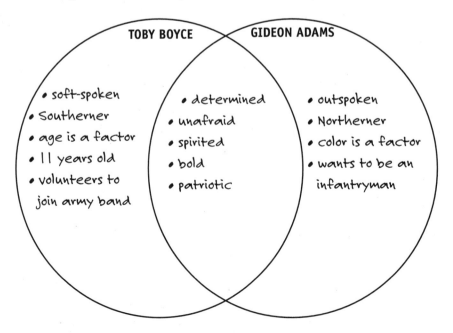

TOBY BOYCE / GIDEON ADAMS

- soft-spoken
- Southerner
- age is a factor
- 11 years old
- volunteers to join army band

- determined
- unafraid
- spirited
- bold
- patriotic

- outspoken
- Northerner
- color is a factor
- wants to be an infantryman

BEFORE YOU READ

Read the introduction to the lesson with students. If you have not already done so, offer information about the Civil War or the battles of Bull Run. Then ask them to complete the prereading activity, a **walk-through**. (Refer to the **Strategy Handbook** on page 40 for more help.)

Motivation Strategy

In "Toby Boyce" and "Gideon Adams," Paul Fleischman tells the story of two soldiers who are eager to serve in the Civil War. Ask students to complete this sentence: "The Civil War was _____." See how many different responses students offer. Make a list on the board and then return to their comments after the reading. What would students like to add to or subtract from the list?

ENGAGING STUDENTS Ask students to summarize or retell their favorite Civil War story. It might be a story that has been passed down through their families, or a story they've seen on TV or read about in a book. Why do they like it? What makes this war, above all others, so fascinating to most people?

Vocabulary Building

Your students will benefit from as much vocabulary work as you can give them. Help them get to the point where they automatically search for **context clues** each time they come to a word they don't recognize or understand. Show them the key vocabulary words for this lesson: *Yankee, miracle, furrowed, regiment,* and *daze.* Have students circle these words in the text. Ask them to try to define each one using context clues. After they've made a guess about the meaning of a given word, they can check the footnote definition to see if their guess is correct. For more practice, have students complete the **Vocabulary** blackline master on page 102.

STRATEGY LESSON: SYNONYMS As an alternate vocabulary strategy, teach a short lesson on synonyms. Explain that sometimes it is easier to memorize the synonym for a word than its full dictionary definition. Show students a list of words from the selection. What synonyms can they come up with? If one or more words cause problems, have students consult a dictionary or a thesaurus. You might include these words from the selection on your list: *limp, ambled,* and *pluck.*

For additional practice on this strategy, see the **Vocabulary** blackline master on page 102.

Prereading Strategies

Although they might not realize it, readers often do a quick **walk-through** before they begin reading almost any story or article. Remind students to take their time as they do their walk-throughs of the Fleischman selection. Be sure to give students enough time to make some thorough notes on page 52. This process of previewing and reflecting will help them become more careful readers.

Spanish-speaking Students

Toby Boyce anhela particpar en la Guerra Civil y vencer a los yanquis del norte. Sabiendo que es demasiado joven para luchar en las batallas, decide tocar un instrumento para el grupo de músico del ejército. A él no le importa que no sabe tocar. La siguiente leyenda también se trata de un joven que quiere luchar en la guerra. Pero éste es un negro que desea vencer el sur, y como Toby Boyce, está dispuesto a hacer cualquier cosa para participar.

II. READ

Response Strategy

Before students begin to read, walk through the process of responding to literature. Introduce the strategy of **questioning** and point out the example given on page 53. Explain to the class that each time a question occurs to them, they should make a note of it in their **Response Notes**. If you like, read the first paragraph of "Toby Boyce" as a group, and then ask volunteers to suggest possible questions about the text. It may help your students to hear several different types of questions that they could ask.

Comprehension Strategies

Using a **double-entry journal** encourages active response to text. Students read or find statements, quotes, ideas, or events in the selection, record them, and then write their thoughts and reactions. Rather than paraphrase, they raise questions about what they're reading and note their reactions. (Remind them to go beyond "I like/don't like this sentence or idea." They can use this as a starting point if they like, but they will need to elaborate a bit and support their opinion.) If you like, work through the first entry on page 54 as a class. Discuss their reactions to and ideas about the quotation from the story. After the discussion, have students make a note of their own ideas in the right-hand column of the journal box.

RECIPROCAL READING Another comprehension strategy that will work well with this selection is a reciprocal reading with a partner. Ask students to take turns reading aloud, switching readers after every page or so. As they read, students should work to 1. clarify the problem, characters, and setting of the story (When and where does the story take place?); 2. predict what will happen (Will Gideon be able to change the recruiter's mind?); 3. summarize the events (What does Toby do when he's told he can't join?); and 4. ask questions about the literature (Which character do you admire most?).

For more help, see the **Comprehension** blackline master on page 103.

Discussion Questions

COMPREHENSION 1. Why is Toby Boyce ineligible to enlist? *(He is too young.)*

2. What does he do to convince the recruiter to find him a place in the army? *(He asks for a place in the band and then shows pluck during his audition.)*

3. Why is Gideon Adams ineligible to enlist? *(He is African American.)*

4. How does he get himself accepted into the army? *(He clips his hair short and buys a bigger cap to cover his hair.)*

CRITICAL THINKING 5. What do Toby Boyce and Gideon Adams have in common? How are they different? *(Invite students to make a comparison between the two characters, using examples from the text to support what they say.)*

Literary Skill

DYNAMIC AND STATIC CHARACTERS You might use the two Fleischman selections as an opportunity to introduce dynamic and static characters. In literature, a *dynamic character* is one who changes over the course of the story. A *static*, or flat, *character* stays the same throughout the story. Usually there are many forces that bring about a change in character. Plot events or action can precipitate a change. Ideas or information from another character can also initiate change. Invite students to discuss changes they see in Toby Boyce and Gideon Adams throughout the stories.

III. GATHER YOUR THOUGHTS

Prewriting Strategies

The **cluster diagram** at the top of page 58 will help students explore one of Fleischman's characters in some detail. Be sure students consult the text as they fill in the circles. They should strive to be as detailed as possible and can write outside of the circles if they run out of room.

Next, students will make a connection between the fictional characters and two people they know from their own lives. Section B shows them how easy it can be to create a bridge between a story and a personal experience. Students who write from personal experience tend to be more focused and direct in their writing.

Students will finish the prewriting activities by creating another cluster. This time they'll describe characteristics of a real person. When they've finished the cluster, they'll have a series of details that they can use in a character sketch. All that will remain is for them to write a topic sentence for the paragraph.

Have students use the **Prewriting** blackline master on page 104.

IV. WRITE

Be sure students understand what's involved in writing a **character sketch**. Explain that a character sketch is a short piece of writing that reveals or shows something important about a real person or a fictional character.

WRITING RUBRIC Use this writing rubric to help you evaluate the quality of students' writing.

Do students' character sketches

- open with a topic sentence that names the person to be described?

- contain details that help the reader get to know this person?

- end with a closing sentence that ties things together?

Grammar, Usage, and Mechanics

After students have written a first draft, have them stop and think carefully about the level of their description. Have they offered enough, or should they add more?

When they are ready to proofread their work, refer them to the **Writers' Checklist.** Remind the class to capitalize proper nouns and the pronoun *I*.

Incorrect: i walked to humboldt park to meet jeremy.

Correct: I walked to Humboldt Park to meet Jeremy.

V. WRAP-UP

Take a moment at the end of the lesson to check the **depth** of students' understanding, using the **Readers' Checklist.** Remind the class that these questions are the kind that good readers ask themselves each time they finish reading a story or article.

Assessment

To test students' comprehension, use the **Assessment** blackline master on page 105.

Name _____

VOCABULARY

Words from the Selection

DIRECTIONS To build vocabulary, answer these questions about five words from the selection.

1. Did a <u>Yankee</u> soldier fight for the North or South during the Civil War?

   _____

2. Is a <u>miracle</u> an amazing or an ordinary thing? _____

3. Is a <u>furrowed</u> brow straight or wrinkled? _____

4. If a military general places a <u>regiment</u> in enemy territory, does that mean that one person or a group of people go? _____

5. If you are in a <u>daze</u>, are you confused or aware of what is going on?

   _____

Strategy Lesson: Synonyms

A *synonym* is a word that has the same or almost the same meaning as another word. For example, *grateful* is a synonym for *appreciative*. Knowing the synonym for a word is like knowing a short cut for the word's definition.

DIRECTIONS Substitute a synonym from the box for the underlined word.

◇impolite   ◇limp   ◇infantry   ◇scowled   ◇commmenced

6. The recruiter <u>frowned</u> at me when he found out I was too young to join.

   _____

7. I felt <u>weak</u> with relief when I saw that help was on the way.

   _____

8. I <u>began</u> playing trumpet when I was ten years old. _____

9. Many patriotic citizens wanted to join the <u>army</u>. _____

10. I was told in a <u>rude</u> manner to stop playing my instrument.

    _____

Name _____

COMPREHENSION
Graphic Organizers

DIRECTIONS Focus on either Toby Boyce or Gideon Adams. What do his words and actions tell you about him? Look over the story again and record some details on this chart.

My inferences about _____

(write character name here)

Things the character says and does	What his words and actions show
1.	
2.	
3.	
4.	
5.	

DIRECTIONS Now look over the chart you just completed. Write five to ten words that describe Toby Boyce or Gideon Adams on the web below.

character name

Name _____

PREWRITING

Writing a Character Sketch

DIRECTIONS Follow these steps to write a character sketch.

STEP 1. Write a topic sentence. Use this formula:

(A specific person) + (a specific feeling about this person) = a good topic sentence.

My topic sentence:

_____

STEP 2. Write three qualities or characteristics of the person you want to describe. (Use your cluster on page 58 for ideas.) Then write one piece of "proof" for each characteristic you name.

characteristic #1: _____

• proof: _____

characteristic #2: _____

• proof: _____

characteristic #3: _____

• proof: _____

STEP 3 Write a concluding sentence that explains how you feel about the person you've described. Try to make your concluding sentence funny or interesting.

My concluding sentence:

_____

_____

Name _____

ASSESSMENT

Multiple-Choice Test

DIRECTIONS On the blanks provided, write the letter of the item that best answers each question or completes each statement.

_____ 1. How old is Toby Boyce when he joins the army?
A. 17   C. 13
B. 15   D. 11

_____ 2. Where does Toby Boyce live?
A. Georgia   C. New York
B. Kentucky   D. California

_____ 3. What plan does Toby Boyce come up with so that he can enlist?
A. He tries to pass as a white soldier.   C. He stands on tiptoe.
B. He decides to join the army band.   D. He puts on a fake beard.

_____ 4. The main problem with Toby's plan is that . . .
A. he is too short.   C. his skin is too dark.
B. he can't play an instrument.   D. all of the above

_____ 5. Whose words inspire Toby Boyce?
A. his father's   C. his grandfather's
B. his grandmother's   D. the enlisting officer's

_____ 6. What is the miracle to which Toby Boyce refers?
A. His plan works.   C. The war ends.
B. His plan doesn't work.   D. The Battle of Bull Run is won.

_____ 7. Why does the enlisting officer refuse to admit Gideon Adams as a soldier?
A. Gideon is African American.   C. Gideon is too young.
B. Gideon is not patriotic.   D. Gideon is too educated.

_____ 8. According to Fleischman, what options did African Americans have if they wanted to help the war effort?
A. They could sign on as cooks.   C. They could sign on as teamsters.
B. They could sign on as ditch   D. all of the above
diggers.

_____ 9. What does Gideon Adams do to become an infantry soldier?
A. He cuts his hair.   C. He changes his name.
B. He buys a bigger cap.   D. all of the above

_____ 10. At the end of the selection, Gideon is nervous about . . .
A. fighting in a war.   C. losing his friends.
B. having his identity revealed.   D. none of the above

Short-essay Test

In what ways are Toby Boyce and Gideon Adams similar? Support your answer with evidence from the text.

Shem Suggs and Judah Jenkins

Skills and Strategies Overview

THEME	Paul Fleischman
READING LEVEL	easy
VOCABULARY	✦hooves ✦legions ✦muskets ✦courier ✦galloped
PREREADING	word chain
RESPONSE	clarify
COMPREHENSION	retell
PREWRITING	brainstorm
WRITING	dialogue / proper form for dialogue
ASSESSMENT	style

BACKGROUND

Paul Fleischman's *Bull Run* is a historical novel comprising a series of brief vignettes, each of which explores the life, thoughts, and feelings of a fictitious man or woman who participated in some way in the Battles of Bull Run.

Bull Run is a stream in northeast Virginia where two Civil War battles took place. The first Battle of Bull Run (1861) was the first great battle of the Civil War. It was devastating for both North and South, with both sides losing in excess of 2,000 troops. More significantly, this battle sounded the warning bell that the Civil War would not be a quick, three-month conflict, as some leaders in the North and South had predicted. The second Battle of Bull Run (1862) was even bloodier than the first. In all, more than 25,000 soldiers were killed or wounded on this small piece of ground in Virginia. After the second Battle of Bull Run, it became more difficult to find men and women willing to risk their lives for a war that was quickly becoming a bloodbath.

General Beauregard, mentioned in line 2 of the second selection, was a Confederate general during the first battle.

UNIT THEME Paul Fleischman explores the fear many soldiers felt on the eve of the first great battle of the Civil War.

GRAPHIC ORGANIZER This main idea/supporting details organizer explores one of Fleischman's main ideas in *Bull Run*.

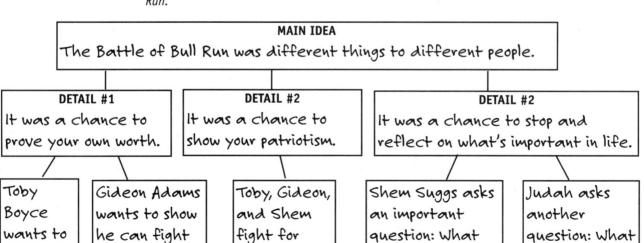

MAIN IDEA
The Battle of Bull Run was different things to different people.

DETAIL #1
It was a chance to prove your own worth.

DETAIL #2
It was a chance to show your patriotism.

DETAIL #2
It was a chance to stop and reflect on what's important in life.

Toby Boyce wants to kill a Yankee.

Gideon Adams wants to show he can fight as well as white men.

Toby, Gideon, and Shem fight for what they believe in.

Shem Suggs asks an important question: What are we doing here?

Judah asks another question: What do I do now to save myself?

BEFORE YOU READ

Remind students of the theme of the unit (Civil War), and then explain that they'll be reading two more selections from Fleischman's *Bull Run*. Then have them complete the prereading activity, a **word chain**. (Refer to the **Strategy Handbook** on page 40 for more help.)

Motivation Strategy

Have students complete this sentence: "War is _____ because _____." If you have time, discuss their responses in some detail. Encourage students to make a connection between the theme of war and their own lives.

ENGAGING STUDENTS Have students tell about war movies they've seen. What are some themes and ideas repeated in several of these movies? What are common storylines or examples of stock characters? Students can keep an eye out for these elements as they are reading "Shem Suggs" and "Judah Jenkins."

Vocabulary Building

Help students pronounce and define the key vocabulary words for this lesson: *hooves, legions, muskets, courier,* and *galloped*. Ask students to circle these words in the text. Although the words may be familiar to students, they may be unsure of the dictionary definition for each and how the words might be used in the context of a discussion about the Civil War. Ask students to use the words together in a paragraph about war. Check to be sure that each of the five words is used correctly. For more practice with these and other words, see page 110.

STRATEGY LESSON: ETYMOLOGIES If you feel students would benefit from an additional vocabulary strategy, you might teach a brief lesson on etymologies. As you know, the etymology of a word is an explanation of the origin and history of the word. For example, *biology* has the base word *bio*, which comes from the Greek word *bios*, meaning "life." Help students learn some common base words and their origins (see the list below). Ask them to make lists of words that use these base words.

- *civ* from the Latin *civis*, meaning "citizen"

- *bio* from the Greek *bios*, meaning "life"

- *chrono* from the Greek *chronos*, meaning "time"

For additional practice on this strategy, see the **Vocabulary** blackline master on page 110.

Prereading Strategies

A **word chain** helps students explore the connotative and denotative definitions of words that are thematically important to a selection. The words on page 61 relate to Fleischman's theme of war. Students will look at the list of words (*retreat, forward, blood,* and *roar*), make a prediction about the story they're about to read, and then use the words together in a "story" of their own about war. If you like, have students work together on this activity. They can consult a dictionary if they don't know a word's meaning, but the four words are simple enough that students should have no trouble coming up with quick definitions on their own.

Spanish-speaking Students

En "Shem Suggs" un soldado en la Guerra Civil espera inquietamente la batalla. Nota la hipocresía de los otros soldados que hablan apasionadamente de la gloria de la guerra antes de leer la Biblia. Al oír la leyenda de *Gulliver's Travels*, que describe un mundo donde no hay guerra, decide que tiene que sobrevivir para poder leer la novela algún día. "Judah Jenkins" es el cuento de un mensajero en la Guerra Civil que aprende del peligro de las batallas cuando apenas evade las balas del enemigo.

When students are ready to begin their close readings, remind them how important it will be for them to make notes that **clarify** the action and events Fleischman describes. These notes will be especially important later, when students will need to remember which character is which. Also encourage them to jot down their questions in the **Response Notes**. You may want to pause after the reading to answer any questions that are still bothering students.

Response Strategy

VISUALIZE Fleischman uses sensory language to help readers visualize the people and places about which he writes. As an alternate response strategy, have students sketch what they "see" in the **Response Notes**. Students can use these sketches later if you decide to ask them to summarize the two selections.

Comprehension Strategies

Be sure students understand that as they are reading, they'll need to stop occasionally in order to **retell** the events described. Retelling a story or article can help readers make connections between events and ideas. Retelling can also help students clarify in their own minds what exactly has occurred. This is a particularly good strategy to use with selections that are challenging or concern a topic that is remote from students' personal experiences. Remind the class that when they retell, they'll need to be thorough but brief. At each **stop and retell**, they should limit themselves to just a sentence or two. In order to do this, they'll need to decide which details are most important to the plot.

For more help, see the **Comprehension** blackline master on page 111.

Discussion Questions

COMPREHENSION 1. Who is Shem Suggs? *(He is a soldier preparing for battle.)*

2. What book does he promise himself he'll read if he makes it out of the war alive? *(Gulliver's Travels)*

3. What impresses him about this book? *(He likes the thought of a land run by horses, a peaceful type of animal. He also likes the fact that there are no wars in this land.)*

4. What is Judah Jenkins's job in the war? *(He is a courier.)*

5. What happens to Jenkins on his trip toward enemy lines? *(His horse is frightened by cannon fire and bolts.)*

CRITICAL THINKING 6. What is the mood in Shem Suggs's camp in the days leading up to the battle? *(Answers will vary. Possible: tense, fearful, reflective.)*

7. How would you describe Shem Suggs and Judah Jenkins? *(Answers will vary. Invite students to compare the two characters using quotations from the text to support their interpretations.)*

Literary Skill

THEME One literary term to introduce with "Shem Suggs" and "Judah Jenkins" is **theme**. Remind the class that *theme* is the main idea or underlying meaning of a literary work. It is what the author wants the reader to remember most about the selection. Some works contain one theme. Others contain several. A theme statement usually expresses an opinion about a topic. For example, Fleischman's topics are the lives of young Civil War recruits. A theme statement might be "Fear was a constant companion to young Civil War soldiers."

III. GATHER YOUR THOUGHTS

Prewriting Strategies

The prewriting activities on page 66 are designed to prepare students to write an imaginary **dialogue** between themselves and one of Fleischman's characters. As a first step, they'll decide to which character they'd most like to "talk." Then they'll work in a small group to **brainstorm** a list of five or more questions they'd like to ask this character. Remind the groups to come up with questions that require more than a simple yes or no response.

Finally, students will write a sample bit of dialogue between themselves and the character. If they like, they can play the role of interviewer and the character can be the "interviewee." Another option is for students to pretend that they too are at the battlefront with the character. What might two soldiers preparing for battle talk about?

Have students use the **Prewriting** blackline master on page 112.

IV. WRITE

Be sure students understand that a **dialogue** is a conversation between two or more people or characters. In dialogue, one person speaks, a second person responds, and then the first person responds to what the second person has said.

WRITING RUBRIC Have students answer the questions on this rubric before submitting a final draft.

Does my dialogue

- involve one of Fleischman's characters?

- make sense?

- sound as if real people are speaking?

Grammar, Usage, and Mechanics

After students have written a first draft, have them stop and think carefully about their work. Be sure they reread the dialogue and check that it flows well. If you like, have students get together in pairs and act out the dialogue. They'll be able to "hear" lines that are not good, and they can revise them later as needed.

When students are ready to proofread their work, refer them to the **Writers' Checklist.** At this point, you might want to introduce a brief lesson on writing dialogue. Show students the example at the bottom of page 66. Then ask them to correct this snippet of dialogue:

Incorrect: I'd like to ride off on my horse and never come back here Shem whispered

Don't do that" his tent mate replied. "You'll miss all the action!

Correct: "I'd like to ride off on my horse and never come back here," Shem whispered.

"Don't do that," his tent mate replied. "You'll miss all the action!"

V. WRAP-UP

Take a moment at the end of the lesson for students to think about what they've read. Ask them to comment on Fleischman's writing **style** using the questions on the **Readers' Checklist** as a starting point.

Assessment

To test students' comprehension, use the **Assessment** blackline master on page 113.

Name _____

VOCABULARY
Words from the Selection

DIRECTIONS Answer the questions by writing one of the words from the list.

> ◆hooves ◆legions ◆muskets ◆courier ◆galloped

Which word would you use to describe

1. how you traveled on a fast horse? _____

2. someone who delivers messages? _____

3. large numbers of soldiers? _____

4. a horse's feet? _____

5. guns with long barrels? _____

Strategy Lesson: Etymologies

An *etymology* is an explanation of the origin and history of a word. For example, *captain* comes from the Latin word *caput* meaning "head."

DIRECTIONS Study the etymology of the word part *civ-*. Then draw a line between each word or phrase on the left and its meaning on the right.

> *civ-* from the Latin *civis*, which means "citizen"

6. civilized   A. war between opposing groups of one nation

7. civilian   B. study of the duties, privileges, and rights of citizens

8. civilization   C. having a highly developed society and culture

9. civics   D. rights guaranteed to all citizens

10. civil war   E. advanced state of development in human society

11. civil rights   F. person who is not in the armed forces

12. civil disobedience   G. refusal to obey civil laws

Name _____

COMPREHENSION
Graphic Organizer

DIRECTIONS Before you can write in the voice of a character, you need to be sure you really understand who the character is.

1. First decide which character you want to focus on: Shem or Judah.

2. Then complete this character diagram. Use specific details from the story.

3. Finish by writing three questions you'd like to ask this character.

How the character acts	How the character talks

Character's name

How I feel about the character	How others feel about the character

Three questions I'd like to ask this character:

1. _____

2. _____

3. _____

Name _____

PREWRITING
Quickwriting

DIRECTIONS   On page 67 of your book, you are asked to write an imaginary conversation with a character. To help you get started, try quickwriting in the voice of one character.

1. First decide which character you want to "become."

2. Then do a three-minute quickwrite in which you say how you feel about war.

3. Try to write exactly how you think your character would write.

Three-minute Quickwrite

_____

_____

_____

_____

_____

_____

_____

_____

_____

_____

_____

_____

TIP: When you finish your quickwrite, read it over. Highlight words, phrases, and ideas that you'd like to use in your dialogue.

Name _____

ASSESSMENT

Multiple-Choice Test

DIRECTIONS On the blanks provided, write the letter of the item that best answers each question or completes each statement.

_____ 1. The selection "Shem Suggs" takes place . . .
   A. before a battle.   C. after a battle.
   B. during a battle.   D. after a peace conference.

_____ 2. What are the soldiers doing while they wait?
   A. They are playing cards.   C. They are reading the Bible.
   B. They are reading letters from family.   D. all of the above

_____ 3. How do the soldiers feel when one father sends a negative note about war?
   A. The letter does not change their minds.   C. The letter makes them fear war.
   B. The letter makes them question war.   D. none of the above

_____ 4. Which commandment are these "whole-souled Christians" so willing to break?
   A. the commandment against bearing   C. the commandment against killing
      false witness
   B. the commandment against stealing   D. none of the above

_____ 5. What book does Suggs promise himself he'll read after the war?
   A. the Bible   C. *Bull Run*
   B. *Gulliver's Travels*   D. *War and Peace*

_____ 6. How does Shem Suggs feel after listening to a part of this book?
   A. happy   C. scared
   B. lonely   D. excited

_____ 7. Judah Jenkins is ordered to . . .
   A. spy on the enemy.   C. fire on the enemy.
   B. ride over to an officer.   D. all of the above

_____ 8. In what direction does Judah Jenkins realize he is going?
   A. He is going toward his house.   C. He is going away from battle.
   B. He is going away from his house.   D. He is going toward battle.

_____ 9. The "tremendous roar" Jenkins hears is . . .
   A. a shot from an enemy cannon.   C. enemy troops marching in.
   B. a cannon shot from his own side.   D. the shout of a wounded soldier.

_____ 10. What happens as a result of this "tremendous roar"?
   A. Jenkins's horse runs away.   C. A fire burns down a tent.
   B. Jenkins is shot and killed.   D. all of the above

Short-essay Test

In what ways are Shem Suggs and Judah Jenkins different?

Memories

Unit Background   MEMORIES (pages 69–82)

Two stories appear in this unit, one by William Brohaugh and one by Joanna Woś. The narrators of both stories recall past experiences, both joyful and painful.

William Brohaugh, author of "A Moment in the Sun Field," is the author of *Write Tight: How to Keep Your Prose Sharp* (1993) and *English Through the Ages* (1998). He edited *Writer's Digest* magazine from 1982 to 1990, when he became editorial director of Writer's Digest Books.

Teaching the Introduction

Photographs on page 69 show a coach holding a bat and explaining a rule or procedure to young players. The bottom photo is of two happy girls—friends or sisters.

1. Ask students to tell about a happy memory that they hope never to forget. Ask them to tell why the memory is a happy one.

2. Ask students whether they have heard older people tell about memories of the past. What kinds of things do the people remember? Are their memories happy, sad, or both? Do family members figure in their memories?

3. At times, older people have memories of the past but refuse to talk about them. Ask why this might be.

Opening Activity

You might have each student record on audiotape the very first thing they can remember as a child. Limit each reminiscence to about a minute.

A Moment in the Sun Field

Skills and Strategies Overview

THEME	Memories
READING LEVEL	average
VOCABULARY	◆grumbled ◆muttzy ◆flubbed ◆earned ◆horizon
PREREADING	picture walk
RESPONSE	visualize
COMPREHENSION	double-entry journal
PREWRITING	word bank
WRITING	descriptive paragraph / compound sentences
ASSESSMENT	meaning

BACKGROUND

William Brohaugh's "A Moment in the Sun Field" is more a snapshot than a short story. It is the kind of writing you might find tucked away in a photo album or paper-clipped to the back of a picture of a dad and two boys playing ball in the backyard.

Brohaugh, who has edited and written several books on writing, uses a kind of backyard-baseball vernacular to tell his story of two boys playing 500 after dinner. The language of this piece is what makes it so unique. Words like *flubbed* and *muttzy* lend a childlike exuberance to the writing that matches exactly the way the two boys feel as they work their way toward 500 points and beyond.

UNIT THEME William Brohaugh uses descriptive language to explore one "perfect" moment in time.

GRAPHIC ORGANIZER A chart like this one can help students keep track of the sensory words in a selection.

Sensory Words: "A Moment in the Sun Field"

sight	sound	touch
muttzy	grumbled	grabbed
shadow	yapping	swinging
horizon	joking	popped
extra white	smacking	double bounced
high sunlight		

BEFORE YOU READ

Read aloud the introduction to the lesson on page 70 to motivate and focus students. When you feel the class is ready to begin reading, ask them to do the prereading activity, a **picture walk** of the selection. (Refer to the **Strategy Handbook** on page 40 for more help.)

Motivation Strategy

Ask students to think of a backyard memory they keep tucked away and only think about every once in awhile. Their memory might involve a game, a conversation, a party, or something else entirely. Ask volunteers to share what they remember and then explain why this memory has stayed with them over the years. What makes this memory, above others, so powerful?

ENGAGING STUDENTS Explain that "A Moment in the Sun Field" is about two 12-year-old boys playing a game with a dad. Ask students to complete this statement: "When you're 12 years old, everything seems _____." The statement will help them begin thinking about one of the selection's themes.

Vocabulary Building

Draw attention to the key vocabulary words for this lesson: *grumbled, muttzy, flubbed, earned,* and *horizon.* Ask students to circle the words in the text, pronounce the words, and then say what they think the words mean. (*Grumbled*, meaning "made a complaint," and *earned*, meaning "gained," are not defined.) Then use the exercise on the **Vocabulary** blackline master on page 120 to give students the opportunity to use the words in sentences.

STRATEGY LESSON: WORD FAMILIES If you feel students would benefit from some additional vocabulary work, teach a brief lesson on word families. Explain that many words in English share common roots. Words that share roots are said to be in the same "family." If you know the definition of the root the words have in common, it is fairly simple to figure out the meaning of all the words in the family. Help students understand the meaning of the root *pos* (from *positur*, "to place"). Then have them make a family of five or more words that contain this root.

For additional practice on this strategy, see the **Vocabulary** blackline master on page 120.

Prereading Strategies

As a prereading activity, students are asked to take a **picture walk** of the selection. Explain that during a picture walk, the reader looks only at the art, photographs, and captions. These elements of a selection can provide valuable clues about the topic and main idea. When they've finished their picture walks, students should work together to explain how the pictures made them feel. In addition, they should use the pictures to make predictions about the topic of the selection. Later, after they've read the piece, you might ask students to return to the pictures and explain the connections they see between the photographs and the mood of the selection. Does the art seem to match the mood? Why or why not? What pictures would students have chosen to accompany this story if they were the designers of the book?

QUICKWRITE As an alternate prereading strategy, ask students to think about an outdoor game they once played with a parent or another adult. Which parts do they remember best? What do they see, hear, smell, and taste when they think about this memory? After you've given them a moment or two to think about a game, have students do a one-minute quickwrite describing the scene. When they've finished, ask them to circle the descriptive words they used. This activity will help prepare students for the writing in Part IV on page 75.

Spanish-speaking Students

"Un momento en el campo de sol" se trata de la magia del verano. Una noche después de cenar, Bobby y su amigo Mike convencen al padre de Bobby que juegue al beísbol en el campo. Los tres juegan y se diviertan por mucho tiempo. Al desaparecer el sol, Bobby piensa en el cielo y el significado de la noche.

READ

Remind students that good readers read actively rather than passively. They read with a pencil in hand so that they can note things that seem interesting or important. Tell the class that as they read "A Moment in the Sun Field," they are to **visualize** the people, place, and events the author describes. Each time they "see" something new, they should make a sketch of it in the **Response Notes** section of their book.

Response Strategy

QUESTION   Questions are bound to come up whenever students read. Tell the class that it is important that they note their questions right away, so they don't lose track of what they want to ask. Have them write the questions they want to ask the author, another reader, or you in the **Response Notes**. When they've finished reading, ask volunteers to read their questions aloud. Work as a class to brainstorm answers.

Comprehension Strategies

In a **double-entry journal,** students note their individual responses to specific phrases, sentences, or lines from a selection. A double-entry journal serves two purposes: it gives readers the chance to do a line-by-line analysis of the text, and it helps readers see that their personal responses to a text can assist them in decoding the author's meaning. Students are asked to respond to one quotation on page 72 and two on page 73. If you like, model a sample response by saying: "This quote reminds me a little of my own dad. Sometimes I'll ask him to play something and he'll complain, but I can still tell he wants to play."

RETELLING   As an alternate comprehension strategy, ask students to stop and retell one or two paragraphs. For example, you might have them pause at the bottom of page 71 and then say what happens in this first part. Retelling a selection can help strengthen the reader's understanding of what the author has said.

For more help, see the **Comprehension** blackline master on page 121.

Discussion Questions

COMPREHENSION   1. Who plays 500 in "A Moment in the Sun Field"? *(Bobby, Mike Pasqui, and Bobby's dad)*

2. Why does the dad do most of the hitting? *(Everyone prefers it that way.)*

3. What happens when it starts getting dark? *(The three keep playing.)*

CRITICAL THINKING   4. Why does the ball remind Bobby of the moon? *(Answers will vary. Possible: As it falls through the sky, Bobby can see just a white slice, or sliver, of it. This reminds him of how the moon sometimes looks.)*

5. What is the mood of this selection? *(Answers will vary. If students have trouble with mood, consider teaching a short lesson on this literary technique. See "Literary Skill" below.)*

Literary Skill

MOOD   To introduce a literary skill with this lesson, you might discuss mood with students. Remind the class that *mood* is the feeling a piece of literature evokes in the reader: happiness, sadness, peacefulness, and so on. Writers create mood through their word choices. Have students identify the mood of "A Moment in the Sun Field." Point out that words such as *flubbed, two-bouncer, smacking,* and *okay* help create a playful, exuberant feel to the piece that may serve to remind the reader of his or her own "moment in the sun field."

III. GATHER YOUR THOUGHTS

Prewriting Strategies

The purpose of the prewriting activities on page 74 is to prepare students to write a **descriptive paragraph** of the setting of "A Moment in the Sun Field." Remind students that setting is the time and place of a story. Then have them begin the first activity, a sketch of the backyard scene Brohaugh describes. Students may want to look over the sketches they made in the **Response Notes** before they begin.

Next, students will brainstorm specific words that describe the setting. On the left side of the chart, they'll build a **word bank** of descriptive words and phrases that Brohaugh uses. On the right side, they'll make their own list of words and phrases that describe the "sun field." Remind students to include sensory words in their descriptions.

Have students use the **Prewriting** blackline master on page 122.

IV. WRITE

Read aloud the directions on page 75 to be sure that students understand the assignment. Remind them that their **descriptive paragraphs** should begin with a topic sentence that tells the topic of the paragraph as well as their thoughts and feelings about the topic.

WRITING RUBRIC You might show students this rubric before they revise their writing. You can also use it later when it comes time to evaluate what they've written.

Do students' descriptive paragraphs

- begin with a topic sentence?
- include details about time and place?
- contain sensory words and images to help the reader visualize the place described?
- stay focused on the setting of the story throughout?

Grammar, Usage, and Mechanics

When they are ready to proofread their work, refer them to the **Writers' Checklist.** At this point, you might want to introduce a brief lesson on compound sentences. Remind the class that a compound sentence must have a comma and a conjunction such as *and, or, but,* or *yet* in order to be correct. For example:

Incorrect: Bobby threw the ball Mike caught it. **(run-on sentence)**

Incorrect: Bobby threw the ball, Mike caught it. **(comma splice)**

Correct: Bobby threw the ball, and Mike caught it.

V. WRAP-UP

Take a moment at the end of the lesson for students to offer their own responses to the story. Ask them to consider what the story **meant** to them. Have them answer the questions on the **Readers' Checklist** aloud so that you have a sense of whether they were able to connect to the story.

Assessment

To test students' comprehension, use the **Assessment** blackline master on page 123.

Name _____

VOCABULARY

Words from the Selection

DIRECTIONS Use these vocabulary words in sentences about a backyard game you once played.

◆ grumbled ◆ muttzy ◆ flubbed ◆ earned ◆ horizon

1. _____

2. _____

3. _____

4. _____

5. _____

Strategy Lesson: Word Families

DIRECTIONS Look at the definition of the word part *pos*. Then look at the sentences in Column 1 and their possible definitions in Column 2. Circle the correct meaning for each.

> *pos* = to place

Column 1	Column 2
6. I <u>positioned</u> myself under the ball.	to put in a proper place to place without thought
7. I will <u>deposit</u> my money in the bank.	to put anywhere to place for safekeeping
8. I will <u>compose</u> a letter to send.	to form by taking apart to form by placing together
9. He was <u>exposed</u> to the cold weather.	placed at risk of a harmful action or condition protected from harmful actions or conditions
10. His <u>posture</u> was very straight.	the positioning or bearing of the body the shape of the body

Name _____

COMPREHENSION
Group Discussion

DIRECTIONS Get together in a small group to discuss "A Moment in the Sun Field." Use the questions on this Discussion Card to guide your discussion.

Discussion Card

1. What is the boys' reaction to the game 500? How do you know?

2. What does it mean that Bobby "suddenly understood the moon"?

3. How did you feel as you were reading this story?

4. To which character did you find it easiest to connect: Bobby or his dad? Why?

5. Rate the story on a scale of 1 to 10, 10 being outstanding. Then explain your rating.

Name _____

PREWRITING

Graphic Organizer

DIRECTIONS Use this chart to show the sensory words that William Brohaugh uses in "A Moment in the Sun Field." (Remember that sensory words are words that appeal to the five senses.) Then add three more sensory words to each column that you come up with on your own.

Sensory Words: "A Moment in the Sun Field"

Write Brohaugh's sensory words here

sight words	sound words	touch words
	grumbled	

Write your own sensory words here

sight words	sound words	touch words

Name _____

ASSESSMENT

Multiple-Choice Test

DIRECTIONS   On the blanks provided, write the letter of the item that best answers each question.

_____ 1. What time of year does the story take place?
   A. winter
   B. spring
   C. summer
   D. fall

_____ 2. What do the boys play with Bobby's dad?
   A. basketball
   B. 500
   C. hockey
   D. cards

_____ 3. Who does most of the batting?
   A. Bobby
   B. Mike
   C. Bobby's mom
   D. Bobby's dad

_____ 4. How do the boys feel about the game?
   A. They hate it.
   B. They love it.
   C. They're bored by it.
   D. They're surprised by it.

_____ 5. How do the boys earn points?
   A. by hitting the ball
   B. by making an out
   C. by catching the ball
   D. by making a basket

_____ 6. What comes up over the house?
   A. a shadow
   B. a plane
   C. a bird
   D. none of the above

_____ 7. What does Bobby assume is millions of miles long?
   A. the sky
   B. all the baseball fields
   C. the shadow
   D. all of the above

_____ 8. When the sun hits the ball, what does Bobby see?
   A. the whole ball
   B. a slice of the ball
   C. a bird
   D. the sun

_____ 9. When Bobby sees the ball falling into his glove, what does he understand?
   A. baseball
   B. the sun
   C. the moon
   D. his father

_____ 10. How does Bobby feel about the time he spends with his father?
   A. content
   B. sad
   C. nervous
   D. bored

Short-essay Test

Why do you think this story is called "A Moment in the Sun Field"?

The One Sitting There

Skills and Strategies Overview

THEME	Memories
READING LEVEL	average
VOCABULARY	◆disposal ◆germs ◆rational ◆peelings ◆perfume
PREREADING	anticipation guide
RESPONSE	react and connect
COMPREHENSION	reciprocal reading
PREWRITING	supporting an opinion
WRITING	review / possessives
ASSESSMENT	understanding

BACKGROUND

Joanna Woś's poignant short story "The One Sitting There" will strike a chord with any reader who has a painful memory. Woś's advice to readers—that they throw the bad memory away and thus get rid of it completely—comes through clearly, although she never actually puts this recommendation into words. Instead, a symbolic act—cleaning out her refrigerator—is a way of cleansing herself of her bad memories.

UNIT THEME Joanna Woś tells the story of a woman coming to terms with a painful memory.

GRAPHIC ORGANIZER An organizer like the one below can help students see the relationship between a main idea and supporting details in a story.

Main idea:
It is important to come to terms with a painful memory.

Detail #1:	Detail #2:	Detail #3:
Bad memories can make you feel sick in the same way that spoiled food can make you feel sick.	Bad memories can make you act irrationally or without reason. Ridding yourself of them can make you "rational" and "reasonable."	Once the bad memory is gone, you can more easily see and hear the good memories. They become "honored" guests in your mind.

BEFORE YOU READ

Read through the introduction to the lesson on page 76 with students. Have students discuss the question of whether it is possible to feel more than one emotion at a time. At the end of the discussion, ask students to complete the prereading activity, an **anticipation guide**. (Refer to the **Strategy Handbook** on page 40 for more help.)

Motivation Strategy

In "The One Sitting There," the author tells about a woman who is having trouble coming to terms with a bad memory. Ask students to think of advice they might give the woman. What has helped students cope with bad memories in their life? What did they do to make the memories go away? A short discussion on this topic will serve as an excellent introduction to the theme.

Vocabulary Building

Introduce the lesson's key vocabulary words to students: *disposal, germs, rational, peelings,* and *perfume.* Ask students to circle these words in the text. After you discuss definitions, ask students to use the words in sentences of their own. The more they use the words, the easier it will be for students to make them a part of their everyday vocabularies. For additional practice with these words, see the **Vocabulary** blackline master on page 128.

STRATEGY LESSON: SUFFIXES If you feel students need some additional vocabulary work, you might teach a short lesson on suffixes. Write this sentence on the board: "The bread, for prosperity, was wrapped in a white linen cloth." Point out that *prosperity* has the suffix *-ity,* which means "state of" or "quality of" and that the root *prosper* means "wealth or plenty." Thus, *prosperity* means "a state of wealth or plenty." Help students separate the suffixes from the root words in *captivity* and *sincerity.* Then have them define the two words. (A *captive* is a prisoner and *sincere* means "genuine, honest.")

For additional practice on this strategy, see the **Vocabulary** blackline master on page 128.

Prereading Strategies

The **anticipation guide** on page 76 will help students begin thinking about the author's message. Tell students that you are interested in their first, off-the-cuff responses to these statements. Since no one else will see their answers, they should be as forthright as possible. After they have finished reading the story, have the class return to the anticipation guide to see which (if any) of their opinions has changed. An anticipation guide shows students that what they read really can impact the way they view the world.

PICTURE WALK If you feel students will benefit from an additional prereading strategy, you might have them do a picture walk of the story. A picture walk can serve as another introduction to the topic—and message—of the selection. From the art, students should be able to make inferences about the mood of the selection. Ask the class: "What do these photographs remind you of? What thoughts and feelings come to mind when you see the girl on page 76 and the doll on page 79?" These inferences about mood will help prepare students for the main idea of "The One Sitting There."

Spanish-speaking Students

En "La que se sienta allí" Joanna Woś escribe de una mujer que lucha entender su propia vida. Cuando un apagón le exige que eche la comida del refrigerador, se acuerda de su juventud. En su familia no se permitía echar ni gastar comida. Sus padres y hermana mayor vivían durante la Segunda Guerra Mundial. Incluso después de la muerte de la hermana, los padres llevaban la vida frugalmente.

. READ

> As students begin to read, walk through the process of responding to literature. Introduce the strategy of **react** and **connect** and point out the example given. Explain that many times a reader's first reactions to a thought or idea are the most genuine of all. For this reason, students should get into the habit of keeping a record of their first reactions.

Response Strategy

VISUALIZE As an alternate response strategy, ask students to visualize the narrator and events of the story. How do they picture the narrator? What expression does she have on her face as she throws out all the food in her kitchen? What do they think the scene would look like to an outside observer? Have students make a few quick sketches in the **Response Notes**. They can use these sketches in Part III, when they are asked to do some in-depth thinking about the story.

Comprehension Strategies

Reciprocal reading is a small-group activity in which students take turns reading aloud and asking each other questions. To get them started, explain that students should work in pairs. Invite one student to read the title and opening paragraph aloud. As a group, discuss the **stop and clarify** question on page 77. Then have student pairs continue reading together. Remind the class that the interrupter questions are meant to help them think carefully about the author's words and ideas.

DOUBLE-ENTRY JOURNAL If you feel students would benefit from an additional comprehension strategy, consider asking them to complete a double-entry journal. Choose two or more quotations from the text to which students can respond. This activity will strengthen personal connections to the story. Quotes that may work well for this activity include these:

- "In our house, growing up, you were never allowed to throw food away."

- "I once saw my father pick up a piece of Wonder Bread he had dropped on the ground. He brushed his hand over the slice to remove the dirt and then kissed the bread."

- "Because I would still be the one sitting there."

For more help, see the **Comprehension** blackline master on page 129.

Discussion Questions

COMPREHENSION 1. Why did the narrator throw away all her food? *(because the power had been off and because she could)*

2. What happened to the narrator's sister? *(She died before the narrator was born.)*

CRITICAL THINKING 3. What is the significance of the title of the story? *(Answers will vary. Have students reread the final paragraph on page 78 before answering this question.)*

4. What is the tone of "The One Sitting There?" *(Answers will vary. Students might suggest there is a tone of defiance mixed with sadness or regret.)*

5. How did the narrator bring her sister back? *(She imagines a different, happier event, one that never actually occurred.)*

Literary Skill

TONE *Tone* is the author's attitude or feeling about a topic or the reader. An author's tone can be serious, humorous, satiric, and so on. In "The One Sitting There," the author's tone reveals the depth of her feelings about her sister's death and how this event continues to affect her years later. She is angry and hurt and not afraid to show it. Work with students to understand the tone of the piece. Since the easiest place to find clues about tone is in the author's word choices, ask students to find words in the essay that reveal the author's feelings.

GATHER YOUR THOUGHTS

The prewriting activities on page 80 are meant to prepare students to write a **review** of the story. Remind the class that a reviewer usually comments on one or more of these elements in a story: plot, character, setting, and theme or main idea. In the first activity, students will rate these elements on a scale of one to ten, ten being excellent.

Next, students will decide whether or not they think "The One Sitting There" is a good story. Then, they'll choose three facts or details that **support the opinion**.

Prewriting Strategies

OPINION STATEMENT If you feel students need help writing an opinion statement for their reviews, you might show them the following formula.

("The One Sitting There") + (my opinion of it) = my opinion statement.

Have students use the **Prewriting and Writing** blackline master on page 130.

WRITE

Read aloud the directions on page 81 to be sure students understand what is expected of them. Remind the class that they will open their **reviews** with a topic sentence or opinion statement. They'll support that opinion with facts and details from the story. Explain that for an opinion to be valid, it must have at least three pieces of support.

After students have written a first draft, have them exchange papers with an editing partner. Student editors should read the review with these two questions in mind:

1. Is the opinion clear?

2. Is the support adequate?

WRITING RUBRIC Use this rubric when assessing the quality of students' writing:

Do students' reviews

- begin with a clear opinion statement?

- include three or more details that support the opinion?

- end with a closing sentence that states the writer's recommendation?

Grammar, Usage, and Mechanics

When students are ready to proofread for grammatical and mechanical errors, refer them to the **Writers' Checklist** and consider teaching a quick lesson on possessives. Review the rules for creating possessives and then have students edit the following sentence for errors:

My fathers grief over my sisters's death was terrible to see.

WRAP-UP

Take a moment at the end of the lesson for students to reflect, using the **Readers' Checklist**. Explain that these are the kinds of questions good readers ask themselves when determining their **understanding** of the selection and the author's message.

Assessment

To test students' comprehension, use the **Assessment** blackline master on page 131.

Name _____

VOCABULARY

Words from the Selection

Directions Choose the word or words in parentheses that best complete each sentence.

1. If you put food in a <u>disposal</u>, you are _____ it. (saving / destroying)

2. <u>Germs</u> can make you _____. (sick / better)

3. A <u>rational</u> decision has been made _____. (quickly / slowly)

4. Lemon <u>peelings</u> are the _____ of the lemon. (outside / inside)

5. <u>Perfume</u> is sold in a _____. (department store / hardware store)

Strategy Lesson: Suffixes

Suffixes are word parts that come at the end of the word. Suffixes can give you clues about the meaning of the word and how it should be used in a sentence. For example, if you add the suffix *-ous* to the noun *grace,* you get the adjective *gracious,* which means "full of grace."

DIRECTIONS Read the suffixes and roots in the box below. Then write the root and suffix of the words numbered 6–10. Finish by writing what you think the word means.

Suffixes	Roots
-ity (state of, quality of)	prosper (wealth, plenty)
-less (without)	scarce (short in supply)
	form (form, shape)
	timid (shy)
	care (caution in avoiding danger)

6. prosperity _____ + _____ = _____
               root   suffix   I think the word means

7. scarcity _____ + _____ = _____
               root   suffix   I think the word means

8. careless _____ + _____ = _____
               root   suffix   I think the word means

9. formless _____ + _____ = _____
               root   suffix   I think the word means

10. timidity _____ + _____ = _____
               root   suffix   I think the word means

Name _____

COMPREHENSION
Graphic Organizer

DIRECTIONS Decide what you liked and didn't like about "The One Sitting There." Use this chart to keep track of your ideas. Be sure to explain your reasons.

"The One Sitting There"

What I liked about the story . . .	What I didn't like about the story . . .	My reasons:

If you had written the story, what would you have done differently?

_____

_____

_____

Name _____

PREWRITING AND WRITING

Writing a Review

DIRECTIONS In a review, you give your opinion, offer support for your opinion, and then say whether or not you could recommend the piece. Follow these steps to write a review.

STEP 1. WRITE AN OPINION STATEMENT. In your opinion statement, say whether you liked the story.

My opinion statement: _____

STEP 2. GATHER SUPPORT FOR YOUR OPINION. Now you will need to support your opinion. Your support should come directly from the story.

fact or detail #1: _____

fact or detail #2: _____

fact or detail #3: _____

STEP 3. PLAN YOUR INTRODUCTION. In the first sentences of your review, you should tell a little about the story. Write some facts about "The One Sitting There" on the fact card.

```
┌─────────────────────────────────────────────┐
│                 FACT CARD                     │
│                                               │
│  story name: _____ │
│  author's name: _____ │
│  what the story's about: _____ │
│  _____ │
│  _____ │
│  _____ │
│  _____ │
│                                               │
└─────────────────────────────────────────────┘
```

STEP 4. PLAN YOUR CLOSING. In your closing sentence, say whether or not you want to recommend the story.

My closing sentence: _____

_____

Name _____

ASSESSMENT

Multiple-Choice Test

DIRECTIONS On the blanks provided, write the letter of the item that best answers each question.

_____ 1. What does the narrator throw away?
A. chicken
C. milk
B. carrots
D. all of the above

_____ 2. Why does the narrator throw food away?
A. She is going on a diet.
C. She doesn't like the food.
B. The food is spoiled.
D. She bought new food.

_____ 3. What was never done in the narrator's house when she was growing up?
A. Food was never thrown away.
C. The sister's name was never mentioned.
B. The children never talked back.
D. The parents never wasted money.

_____ 4. What did her parents do with rotten food and peelings?
A. fed them to the dogs
C. put them on the compost heap
B. made soup with them
D. all of the above

_____ 5. In the narrator's childhood home, what were leftover meat and potatoes used for?
A. stew
C. soup
B. meat pie
D. all of the above

_____ 6. What did the narrator's dad do when he dropped bread on the floor?
A. kissed it
C. threw it away
B. brushed it off
D. A and B

_____ 7. What did her sister do with the bread when she was a baby?
A. threw it
C. played with it
B. squeezed it between her fingers
D. none of the above

_____ 8. What does the narrator do with the bread in her kitchen?
A. bakes it
C. throws it away
B. slices it
D. gives it away

_____ 9. Why does the narrator put salt on the table?
A. to represent tears
C. to represent death
B. to represent prosperity
D. to represent forgiveness

_____ 10. At the end of the selection, who does the narrator "bring back"?
A. her mom
C. her brother
B. her dad
D. her sister

Short-essay Test

How does the narrator feel at the end, when her sister "arrives" for a visit?

Mythology

Unit Background   **MYTHOLOGY** (pages 83–102)

Two Greek myths are included in this unit. "Pandora" is retold by Bernard Evslin and "Hera" is retold by Ingri and Edgar Parin d'Aulaire.

Bernard Evslin (1922–1993) was born in Philadelphia. He attended Rutgers University and became a screenwriter, playwright, and producer of documentaries. He later began to write about gods and heroes and produced a steady stream of books for young people, many of which are still in print. In 1975 *The Green Hero: Early Adventures of Finn McCool* was nominated for a National Book Award. Among his many books are *Heroes, Gods and Monsters of the Greek Myths* (1967), *Adventures of Ulysses* (1969), *The Trojan War* (1971), and *Jason and the Argonauts* (1986).

Edgar Parin d'Aulaire (1898–1986) was born in Munich. He married Ingri Mortenson, who was born in 1904 in Konigsberg, Norway, and they came to the United States in 1929. Together they wrote and illustrated many children's books, including *D'Aulaire's Book of Greek Myths*, from which "Hera" is taken.

According to Greek myth, Pandora was the first mortal woman. Hera was a goddess and Zeus's wife.

Teaching the Introduction

Images on page 83 show Hera and two peacocks, with whom she endowed, in their tails, the eyes of Argus. The mighty Zeus is shown at the bottom, and in the upper left is Pandora kneeling on the box from which all the world's troubles have escaped.

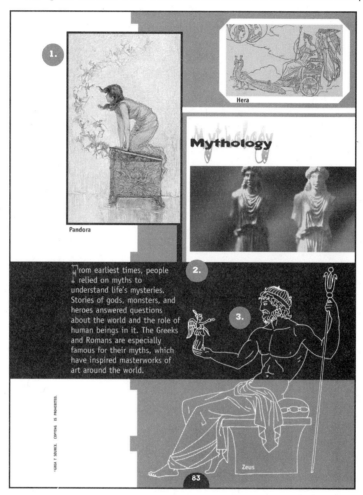

1. Read the introduction on page 83 with students, and ask how many have read or heard a myth and whether they know the story of Pandora. If they have no experience with myths, tell them that the story of Pandora is a mythical explanation of something that people have wondered about for centuries: why humans are plagued with so many troubles.

2. Tell students that nearly all peoples have had myths or legends about the beginnings of the world and about magical or supernatural beings and events. (Students may have heard or read tales of Paul Bunyan or John Henry, or Native American or African tales and legends, in grade school.)

3. Ask students to tell where they can find superheroes and fantastic situations today. *(They may mention comic strips or comic books, computer games, books, or movies.)*

Opening Activity

Ask students to talk about the appeal of supernatural events and superheroes in films, video games, and books.

Pandora

Skills and Strategies Overview

THEME	Mythology
READING LEVEL	challenging
VOCABULARY	✦torment ✦scheme ✦grieves ✦scorch ✦rustling
PREREADING	preview
RESPONSE	question
COMPREHENSION	predict
PREWRITING	storyboard
WRITING	tale or story / verbs
ASSESSMENT	enjoyment

BACKGROUND

In classical mythology, the story of Pandora is tied to the story of Prometheus, who was known as the champion of humankind. As the story goes, the gods of Mount Olympus became convinced that the people on earth had become indifferent to the gods' tremendous powers. As punishment, Zeus (the ruler of the universe) took fire away from humans and said he would never give it back.

Prometheus went up to Mount Olympus and stole the fire back again. As punishment, Zeus chained him to a rock for all eternity. To punish the humans for accepting the fire from Prometheus, he ordered Hephaestus to create Pandora and Hermes to give her a box that contained all the troubles and diseases that the world now knows. To make the situation worse, she was given the curse of curiosity.

UNIT THEME The myth "Pandora" answers the question: Why do so many ills plague humankind?

GRAPHIC ORGANIZER This organizer shows the chain of events described in "Pandora."

Zeus takes fire from humans and locks it away on Mount Olympus. → Prometheus steals it back. → Zeus chains Prometheus to a rock and orders Hephaestus to mold a girl from clay. → Hermes gives Pandora a beautiful box but tells her not to open it.

He takes Pandora to Epimetheus, Prometheus's brother, and offers her as a wife. → Pandora creates a home for herself and her husband. → Although she's happy, Pandora can't stop thinking about the box. → She hides the box, locks it in a trunk, and eventually buries it in her garden.

Feeling that she must look inside the box or die, she digs it up and opens it. → Horrible creatures fly out of the box. → Pandora slams the box shut before the last creature can fly out. → As a result of Pandora's actions, humankind is forced to live with famine, insanity, diseases, and all kinds of pain, sorrow, and death.

BIBLIOGRAPHY Students might enjoy reading myths from one of these engaging and easy-to-read books: *One Hundred and One Read-Aloud Myths and Legends* by Joan C. Verniero and *D'Aulaire's Book of Greek Myths* by Ingri and Edgar Parin D'Aulaire.

⌐. BEFORE YOU READ

Read aloud the introduction to the lesson on page 84. Ask the class what they know about Greek and Roman mythology. See how many different myths they can name. Then introduce the prereading activity, a **preview**. (Refer to the **Strategy Handbook** on page 40 for more help.)

Motivation Strategy

Tell students that the Greek and Roman gods and goddesses were immortal; that is, they were supposed to be able to live forever. Pandora, however, was mortal and, according to some stories, was the first woman created.

ENGAGING STUDENTS Tell the class that the main character in "Pandora" is so curious that she can't stop herself from doing something she knows she's not supposed to do. Ask students to tell about a time they felt this way. What happened? Did anything bad happen? Why or why not? A short discussion about curiosity will serve as an excellent warm-up to the theme of the selection.

Vocabulary Building

Point out the key vocabulary words for this lesson: *torment, scheme, grieves, scorch,* and *rustling.* Ask students to circle these words in the text. These words appear in an exercise on the **Vocabulary** blackline master on page 138. Encourage students to learn the definitions for these words so that they can begin incorporating the words into their own vocabularies.

STRATEGY LESSON: NEGATIVE PREFIXES If students would benefit from an additional vocabulary strategy, consider teaching a brief lesson on negative prefixes. Remind the class that when a negative prefix such as *dis-, in-, mis-,* or *un-* is added to a word, the meaning of the word changes. Ask students to practice using these prefixes with words of their own. Have them come up with at least five words using one of the negative prefixes above.

For additional practice on this strategy, see the **Vocabulary** blackline master on page 138.

Prereading Strategies

Before they read, students will do a **preview** of "Pandora." A preview is a helpful prereading strategy. Thumbing through the pages they are about to read can help students learn about the subject and anticipate any comprehension problems they might have. To that end, you might have students note any glossed words that are unfamiliar. You can help with problem words later, in a brief vocabulary lesson.

PICTURE WALK As an alternate strategy, ask students to do a picture walk of the selection. A picture walk is similar to a preview in that it asks students to take a quick look through the selection they're about to read. A picture walk can also reveal valuable clues about the topic of the story and, in some cases, the author's main idea. These clues can help readers later, when it is time to understand the plot, characters, and setting of the selection.

Spanish-speaking Students

"Pandora" es un mito que explica las maneras del mundo y la naturaleza humana. El dios Zeus crea Pandora para castigar al mundo. Él y otros dioses le dan a Pandora muchos regalos, que incluyen una caja misteriosa, y la caracteriística de la curiosidad. Inevitablemente, Pandora ignora los avisos de no abrir la caja. Al abrirla, libera todas las maldades del mundo, menos el presentimiento. Por eso, los seres humanos incluso hoy en día luchan contra muchas dificultades. Afortunadamente, mantienen la esperanza.

READ

Response Strategy

The directions at the top of page 85 ask students to read with a partner. Remind students to note their **questions** in the **Response Notes**. They may find that some of these questions are answered later in the story. Consider discussing remaining questions with the whole class.

Comprehension Strategies

Be sure students know that they will need to stop occasionally in order to **predict** the events of the myth. Your goal is to get students to make predictions automatically as they read.

GRAPHIC ORGANIZER As an alternate comprehension strategy, ask students to create a sequence organizer that helps them keep track of what happens first in the myth, what happens next, and so on. When they have finished, make a whole-class organizer that students can add to from their notes in the book. Students may want to consult this organizer when they are working on the **Prewriting** blackline master on page 140.

For more help, see the **Comprehension** blackline master on page 139.

Discussion Questions

COMPREHENSION 1. Where does Pandora come from? *(Hephaestus made her out of clay.)*

2. What is Pandora's relationship to Epimetheus? *(They are husband and wife.)*

3. Why is Pandora sent to earth? *(as a punishment to humans)*

4. Why does Pandora open the box? *(She is so curious that she can't stand not to.)*

CRITICAL THINKING 5. How would you describe Pandora? Explain. *(Answers will vary. Ask students to support what they say with evidence from the selection.)*

6. If you had been in Pandora's place, would you have opened the box? *(Answers will vary.)*

Literary Skill

PLOT *Plot* is the action or sequence of events in a story. A plot can be diagrammed on a plot line. A plot line for "Pandora" might look something like this:

CLIMAX (crisis)
Pandora opens the box.

Pandora's curiosity increases.

RISING ACTION (complications)

FALLING ACTION (complications)

Little monsters fly out of the box. Pandora slams it shut.

The gods create Pandora.
EXPOSITION

Storyteller explains the significance of the monsters.
RESOLUTION (denouement)

III. GATHER YOUR THOUGHTS

The purpose of the prewriting activities is twofold. First, students will complete a **storyboard** that will help them understand the plot of "Pandora." Next, students will complete an **organizer** that helps prepare them to write a continuation of Pandora's story. Both activities encourage students to think more critically about the characters and events.

Prewriting Strategies

BRAINSTORMING If students need an additional prewriting activity, have the class work as a group to think up ideas for a continuation of Evslin's story. Use the organizer at the bottom of page 91 to help them get started. Then ask the class to think about answers to these questions:

1. What other conflict can you think of that would involve Pandora?

2. Which characters besides Pandora might be involved in this conflict? What will they do and say?

3. How will the conflict be resolved?

4. How will the continuation end?

Have students use the **Prewriting** blackline master on page 140.

IV. WRITE

Be sure students understand that their assignment is to write a **tale** that continues the story of Pandora. Read aloud the directions at the top of page 92 and then ask a volunteer to summarize what the class is supposed to do. Be sure to remind the class to use their prereading notes when writing their stories.

WRITING RUBRIC Use this writing rubric to help students focus on the assignment requirements and for assistance with a quick assessment of their writing.

Do students' tales

- read as if they are natural continuations of the Pandora story?

- include plot elements such as conflict, climax, and resolution?

Grammar, Usage, and Mechanics

After students have written a first draft, have them read what they have written and check that it makes sense. Then ask them to proofread their work, using the **Writers' Checklist** as a guide. At this point, you might want to introduce a mini-lesson on verbs. Explain how important it is for students to use correct verb tenses. Also reiterate how confusing it can be when a writer mixes verb tenses in a single piece of writing. For practice, ask students to edit these sentences for verb errors:

Pandora was a curious girl. Hermes gave her a box and she ~~opens~~ *opened* it. Monsters ~~flies~~ *flew* out of the box and Pandora ~~shutted~~ *shut* it tight.

V. WRAP-UP

Take a moment for students to reflect using the **Readers' Checklist**. Its intent is to help students ask the questions good readers ask of themselves after finishing a reading. Then ask the class to discuss their **enjoyment** of the story.

Assessment

To test students' comprehension, use the **Assessment** blackline master on page 141.

Name _____

VOCABULARY

Words from the Selection

DIRECTIONS Write the word from the list below that best fits each of the following descriptions.

> ◆torment   ◆scheme   ◆grieves   ◆scorch   ◆rustling

1. A kind of suffering. _____

2. A clever plan. _____

3. Feels sad because of a death. _____

4. To burn something. _____

5. Making a soft sound. _____

Strategy Lesson: Negative Prefixes

DIRECTIONS On the blanks below, write the underlined word from each sentence. Then add the prefix *dis-*, *un-*, *in-*, or *mis-* to the word, and write the meaning of the new word.

6. She will <u>appear</u> before dinner.

_____

7. I think he is a (an) <u>grateful</u> boy.   .

_____

8. The dog was <u>shackled</u> by its owner.

_____

9. The movie character was obviously <u>sane</u>.

_____

10. At an early age, <u>fortune</u> came to him.

_____

Name _____

COMPREHENSION
Graphic Organizer

DIRECTIONS Use this character map to show what you know about Pandora. Feel free to check details in your book if you need to.

What she looks like	What she likes and dislikes	How she acts toward other characters
Her best qualities	Pandora Her worst qualities	How I feel about her

Name _____

PREWRITING
Storyboard

Good writers make a plan for their stories. (Sometimes they make a plan on paper, and sometimes they keep the plan in their heads.)

DIRECTIONS Make a plan for your tale about Pandora. Focus on the plot. What will happen first? What will happen next? How will things turn out in the end?

1. Sketch the events of your tale.

2. Underneath each sketch, write a one- or two-sentence explanation of the event.

3. Give your tale a title.

Storyboard for _____

(title of your tale)

1.	2.	3.

4.	5.	6.

Name _____

ASSESSMENT

Multiple-Choice Test

DIRECTIONS On the blanks provided, write the letter of the best answer for each question.

_____ 1. Why was Prometheus punished by Zeus?
   A. He killed a man.   C. He gave man fire.
   B. He insulted Zeus.   D. He married Zeus's daughter.

_____ 2. What did Hephaestus use to make the girl?
   A. dirt   C. flesh
   B. clay   D. water

_____ 3. What gift or gifts did Pandora receive?
   A. beauty   C. a puppy
   B. curiosity   D. A and B

_____ 4. What one thing did Pandora wonder about?
   A. her golden box   C. her home
   B. her husband   D. her garden

_____ 5. What did Hermes say when he gave Pandora the box?
   A. Put it in a special place.   C. Give it to your daughter.
   B. Never open it.   D. Hide it carefully.

_____ 6. Where did Pandora *not* put the box?
   A. in an oak chest   C. in a neighbor's house
   B. in the garden   D. in a storeroom

_____ 7. Why were Pandora's hands bloody and her clothes stained?
   A. She had been planting   C. She had buried the box in the garden.
        in the garden.
   B. She had been in a fight.   D. She had fallen in the street.

_____ 8. What kept Pandora awake and pulled her outside in the night?
   A. her husband   C. the gods
   B. the golden box   D. all of the above

_____ 9. What came out of the box when it was opened?
   A. lizardlike creatures   C. screams
   B. a foul smell   D. all of the above

_____ 10. According to the myth, what can humans not live without?
   A. endless trouble   C. hope
   B. insanity   D. sorrow

Short-essay Test

How did Zeus get revenge on humankind through Pandora?

STUDENT PAGES 94–102

Skills and Strategies Overview

THEME Mythology

READING LEVEL challenging

VOCABULARY
✦distress ✦inherit ✦wrath ✦dainty ✦mournful

PREREADING think-pair-and-share

RESPONSE mark or highlight

COMPREHENSION graphic organizer

PREWRITING clustering

WRITING descriptive paragraph / subject-verb agreement

ASSESSMENT ease

BACKGROUND

As the Greek goddess of marriage and childbirth, Hera expected that her husband and children would bring her great joy. Instead, her unfaithful husband, Zeus, caused her so much grief and torment that she could never really enjoy her children or her status as the queen of Mount Olympus. Zeus had so many wives that Hera was afraid to turn her back on him for even a moment. Not surprisingly, she soon earned a reputation as the most temperamental and vengeful of all the goddesses.

UNIT THEME Jealousy, revenge, and retribution are all part of the myths involving Hera, the Greek goddess of marriage and childbirth.

GRAPHIC ORGANIZER A cluster diagram like this one can help students organize details for an in-depth analysis of a single character.

BEFORE YOU READ

Read the introduction to the lesson with students. Offer additional background on Hera if you think students will benefit. Then have them complete the prereading activity, a **think-pair-and-share**. (Refer to the **Strategy Handbook** on page 40 for more help.)

Motivation Strategy

ENGAGING STUDENTS Explain that this myth is about the Greek goddess Hera, one of Zeus's wives. Ask students to complete this sentence: "I think Hera was known for her _____." Students' predictions may pique their curiosity about this queen of Olympus.

Vocabulary Building

Draw attention to key vocabulary words for this selection: *distress, inherit, wrath, dainty,* and *mournful.* Have students circle these words in the text. Some of these words will be familiar, although students may be a little uncertain about definitions and pronunciations. Help students learn the new words and reinforce their understanding of the words they already know. For more practice, turn to the **Vocabulary** blackline master on page 146.

STRATEGY LESSON: ETYMOLOGIES If you feel students would benefit from an additional vocabulary strategy, you might teach a brief lesson on etymologies. The etymology of a word tells its history and origin. For example, *biology* has the base word *bio,* which comes from the Greek word *bios,* meaning "life." Help students learn some common word parts and their origins. Ask them to suggest words that use these word parts.

mort- from a Latin word meaning "death" *(mortal, immortal, immortality)*

geo- from a Greek word meaning "earth" *(geography, geometry, geology)*

mono- from the Latin word meaning "single" *(monorail, monologue, monotone)*

For additional practice on this strategy, see the **Vocabulary** blackline master on page 146.

Prereading Strategies

Students are asked to complete a **think-pair-and-share** before reading "Hera." A think-pair-and-share can help students become actively involved in a selection even before they begin the first page. In addition, this activity can help refine students' ability to work cooperatively in a group. During the "pair" part of the exercise, students should build upon other's ideas and help the group reach consensus on the ordering of the statements from the text. Finish the activity by asking each group to share their ideas with the rest of the class.

QUICKWRITE As an alternate prereading strategy, ask students to do a quickwrite. Read the first paragraph of the myth aloud while students follow along in their books. Then, have them do a one-minute quickwrite about a topic you assign. For example, you might have them write about "marriage," "jealousy," or "deception." Quickwrites are meant to help readers begin connecting their own thoughts and ideas to a piece of writing.

Spanish-speaking Students

"Hera" es un mito griego que demuestra las maneras engañosas de los dioses. Cuando Zeus se enamora de una mujer mortal, Io, le convierte en una vaca para engañar a Hera y evadir su ira. Pero Hera sabe que Zeus ha sido infiel. Hace todo lo posible para asegurar que Io y Zeus estén separados.

II. READ

Before students begin reading, have a volunteer read aloud the directions at the top of page 95. Be sure every student understands the response strategy of **mark** or **highlight**. Remind students to pay careful attention to any character clues they find as they are reading the myth.

Response Strategy

VISUALIZE How do students picture Hera? How do they picture Zeus? As an alternate response strategy, ask them to visualize these two characters as they are reading. Have them make quick sketches of each in the **Response Notes**. Students might return to their sketches when it comes time to write their descriptive paragraphs (Part IV).

Comprehension Strategies

Graphic organizers keep students organized and on task as they read. For this selection, students will complete two different character trait organizers that will help them make inferences about Zeus and Hera. Tell the class that these organizers are meant to help them keep track of important facts and details about the characters. As an added benefit, students can use their organizers to help with the assignments in Part III and Part IV.

DIRECTED READING As an alternate comprehension strategy, you might do a directed reading of "Hera." Directed reading can help reluctant or low-level readers better understand what they are reading. In a directed reading, the teacher or group leader reads the selection aloud, pausing occasionally to ask comprehension questions that can assist students in understanding the sequence, characters, setting, and so on. Even the simplest questions, such as "What is Hera doing here?" or "Which characters are involved in this scene?" can help clear up student confusion.

For more help, see the **Comprehension** blackline master on page 147.

Discussion Questions

COMPREHENSION 1. How did Zeus convince Hera to marry him? *(He turned himself into a little bird and she took pity on him.)*

2. Why is Hera so angry with Zeus? *(because he is unfaithful to her)*

3. Who is Io? *(a beautiful young girl whom Zeus loves)*

4. What trick does Hera play on Io and Zeus? *(After Zeus turns Io into a cow in order to protect her from Hera's wrath, Hera tricks them both by insisting that she keep the cow for herself.)*

CRITICAL THINKING 5. What advice do you have for Hera? *(Encourage students to imagine how they would feel if they were Hera.)*

6. What are the two instances in this story of something being changed into something else? *(Io is changed into a cow, and the eyes of the dead Argus become part of the peacock's tail.)*

Literary Skill

CHARACTERIZATION You might use "Hera" as the basis for a brief lesson in characterization. *Characterization* is the method by which an author describes a character in a written work. A writer can describe a character's physical appearance, personality, behavior, thoughts, feelings, and speech. Sophisticated readers know that clues about character can be found in all parts of a story. Help students see that Hera's actions, speech, and interactions with other characters reveal a wealth of information about her.

III. GATHER YOUR THOUGHTS

Prewriting Strategies

The prewriting activities on page 101 will help prepare students to write a **descriptive paragraph** about Zeus or Hera. They begin by completing a **cluster** about both characters. Encourage them to concentrate on listing a variety of traits that explore the characters' appearance, personality, relationship with other characters, and so on.

Next students will complete a **graphic organizer** about the character they'd like to describe. Ask them to be as thorough as possible when responding to the queries in the boxes. Also remind them to refer to their during-reading graphic organizers as necessary.

Have students use the **Prewriting and Writing** blackline master on page 148.

IV. WRITE

Read aloud the directions on page 102 to be sure that students understand that their assignment is to write a **descriptive paragraph** about either Zeus or Hera. Ask them to keep their prewriting work close at hand so that they can refer to it as they write. If necessary, review the characteristics of a descriptive paragraph with students. Explain that in this type of writing, the sentences work together to present a single, clear picture (description) of a person, place, or thing.

WRITING RUBRIC Use this writing rubric to help students focus on the assignment requirements and for assistance with a quick assessment of their writing.

Do students' descriptive paragraphs

- begin with a topic sentence that names the character and says how the writer feels about him or her?

- include relevant facts and details from the text about the character?

- stay focused on this one character throughout?

Grammar, Usage, and Mechanics

When they are ready to proofread their work, refer students to the **Writers' Checklist.** At this point, you might want to introduce a mini-lesson on subject-verb agreement. Remind the class that the subject and verb of a sentence have to "agree." A singular subject needs a singular verb. A plural subject needs a plural verb. For example:

Incorrect: Hera and Zeus fights a lot.

Correct: Hera and Zeus fight a lot.

V. WRAP-UP

Take a moment at the end of the lesson for students to think about the myths. Point out the **Readers' Checklist,** and ask students to answer both questions. Have the class explain what they found **easy** or challenging about the selection. Listen to their comments carefully and then modify future lessons and strategies as needed.

Assessment

To test students' comprehension, use the **Assessment** blackline master on page 149.

Name _____

VOCABULARY
Words from the Selection

DIRECTIONS Context clues can help you figure out the meaning of a word without looking in the dictionary. Use context clues to figure out what the underlined words mean. Write the meaning of the word on the line.

1. ". . . pretending to be in <u>distress</u>, he flew into Hera's arms for protection."

   _____

2. "All of his children would <u>inherit</u> some of his greatness and become great heroes and rulers." _____

3. "He had seen Hera coming and, to protect his newest bride Io from her <u>wrath</u>, he had changed the girl into a cow." _____

4. ". . . she pretended to suspect nothing and begged Zeus to let her have the <u>dainty</u> cow."

   _____

5. "She raised her <u>mournful</u> eyes to Olympus, but Zeus was so afraid of Hera that he did not dare to help her." _____

Strategy Lesson: Etymologies

DIRECTIONS Study the word parts and their meanings in Box A. Then choose words from Box B to answer questions 6–10. Write your answers on the lines.

Box A

> *mort-* from the Latin word meaning "death"
>
> *geo-* from the Greek word meaning "earth"
>
> *mono-* from the Greek word meaning "single"

Box B

> immortality   mortal   geology   monorail   monologue

6. Which word means "study of the origin and history of the Earth"?

   _____

7. Which word means "having a single track"? _____

8. Which word means "living forever"? _____

9. Which word means "human"? _____

10. Which word means "a continuous series of jokes delivered by one comedian"?

    _____

Name _____

COMPREHENSION
Directed Reading

DIRECTIONS With a partner, work through the answers to these questions.

1. Who is Hera and what is special about her?

_____

_____

_____

2. What three words would you use to describe her?

_____

_____

_____

3. Why do Hera and Zeus fight so much?

_____

_____

_____

4. How does Hera get even with Io and Zeus?

_____

_____

_____

5. What is the myth "Hera" about? Summarize it here.

_____

_____

_____

_____

Name _____

PREWRITING AND WRITING
Writing a Topic Sentence and Details

DIRECTIONS The first sentence of a paragraph should set the stage for what you want to tell readers. The first sentence is your topic sentence. Follow these steps to write a topic sentence and supporting details.

STEP 1. List six details about Hera or Zeus. Don't worry about writing complete sentences—just list words that you think describe the character.

detail #1: _____   detail #2: _____

detail #3: _____   detail #4: _____

detail #5: _____   detail #6: _____

STEP 2. Look at your list. Circle the words that you think best describe your character. Then imagine someone has never heard of your character. What three words would you use to describe him or her?

Three words: _____   _____   _____

STEP 3. Write a topic sentence using these words.

My topic sentence: The character _____ is _____ ,

_____ , and _____ .

STEP 4. Now plan the rest of your paragraph. Give facts and details from the story that support your topic sentence.

detail #1: _____

_____

detail #2: _____

_____

detail #3: _____

_____

Use your supporting details as you write your paragraph. Each sentence after the topic sentence should include one detail.

Name _____

ASSESSMENT

Multiple-choice Test

DIRECTIONS On the blanks provided, write the letter of the item that best answers each question or completes each statement.

_____ 1. To whom was Hera married?
- A. Echidna
- B. Argus
- C. Zeus
- D. Hermes

_____ 2. What gift did Mother Earth give Hera?
- A. a garden
- B. an apple tree
- C. a dragon
- D. a nymph

_____ 3. What did Zeus want a lot of?
- A. children
- B. power
- C. wives
- D. all of the above

_____ 4. What did Zeus turn his new wife into to protect her from Hera?
- A. a cow
- B. a dog
- C. a queen
- D. a thundercloud

_____ 5. Argus had 100 . . .
- A. arms.
- B. eyes.
- C. hairs.
- D. toes.

_____ 6. Who came down to help Io?
- A. Hera
- B. Zeus
- C. Hermes
- D. Inachos

_____ 7. How did Hera feel about Io?
- A. She was jealous of her.
- B. She was angry with her.
- C. A and B
- D. She admired her.

_____ 8. How does Io communicate with her father?
- A. through words
- B. with sign language
- C. by writing in the dirt
- D. by using body language

_____ 9. What was Io chased by?
- A. a gadfly
- B. Hera
- C. Argus
- D. a peacock

_____ 10. Io became the goddess-queen of . . .
- A. Egypt.
- B. Olympus.
- C. Rome.
- D. Greece.

Short-essay Test

Why do you think Hera permitted Zeus to change Io back into a human?

John Christopher

Unit Background   JOHN CHRISTOPHER (pages 103–130)

This unit contains two excerpts from chapters one and two of John Christopher's novel, *When the Tripods Came* (1988).

Born in Lancastershire, England, in 1922, Christopher was a freelance writer at the beginning of his career and wrote stories for science-fiction magazines. He turned to writing full time in 1958. He has written for adults and children under various names. *The Tripods Trilogy* has been published in 13 languages and is well loved by young people all over the world. His other books for young people include *The Sword Trilogy* (1970, 1971, 1972, 2nd edition, 1989) and *The Fireball Trilogy* (1981, 1982, 1986).

Teaching the Introduction

The cover of Christopher's book is shown on page 103, along with a surrealistic rendering of a tripod.

When the Tripods Came

JOHN CHRISTOPHER

Born in 1922, Samuel Youd has published more than 70 novels under 7 different names. He has enjoyed the most success as John Christopher, an author of science-fiction novels and children's adventure stories. His most famous work is the *Tripods* trilogy. It was made into a film for British television.

103

1. Ask for a show of hands from students who like science fiction and from those who don't. Then ask them to give reasons for their likes and dislikes.

2. Read the unit introduction on page 103 with students, and ask whether anyone has read Christopher's books and, if so, what they think of them.

3. Ask students to speculate about how writers get ideas for science fiction.

Opening Activity

Ask students to talk about what science fiction is usually about. Do they think that we have already had visitors from outer space, or do they think that such visitors are even possible, given the vast distances in space? Then ask students to draw what they think a visitor from outer space might look like.

Skills and Strategies Overview

THEME John Christopher

READING LEVEL average

VOCABULARY ◇ ancient ◇ volunteering ◇ intervals ◇ digesting ◇ demolition

PREREADING web

RESPONSE clarify

COMPREHENSION predict

PREWRITING graphic organizer

WRITING compare and contrast paragraph / contractions

ASSESSMENT style

BACKGROUND

John Christopher (a pen name for the writer C. S. Youd) is one of today's most famous science-fiction writers. Although all science-fiction stories are different, many share common themes, including these: time travel, life in other worlds, space travel, the invasion of Earth by beings from other planets, and incredible scientific or technological inventions.

Most science-fiction writers hope to persuade readers that the world they have created is theoretically possible. As such, even the most fantastic inventions in science fiction are somehow rooted in scientific fact. Although science fiction presents worlds that are radically different from the reader's world, they also use "markers" (language, music, people, locations, and so on) that remind readers of real life. These markers are what make science fiction believable.

UNIT THEME John Christopher explores themes of courage and growing up in "Arrival."

GRAPHIC ORGANIZER You might use this web to offer background information about science fiction.

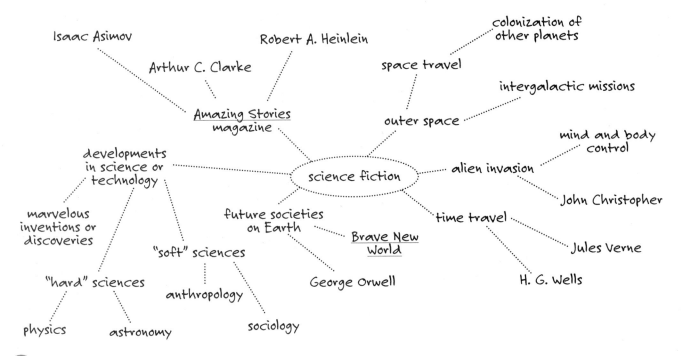

BEFORE YOU READ

Read through the introduction to the lesson with students. If you have not already done so, offer information about John Christopher and the genre of science fiction. Tell students that the story takes place in England. Then have students complete the prereading activity, a **word web**. (Refer to the **Strategy Handbook** on page 40 for more help.)

Motivation Strategy

Ask students to describe the most fantastic aliens they can think of. What do they look like? How do they act? A brief discussion on this topic will pique students' interest in Christopher's story.

ENGAGING STUDENTS Explain that in the story students are about to read, two young people must be braver than they have ever been in their lives. Ask students to tell about a time they had to show courage. What happened? Give students the opportunity to connect one of Christopher's themes to their own lives.

Vocabulary Building

Help students use **context clues** as they read to figure out the meanings of difficult or unknown words. Ask them to pay particular attention to the key vocabulary words for this lesson: *ancient, volunteering, intervals, digesting,* and *demolition.* Have students circle these words in the text. Although the footnotes define these words for students, you'll want to model using context clues and then checking your ideas against the footnote: "I'm not sure of the meaning of the word *ancient*. I notice that it is used to describe a 'rusting' tractor. I also see in the preceding sentence that a blaze of orange lights up some 'old' farm equipment. Could *ancient* be another word for *old*? I can look at the footnote to see if my idea is correct." For additional practice, see the **Vocabulary** blackline master on page 156.

STRATEGY LESSON: PREFIXES As another vocabulary strategy, write the following prefixes and their meanings on the boards: *tri-* ("three") and *quadri-* ("four"). Then ask someone to tell what a *tripod* is. (Something that has three legs or feet; *podos* is Greek for "foot") Ask for other words with the prefix *tri-*. (*triple; tricycle; triceratops*)

For additional practice on this strategy, see the **Vocabulary** blackline master on page 156.

Prereading Strategies

Webs give students the chance to explore abstract words or concepts that are important to a selection. Creating a web can help make the abstraction or concept more concrete. In a word web, the writer lists phrases, situations, experiences, and emotions that they associate with the word or words to be defined. The things they write on their webs can come from what they've read or seen or from their own ideas and experiences. When they've finished, students will have created their own definitions. They'll understand what the word or concept means to them, which in turn will help them understand an author's main idea.

Spanish-speaking Students

"La llegada" viene de la novel famosa *When the Tripods Came,* escrito por John Christopher. En esta selección Laurie y Andy se encuentran refugio en un cobertizo abandonado después de una expedición fracasada. Se despiertan cuando oyen una gran explosión. Están sorprendidos y asustados al ver una máquina grandísima con tentáculos largos destruir las casas y la gente en la finca. Laurie y Andy no saben qué hacer para salvarles la vida.

II. READ

Before students begin "Arrival," remind them of how important it is to keep track of their during-reading comments. Ask them to make notes that help **clarify** the setting, characters, and especially the action of the story. They can record their notes in the **Response Notes** section of each page. If you feel it would be helpful, read aloud the sample note in the margin on page 105. Explain that this is the type of comment they should make when reading Christopher's story. (You may want to tell students that Laurie is a boy.)

Response Strategy

VISUALIZE Students will naturally try to visualize the setting and action of "Arrival." As an alternate response strategy, have the class make sketches of what they "see" as they are reading. Their sketches will come in handy later, when it comes time to make inferences about the story.

Comprehension Strategies

At several different points in the story, students will need to **stop and predict** what they think will happen next. Making predictions can help readers feel more directly involved in what they're reading. Predictions can also help readers make inferential-type responses to a text. In order to predict, a reader needs to think interpretively about character, plot, and perhaps even theme.

GRAPHIC ORGANIZER As an additional comprehension strategy, ask students to create a sequence organizer that helps them keep track of the chain of events Christopher describes. On the board, draw a model of an organizer, with "A noise awakens Laurie" written in the first of six to eight boxes. Have students copy the organizer onto a sheet of paper that they keep in front of them as they are reading. Each time something new happens, students can make a note of it on their organizers.

For more help, see the **Comprehension** blackline master on page 157.

Discussion Questions

COMPREHENSION 1. What is the setting of "Arrival"? *(an isolated farm at night and at dawn)*

2. Who are the main characters in the story? *(Laurie—the narrator—and his friend, Andy)*

3. What do the boys see in the field that frightens them so badly? *(a huge, mechanical creature with three stiltlike legs)*

CRITICAL THINKING 4. How are Laurie and Andy's responses to the creature similar? How are they different? *(Accept reasonable responses. Have students support what they say with specific evidence from the story.)*

5. What do you predict the capsule will do after it stops rotating? *(Ask students to predict what will happen in the continuation of "Arrival," which they'll read in Lesson 12 of their Sourcebook.)*

Literary Skill

INFERENCES Students should know that no writer will spell everything out in a story. Readers are expected to make *inferences* (reasonable guesses) based on the evidence provided. Remind students that inferences should not be judged in terms of "right" or "wrong." When we test the validity of an inference, we do so in terms of the quantity and quality of the evidence provided. Can the reader provide adequate evidence to support the assertion? This is the question students should ask themselves during an inferential discussion about a character (Andy or Laurie, for example), plot, or main idea. Ask students to infer the source of the capsule.

III. GATHER YOUR THOUGHTS

Prewriting Strategies

The prewriting activities on pages 114 and 115 will help students think interpretively about Christopher's story. In addition, they will prepare students to write a **compare and contrast paragraph** about the two main characters. Students will begin by completing a character analysis of Andy and Laurie. For this activity, students will need to make inferences using what the author says as support for their ideas.

Next students will compare the two characters using the **graphic organizer** (a Venn diagram) on page 115. Remind students that the purpose of a Venn is to help them explore both similarities and differences. Encourage them to transfer some of the comments they made on page 114 to the Venn on page 115. When they write their paragraphs, they should use their notes on the Venn diagram as a starting point.

Have students use the **Prewriting** blackline master on page 158.

IV. WRITE

Read aloud the directions on page 116 to be sure that students understand the assignment. Remind them that their **compare and contrast paragraphs** should begin with a topic sentence that sets up the comparison. In the next sentence, they might want to briefly introduce their support.

WRITING RUBRIC Use this writing rubric to help students focus on the assignment requirements and for assistance with a quick assessment of their writing.

Do students' compare and contrast paragraphs

- thoroughly explore the similarities and differences between the two characters?
- include adequate supporting details?
- stay focused on the comparison named in the topic sentence?

Grammar, Usage, and Mechanics

When students are ready to proofread their writing, refer them to the **Writers' Checklist.** At this point, you might want to introduce a brief lesson on contractions, since many of your students will not have studied them since elementary school. Remind students that in a contraction, an apostrophe replaces the letter or letters that have been taken out. For practice, ask students to form contractions for these words: *there is, it is, will not,* and *you would (there's, it's, won't,* and *you'd).*

V. WRAP-UP

Take a moment at the end of the lesson for students to reflect on John Christopher's writing **style.** Have them use the **Readers' Checklist** as a starting point. They can begin by answering the three questions on the checklist and then elaborating on their answers orally during a brief class discussion.

Assessment

To test students' comprehension, use the **Assessment** blackline master on page 159.

Name _____

VOCABULARY

Words from the Selection

DIRECTIONS To build vocabulary, answer these questions about five words from the selection.

1. If something is considered <u>ancient</u>, is it old or new? _____

2. When you are <u>volunteering</u>, are you offering to do something or turning down a request?

   _____

3. If something happens in <u>intervals</u>, does it happen all at once or over time?

   _____

4. When your stomach is <u>digesting</u>, does it mean that you have just eaten or need to eat?

   _____

5. When there is a <u>demolition</u> of a building, is it being rebuilt or destroyed?

   _____

Strategy Lesson: Prefixes

DIRECTIONS Study the prefixes and their meanings in the box. Then answer the questions.

tri- = three	*quadri-* = four

6. How many people sing in a trio?

   _____

7. What is a quartet?

   _____

8. How many angles does a triangle have?

   _____

9. What is a quadruped?

   _____

10. What is a triple play in baseball? (Find the term in a dictionary, if you don't know what it means.)

   _____

Name _____

COMPREHENSION
Graphic Organizer

DIRECTIONS Make inferences on this chart about Laurie and Andy. Use direct quotations from the text as often as possible.

	Examples	What this tells me about the character
Andy's words	• "I think we ought to get away from here. . . ." (page 111) • •	Andy is action-oriented.
Andy's actions	• • •	
Laurie's words	• • •	
Laurie's actions	• • •	

Name _____

PREWRITING
Comparing and Contrasting

DIRECTIONS Use your chart and Venn diagram to help you write a paragraph that compares and contrasts Andy and Laurie.

STEP 1. WRITE A TOPIC SENTENCE. Write a topic sentence that prepares the reader for the comparison you want to make. Use this as your topic sentence:

The episode with the Tripods shows that Laurie and Andy are very similar / very different.

(circle one)

STEP 2. LIST SIMILARITIES. List three important similarities between the two characters here.

similarity #1: _____

similarity #2: _____

similarity #3: _____

STEP 3. LIST DIFFERENCES. List three important differences between the two characters here.

difference #1: _____

difference #2: _____

difference #3: _____

STEP 4. WRITE A CLOSING SENTENCE. Write a closing sentence that sums up the comparison and leaves your readers with something to think about.

My closing sentence: _____

_____

```
WRITING TIP
If you want to emphasize the similarities between the two
characters, discuss them first. If you want to emphasize the
differences between the two, then you should discuss them
last.
```

Name _____

ASSESSMENT

Multiple-Choice Test

DIRECTIONS On the blanks provided, write the letter of the item that best answers each question.

_____ 1. Where were Andy and Laurie sleeping?
   A. in a farmhouse   C. at a campground
   B. in a shed   D. outside

_____ 2. What do they do after they hear the first noise?
   A. go back to sleep   C. continue their expedition
   B. find better shelter   D. make breakfast

_____ 3. What are they sleeping on?
   A. straw   C. cots
   B. dirt   D. sleeping bags

_____ 4. What awakens them the second time?
   A. loud thumpings   C. mechanical sounds
   B. the ground shaking   D. all of the above

_____ 5. How does the mechanical capsule move?
   A. It floats.   C. It flies.
   B. It walks on stiltlike legs. D. It slides on the ground.

_____ 6. What does Andy guess the machine is for?
   A. farming land   C. making a science-fiction movie
   B. destroying houses   D. helping others

_____ 7. What happens to the man at the farm?
   A. He is put inside the machine. C. He runs away.
   B. He is rescued.   D. He is thrown by the machine.

_____ 8. What is taken inside the machine?
   A. a double bed   C. a television
   B. a bathtub   D. a chair

_____ 9. What does this monster of a machine remind Laurie of?
   A. a roller coaster   C. a farm
   B. the Eiffel Tower   D. the Statue of Liberty

_____ 10. Why does time seem to move so slowly for Laurie?
   A. because Laurie is bored   C. because Laurie is hungry
   B. because Laurie is tired   D. because Laurie is scared

Short-Essay Test

What advice do you have for Andy and Laurie? Explain.

Arrival, continued

Skills and Strategies Overview

THEME	John Christopher
READING LEVEL	average
VOCABULARY	◇demonstrate ◇probing ◇tendency ◇anticipated ◇inefficient
PREREADING	anticipation guide
RESPONSE	prediction
COMPREHENSION	story frame
PREWRITING	supporting an opinion
WRITING	point of view paragraph / commas
ASSESSMENT	depth

BACKGROUND

John Christopher is a successful and enormously popular science-fiction writer for children and young adults. In the *Tripods Trilogy*, a number of gigantic three-legged creatures from outer space invade the Earth and take control of the human population. The aliens are able to subdue humans by "capping" them with a metal helmet that prevents rebellious thoughts. For technical reasons, however, no human is capped until he or she reaches puberty. Thus, children are the only humans capable of thinking independently and resisting the aliens.

For many years, readers begged Christopher for another Tripod book. He resisted the idea of writing a sequel because he felt he had ended the story of the Tripods in the right place. He did decide, however, to write a prequel—a book set before the first one in the series. In *When the Tripods Came* (1988), Christopher offers a frightening explanation of how the Tripods were able to take over most of the world. The excerpts in the *Sourcebook* are from the first two chapters of this book.

UNIT THEME John Christopher explores the themes of courage and growing up in this story of an alien invasion.

GRAPHIC ORGANIZER This sequence organizer shows the events of the stand-off on the farm and the pulverization of the Tripod.

A noise and thumpings awaken Laurie and Andy. →	They catch sight of an enormous Tripod. →	A "tentacle" from the Tripod destroys the chimney of a farmhouse.
Laurie and Andy frantically try to figure out a way to escape the wrath of the Tripod. ←	The Tripod destroys the house. ←	A man comes outside the house and is seized by a second tentacle. The man is taken into the ship.
Army planes, a helicopter, and an armored brigade appear. →	A single tank approaches the Tripod waving a white flag. →	The tank plays classical music and the tentacles keep time.
A wave of fighter planes destroys the Tripod. ←	A second tank fires uselessly on the creature. The tank is destroyed.	

BIBLIOGRAPHY Students might enjoy the original three books in the Tripod series: *The White Mountains* (1967), *The City of Gold and Lead* (1967), and *The Pool of Fire* (1968).

I. BEFORE YOU READ

As a class, review the plot and characters of the first part of "Arrival." Then ask the class to complete the prereading activity for the story continuation, an **anticipation guide**. (Refer to the **Strategy Handbook** on page 40 for more help.)

Motivation Strategy

ENGAGING STUDENTS Ask students to reread the final two paragraphs of the first part of "Arrival" (page 113). Then ask them to predict what they think will happen to the Tripod, Laurie and Andy, the United Kingdom, and the world.

Listening to others' predictions and making some of their own may spark students' interest in reading the second half of the story.

Vocabulary Building

Draw attention to the key vocabulary words for this selection: *demonstrate, probing, tendency, anticipated,* and *inefficient*. Some of these words will be familiar to students, although they may be a little uncertain about definitions and pronunciations. Ask students to circle these words in the text. Help students learn the new words and reinforce their understanding of the words they already know. For more practice, turn to the **Vocabulary** blackline master on page 164.

STRATEGY LESSON: ANTONYMS As an alternate vocabulary strategy, teach a lesson on antonyms. Knowing the antonym for a word can help reinforce the reader's understanding of the definition. To make things interesting, have students see how many antonyms they can think of for words from the selection, such as *emerged, reluctantly,* and *civilized*.

For additional practice on this strategy, see the **Vocabulary** blackline master on page 164.

Prereading Strategies

An **anticipation guide** is the perfect prereading strategy to use with long selections that you need to divide between several class periods or with stories that contain quite a bit of suspense, such as "Arrival." This strategy encourages students to become interested in the outcome of the story and helps involve them directly in the topic or theme. For the anticipation guide on page 118, students will need to decide how they feel about life on other planets. Does it exist, or is it all in the minds of science-fiction writers? Ask them to rate each statement carefully, and then return to the guide after they finish the story. "Arrival" may influence them to change their minds about one or more of their ratings.

QUICKWRITE As an alternate prereading strategy, ask students to quickwrite about the topic of life on other planets. Ask them to think about books they've read, movies they've seen, and stories they've read in the newspaper. Then, have them write for one minute about their opinion of the topic. When they have finished, ask them to read what they've written, circling the most important or interesting ideas.

Spanish-speaking Students

En la continuación de "La llegada" los militares de Inglaterra, los Estados Unidos, y la Unión Soviética han destruido las máquinas que vinieron a sus países respectivos. Laurie y Andy se han vuelto seguros a casa y ahora intentan continuar sus vidas normalmente. Como había poca gente que vío las máquinas, tienen que contestar muchas pregunats sobre lo que presenciaron. La experiencia les ha afectado mucho, y no ven la gracia en las burlas de sus compañeros de clase.

II. READ

Response Strategy

Ask a volunteer to read the directions at the top of page 119 aloud, and then have another student explain the response strategy. Reiterate how important it will be for students to make **predictions** as they are reading. Remind the class that their predictions can keep them involved and interested in the story.

Comprehension Strategies

Students are asked to fill in **story frames** as they are reading the continuation of "Arrival." Story frames can help students understand the sequence of events in a story. As an added benefit, story frames can prod the reader into thinking carefully about elements of setting, character, and plot. Encourage students to reread their story frame notes once they've finished the selection. Once they know the ending of the story, they may want to make small additions or changes to their story frames.

DIRECTED READING As an alternate comprehension strategy, conduct a directed reading of Christopher's story. Allow students to read at their own pace, but have them look for answers to a set of questions as they read. When they spot an answer, they can make a note in the margin of the book. You might have students watch for answers to these factual and inferential questions as they read: "What frightens Laurie and Andy most about the Tripod? What is the government's plan in dealing with the Tripod? Is the plan successful? Why or why not?"

For more help, see the **Comprehension** blackline master on page 165.

Discussion Questions

COMPREHENSION 1. What do the first and second tanks do to the Tripod? *(The first waves a white flag and then plays music. The second comes to explore the Tripod and is summarily crushed.)*

2. Why don't Andy and Laurie run away from their hiding spot? *(They're afraid of being killed outright, like the farmer's dog.)*

3. What ends the standoff in the farmer's field? *(The military "pulverizes" the Tripod.)*

CRITICAL THINKING 4. What is Wild Bill's attitude toward the Tripods? *(Answers will vary. Possible: He scoffs at them a bit and feels superior to the whole event.)*

5. Explain why Laurie and Andy feel so reluctant to discuss the whole adventure. *(Accept reasonable responses. Possible: They are badly frightened and know the Tripods are nothing to laugh about.)*

Literary Skill

SIMILE A *simile* is a figure of speech in which two basically unlike things are compared, usually with the words *like* or *as*. Point out the following similes: ". . . the machine had the look of an insect digesting its prey." (page 110); ". . . armorplate crumpled like tinfoil." (page 122); ". . . the tank dropped like a toffee paper." (page 122). Have students note that these similes help the reader visualize the look and strength of the Tripod.

III. GATHER YOUR THOUGHTS

The prewriting activities on page 129 show students how to form an **opinion** and then **support** that opinion. Before they begin, remind the class of one important point: When writing an opinion paragraph or point of view paper, the writer uses his or her own thoughts and ideas to create the opinion statement but supports that opinion with *facts and details*. The strongest, most convincing opinions are supported with evidence from books, magazines, newspapers, or Internet articles; expert testimony (someone who knows about the topic); and personal experience.

Prewriting Strategies

OPINION STATEMENT Your students may need some help writing their opinion statements. If so, explain that an opinion statement is similar to a topic sentence. Writers can use this formula:

(A specific topic) + (a specific opinion about that topic) = a good opinion statement.

Have students use the **Prewriting** blackline master on page 166.

IV. WRITE

Read aloud the directions on page 130. Remind the class that a **point of view paragraph** (or persuasive paragraph) is one that presents information to support or prove a point. It expresses an opinion and tries to convince the reader that the opinion is correct or valid.

WRITING RUBRIC Use this rubric when you are ready to evaluate students' writing.

In their point of view paragraphs, do students

- present a clearly worded opinion?

- provide adequate facts and details to support the opinion?

- stay focused on one topic and opinion throughout?

Grammar, Usage, and Mechanics

After students have written a first draft, have them stop and reflect on what they've written. They should ask themselves this: "Is my opinion statement clear? Have I provided adequate support?"

When they are ready to proofread, have them review the **Writers' Checklist**. Consider teaching a brief lesson on commas. Explain that commas are used to separate items in a series, in dates, and between the city and state name in an address. Ask students to add commas to these sentences:

The Tripod was big solid and menacing. It touched down in Albany New York on Feb. 1 2001.

V. WRAP-UP

Take a moment at the end of the lesson for students to reflect on what they've read, using the **Readers' Checklist**. Ask them to explain what Christopher's writing made them think about and the connections they found themselves making to their own lives. Questions like the ones on the checklist can help students measure the **depth** of their understanding of the reading.

Assessment

To test students' comprehension, use the **Assessment** blackline master on page 167.

Name _____

VOCABULARY

Words from the Selection

DIRECTIONS Use the vocabulary words in a paragraph about Laurie, Andy, and the Tripod. Write your paragraph on the lines below.

◇demonstrate ◇probing ◇tendency ◇anticipated ◇inefficient

1–5 _____

_____

_____

_____

_____

Strategy Lesson: Antonyms

An *antonym* is a word that means the opposite of another word. For example, *dark* is an antonym for *light*.

DIRECTIONS Find the word in Column B that is the opposite of a word in Column A. Then draw a line between the two words. If there is a word you don't know, skip it and come back to it when you've finished the whole column.

Column A	Column B
6. reluctantly	wild
7. civilized	building
8. emerged	willingly
9. pulverizing	strong
10. sarcastic	disappeared
11. pushover	sincere

12. Use *civilized* in a sentence that shows you know what it means.

_____

_____

Name _____

COMPREHENSION
Directed Reading

DIRECTIONS Answer these questions with a partner. Be as detailed as possible in your answers.

1. Why do you think the Tripods came to Earth? _____

_____

_____

2. Would you say Andy and Laurie were courageous or cowardly? Support your answer.

_____

_____

3. What is Wild Bill's attitude toward the Tripods? _____

_____

_____

4. Why do you think he feels this way? _____

_____

_____

5. How does Laurie feel about the incident with the Tripods once it is over?

_____

_____

6. What is the significance of the final line of "Arrival"? _____

_____

_____

Name _____

PREWRITING
Writing a Point of View Paragraph

DIRECTIONS Follow these steps to write a point of view paragraph.

STEP 1. WRITE AN OPINION STATEMENT. Use this formula to help you write your opinion statement:

MY OPINION STATEMENT:
c r o s s   o u t   o n e It's (very likely / very unlikely) that a spaceship from another planet will land in the United States.

STEP 2.

SUPPORT YOUR OPINION. Now gather support for your opinion. Use facts and details from these sources:

1. John Christopher's *When the Tripods Came* or another book

2. an "expert" (your teacher, a friend, a family member, or anyone else who knows something about the topic)

3. personal observations or experiences

SUPPORT #1	SUPPORT #2	SUPPORT #3

STEP 3. WRITE. Write your point of view paragraph in your book.

⇒ Open with your opinion statement.

⇒ Then give your support.

⇒ End with a closing sentence that expresses your opinion statement in a slightly different way.

My closing sentence: _____

_____

_____

_____

Name _____

ASSESSMENT

Multiple-Choice Test

DIRECTIONS On the blanks provided, write the letter of the item that best answers each question.

_____ 1. The government sent which of the following to fight the Tripod?
- A. a helicopter
- B. a fighter plane
- C. tanks
- D. all of the above

_____ 2. What did Andy suggest the boys do once the army arrived?
- A. wave a white flag
- B. stay in the shed
- C. make a run for it to the tanks
- D. radio for help

_____ 3. What approached the Tripod with a white flag?
- A. a plane
- B. a tank
- C. a soldier
- D. a television truck

_____ 4. What surprise came out of the tank?
- A. classical music
- B. guns
- C. a dog
- D. an alien

_____ 5. What did the Tripod's tentacles do?
- A. pick up the tank
- B. keep time
- C. move in rhythm
- D. all of the above

_____ 6. What finally destroyed the Tripod?
- A. the tank
- B. machine guns
- C. fighter-bombers
- D. a challenger

_____ 7. Who made Laurie talk about his experience with the Tripod even though he didn't want to?
- A. Wild Bill
- B. Andy
- C. television reporters
- D. newspaper reporters

_____ 8. Where did a Tripod not land?
- A. Montana
- B. Kazakhstan
- C. Paris
- D. Dartmoor

_____ 9. What did the Tripods use at night so they could see?
- A. laser beams
- B. searchlight beams
- C. moon light
- D. infrared light

_____ 10. What emotion does Laurie feel when he thinks about the Tripods?
- A. humor
- B. excitement
- C. fear
- D. boredom

Short-essay Test

What inferences (reasonable guesses) can you make about the Tripods?

Facing Adversity

Unit Background

FACING ADVERSITY (pages 131–144)

A poem by Maya Angelou and a novel excerpt from Louis Sachar's *Holes* (1998) make up this unit.

Maya Angelou (born 1928) has had a remarkable and successful career as a poet, short-story writer, playwright, and performer. She has also written her autobiography and composed musical scores, appeared on television, taught dance and writing, and won honorary degrees. Recent works include *I Shall Not Be Moved* (poetry, 1990) and "On the Pulse of Morning" (inaugural poem, 1993).

Louis Sachar was born in East Meadow, New York, in 1954, and is one of the most successful writers of fiction for young people today. A popular and award-winning book is *There's a Boy in the Girl's Bathroom* (1987), but *Holes* has begun to top that in popularity. He lives in Austin, Texas.

Teaching the Introduction

Images on the top of page 131 show animals that tend to frighten and repulse people. The photograph below depicts a prison camp for troubled teens.

Facing Adversity

Most people are afraid of one thing or another. Life is full of frightening challenges that we must confront every day. When facing adversity, President Franklin Delano Roosevelt had the best advice. He said: "The only thing we have to fear is fear itself."

131

1. Ask the class for some suggestions about the meaning of the word *adversity* (an unfortunate event or circumstance) in the unit title.

2. Ask students to tell what they were frightened of when they were young. How many students were frightened by the same types of things? Can they laugh at those fears now?

3. Have students suggest some good ways of dealing with adversity. With some classes, you may want to read the following by the seventeenth-century American poet Anne Bradstreet and ask students to comment on her words: "If we had no winter, the spring would not be so pleasant: if we did not sometimes taste of adversity, prosperity would not be so welcome."

Opening Activity

"Life Doesn't Frighten Me" lends itself well to choral reading. Lines 1, 2, 4, and 5, for example, can be spoken by individual voices, and the repeated lines 3, 6, 9, and so on can be spoken in unison, as can the entire last stanza. Assign lines now, and sometime during study of the poem, have students practice their reading aloud.

Life Doesn't Frighten Me

STUDENT PAGES 132–136

Skills and Strategies Overview

THEME	Facing Adversity
READING LEVEL	easy
VOCABULARY	◇shadows ◇loose ◇counterpane ◇strangers ◇charm
PREREADING	read-aloud
RESPONSE	visualize
COMPREHENSION	directed reading
PREWRITING	graphic organizer
WRITING	expository paragraph / capitalization
ASSESSMENT	understanding

BACKGROUND

Maya's Angelou's poem "Life Doesn't Frighten Me" was originally published as a children's book, but the poem speaks to anyone with fears, whether real or imagined.

Maya Angelou is a writer, poet, playwright, performer, and educator who garnered the admiration of the general public when she stood before the nation to deliver her eloquent poem "On the Pulse of Morning" at President Bill Clinton's 1993 inauguration. In this poem and in most of her other works, Angelou reminds the world that all humans are essentially the same, regardless of the color of their skin. Her messages of hope, perseverance, and triumph over adversity make her a popular writer with children and adults alike.

UNIT THEME Maya Angelou explores themes of fear and courage in this rhythmic poem.

GRAPHIC ORGANIZER An organizer like this one can help students clearly see the series of problems and solutions Angelou presents in her poem.

PROBLEM

shadows
noises
barking dogs
ghosts
Mother Goose (fairy tales?)
lions
dragons
tough guys
being alone at night
panthers
strangers
new classrooms
frogs and snakes

SOLUTION

talk back to your fears
make fun of your fears
smile instead of crying
realize the fears are imaginary
use a "magic charm"
believe in yourself
celebrate your triumph over scary things

BIBLIOGRAPHY Your more-advanced readers might enjoy reading Angelou's poem "On the Pulse of Morning" or the first volume in her multi-volume autobiography, *I Know Why the Caged Bird Sings* (1970).

I. BEFORE YOU READ

Read aloud the introduction to the lesson (page 132). Be sure students understand what it means to **visualize** something as they're reading or listening. (Remind them that visualizing should be something they do automatically.) Then ask students to complete the prereading activity, a **read-aloud**. (Refer to the **Strategy Handbook** on page 40 for more help.)

Motivation Strategy

Ask students to think about the title of Angelou's poem. Explain that the speaker names some of the things in life that scare other people but don't scare her. Ask students: "What were three things that scared you as a child? Do the same three things scare you now? Why or why not?" Have students tell you what they did to overcome their childhood fears. Then tell them to keep these coping strategies in mind as they read the poem.

Vocabulary Building

Help students use **context clues** as they read to figure out the meanings of difficult words, especially the key vocabulary: *shadows, loose, counterpane, strangers,* and *charm.* (Only *counterpane* is footnoted.) Model using context clues and then checking your ideas against a dictionary definition: "I don't know the word *charm.* I see, though, that it is something magical and that it is small enough to fit up a sleeve. I also remember the word being used to describe something that hangs on a bracelet. Could a *charm* be some type of small ornament? And could *magic charm* be like a small ornament that has magical powers to prevent harm? I can check the dictionary to see if my guess is correct." Have students circle the five words in the text.

STRATEGY LESSON: PREFIXES Tell students that the prefix *self-* means "oneself." For example, *self-satisfied* means "content with oneself." Have students practice adding the prefix *self-* to a set of words. Then have them define each of the words.

For additional practice on this strategy, see the **Vocabulary** blackline master on page 174.

Prereading Strategies

The purpose of a **read-aloud** is to ease reluctant readers into a long or intimidating text. (As you know, many students find poetry quite intimidating.) For many readers, listening while a selection is read aloud can make the text seem less forbidding and easier to understand. After they listen to the opening stanza of Angelou's poem, students will fill out a **listener's guide** that encourages them to reflect on what they have heard so far and make predictions. When it is time to read the rest of the poem, do a round-robin reading while the class follows along in their books.

SKIM As an alternate prereading strategy, ask students to skim the selection. A skim is another good way to ease reluctant readers into a text. To make the most of the strategy, have students skim with some questions in mind. You might post these and others questions on the board:

1. What is the poem about?

2. What repeated words or phrases did you notice while you were skimming?

3. Is there rhyme in the poem?

4. Is there rhythm?

Spanish-speaking Students

Se conoce a Maya Angelou como una de los poetas más aclamadas de hoy día. En "La vida no me asusta" Angelou describe todas las cosas que no le asustan a la narradora joven. Se sospecha que en realidad, intente a convenecer a sí misma que no haya razón para tener miedo. Usando las herramientas clásicas de la poesía—la rima, la repeticion, y las palabras descriptivas—Angelou logra vitalizar el poema.

II. READ

Response Strategy

Remind students that you want them to be active rather than passive listeners. Active listeners take notes as they listen. They note words and phrases that they think are important or confusing. They also **visualize** the people, places, and events the writer describes. Be sure students make sketches of the pictures that come to mind. If you do a second reading of the poem, ask them to make a second set of sketches. Students might be surprised that they can "see" a whole new group of pictures on a second reading.

Comprehension Strategies

Directed reading can aid in comprehension of a text. The **stop and think** questions that interrupt Angelou's poem are written with the aim of helping students move beyond a literal understanding of the poem. Questions such as "why does the speaker name all the things she's *not* afraid of" prompt students to think inferentially. If you like, save these questions for a second reading of the poem. Have a volunteer read the poem once to give students an idea of what the poem is about and how it sounds. Then, on a second reading, pause at each interrupter question and discuss it as a class.

RETELL As an alternate comprehension strategy, ask students to retell the poem either orally or in writing. Have them explain who or what the poet describes and then say what they think the poet's message is. Retelling is a terrific strategy to use with poetry because it allows students to take a break from thinking about poetic form. Students who are frustrated because they can't decipher the rhythm or rhyme scheme will jump at the chance to simply discuss what the poem says.

For more help, see the **Comprehension** blackline master on page 175.

Discussion Questions

COMPREHENSION 1. What are some of the things the speaker is not afraid of? *(life, including the dark, barking dogs, ghosts, panthers, lions, new situations, and so on)*

2. What does the speaker do to allay her fears? *(She shouts at them, makes fun of them, laughs at them, and so on.)*

3. What does the speaker keep with her to ward off fear? *(a magic charm)*

CRITICAL THINKING 4. What is the effect of the repetition of the line, "Life doesn't frighten me at all"? *(Remind students that poets often use repetition in order to emphasize meaning and/or create a sense of rhythm. Angelou seems to have both purposes in mind.)*

5. How old do you think the speaker of the poem is? *(Accept reasonable guesses so long as they are supportable with evidence from the selection. Many students will suggest that the speaker is quite young, since she names fears a very young child would have.)*

Literary Skill

RHYTHM You might teach a brief lesson on rhythm. Explain that *rhythm* is the pattern of stressed and unstressed sounds in poetry. Rhythm can affect tone and greatly increase the pleasure with which we read a poem. Ask: "How is the rhythm of stanza 3 different from the rhythm of the rest of the poem?" Students might suggest that this abrupt change of rhythm varies the mood. Point out that in the first two stanzas, lines 1, 2, 4, 5, 7, 8, 10, and 11 each have three stresses. You might have students tap out the rhythm of other stanzas.

III. GATHER YOUR THOUGHTS

The **graphic organizer** on page 135 will help students gather the information they will need to write an **expository paragraph** about Maya Angelou and "Life Doesn't Frighten Me." If you have time, send one or two students to the library or Internet to search for information about the poet. Then ask students to report on what they find. Students can make notes about this information in the "What I know about this poet" section of the fact sheet.

Be sure students write what they think the main idea of the poem is. If they get stuck, ask: "What do you think Angelou wants you to remember most?"

Prewriting Strategies

QUICKWRITE If you feel students would benefit from another prewriting strategy, you might ask them to do a one-minute quickwrite about Angelou's poem. A quickwrite can help students who are stuck trying to think of a first sentence. Ask them to write whatever comes to mind about the poem without worrying about sequence, grammar, or punctuation. When they've finished, ask them to read what they've written and circle words or sentences that they would like to use in their expository paragraph.

Have students use the **Prewriting** blackline master on page 176.

IV. WRITE

Read aloud the directions on page 136 to be sure that students understand the assignment requirements. If necessary, review the characteristics of an **expository paragraph**. Explain that an expository paragraph is one that presents facts, gives directions, defines terms, and so on. This type of writing is used when the writer wants to explain facts or ideas.

When they have finished a rough draft, have students read their writing and check to be sure that they've included information about the poet; information about the poetic style: rhyme, rhythm, language, and so on; and a discussion of the main idea of the poem.

WRITING RUBRIC You might use this rubric to help assess students' writing:

In their expository paragraphs, do students

- name the poem and poet and discuss what the poem is about?

- include specific details about length, rhyme, rhythm, and word choice?

- discuss the poem's main idea?

Grammar, Usage, and Mechanics

Ask students to review the questions on the **Writers' Checklist** and then edit this sentence for capitalization errors:

maya angelou recited "on the pulse of morning" at the 1993 presidential inauguration in washington.

V. WRAP-UP

Take a moment at the end of the lesson for students to think about Angelou's writing and their **understanding** of the poem. Ask volunteers to read the **Readers' Checklist** aloud and answer each question.

Assessment

To test students' comprehension, use the **Assessment** blackline master on page 177.

Name _____

VOCABULARY

Words from the Selection

DIRECTIONS Using context clues, figure out the meaning of the underlined word in each sentence. Write the meaning on the blank.

1. The summer sun was hot, but we sat in the shadows under a tree.

_____

2. We were quite comfortable sitting on an old counterpane we had taken from a bed.

_____

3. Suddenly, two unfamiliar people appeared; they were strangers to us.

_____

4. They each had a big dog. One dog was tied, but the other was loose.

_____

5. It was probably time to get out my magic charm to keep from being bitten.

_____

Strategy Lesson: Prefixes

DIRECTIONS The prefix *self-* means "oneself." Write the word from the list below that fits in each sentence.

> ❖self-centered   ❖self-respect   ❖self-assured   ❖self-control

6. It is _____ of you to think only of yourself instead of others.

7. If you raise your hand instead of calling out, you are using

   _____.

8. The speaker was _____ when he gave his speech.

9. Show a little _____ and dress nicely for your interview.

10. Think of a word with the prefix *self-* and use it in a sentence that shows you know what it means.

Name _____

COMPREHENSION
Reader's Log

DIRECTIONS Answer these questions about "Life Doesn't Frighten Me." Then say how you feel about the poem.

1. The poem is about _____

and _____

2. I think the speaker of the poem is _____

_____

_____

3. My favorite part of the poem is _____

_____

_____

4. My least favorite part of the poem is _____

_____

_____

5. This poem reminds me of _____

_____

_____

I WOULD / WOULD NOT like to read another poem by Maya Angelou.

  (circle one)

Here's why: _____

_____

_____

Name _____

PREWRITING

Fact and Opinion

Sometimes it is hard to tell a fact from an opinion. An **opinion** is a view or belief held by someone. A **fact** is a statement that can be proven true or untrue. For example,

FACT: Maya Angelou wrote "Life Doesn't Frighten Me."

OPINION: It is an excellent poem.

DIRECTIONS Look at these facts and opinions about the poem. Write F next to the facts and O next to the opinions.

_____ 1. The speaker fears nothing.

_____ 2. Everyone is afraid of lions.

_____ 3. The speaker doesn't cry when she's scared.

_____ 4. It is silly to be afraid of strangers.

_____ 5. The panthers in the park might be a little scary.

Supporting Details

DIRECTIONS Read the main idea statement in the box. Then read five facts from the poem. Decide which facts best support the main idea. Write them in the organizer.

FACT: The poet is Maya Angelou.

FACT: The speaker of the poem names things that might frighten people.

FACT: She tells what she does if she feels scared.

FACT: The poem has rhyming words.

FACT: She says that if she smiles at her fears, they go away.

Main Idea:		
In this poem, Angelou explores the theme of courage.		
Fact 1	**Fact 2**	**Fact 3**

Name _____

ASSESSMENT

Multiple-Choice Test

DIRECTIONS On the blanks provided, write the letter of the item that best answers each question or completes each statement.

_____ 1. What type of writing is "Life Doesn't Frighten Me"?
A. It is historical fiction.   C. It is a fairy tale.
B. It is a poem.   D. It is a fable.

_____ 2. What does the speaker see on the wall?
A. shadows   C. ghosts
B. dogs   D. dragons

_____ 3. The speaker is *not* frightened by . . .
A. strangers.   C. life.
B. being alone.   D. all of the above

_____ 4. To what children's book character does the speaker refer?
A. Humpty Dumpty   C. Jack and the Beanstalk
B. Mother Goose   D. Cinderella

_____ 5. Which words are examples of rhyming words?
A. ghosts / cloud   C. boo / shoo
B. lions / loose   D. fly / smile

_____ 6. Who or what is breathing fire in the poem?
A. Mother Goose   C. panthers
B. lions   D. dragons

_____ 7. Who pulls the speaker's hair?
A. boys   C. kissy girls
B. strangers   D. ghosts

_____ 8. Where is the only place the speaker might be afraid?
A. in the hall   C. in the park
B. in her dreams   D. at school

_____ 9. What does the speaker have that helps her?
A. a rabbit's foot   C. a magic charm
B. a pet dog   D. a special friend

_____ 10. What is the tone of this piece?
A. timid   C. angry
B. fearful   D. self-confident

Short-essay Test

Explain the title of the poem.

Stanley Yelnats

Skills and Strategies Overview

THEME	Facing Adversity
READING LEVEL	easy
VOCABULARY	✦hammock ✦scorpions ✦stationery ✦stifling ✦ratios
PREREADING	walk-through
RESPONSE	react and connect
COMPREHENSION	double-entry journal
PREWRITING	choosing a subject
WRITING	journal entry / easily confused words
ASSESSMENT	meaning

BACKGROUND

"Stanley Yelnats" is an excerpt from Louis Sachar's Newbery-award-winning novel, *Holes* (1998). *Holes* is the story of a good boy who makes a small mistake and is sent to Camp Green Lake, a juvenile detention facility in the middle of Texas. The philosophy of the camp—"If you take a bad boy and make him dig a hole every day in the hot sun, it will turn him into a good boy"—helps guarantee that Stanley's stay at Green Lake will be anything but pleasurable.

Sachar uses a combination of humor and irony in this compelling story of an honest boy who is surrounded by some very dishonest adults. In the novel as a whole, Sachar's topics include family, friendship, the underdog, and growing up.

UNIT THEME The main character in "Stanley Yelnats" faces adversity by making the best of a bad situation.

GRAPHIC ORGANIZER A story pyramid can help readers think about the characters, setting, and events of a story.

1. _Stanley_
Name of main character

2. _lonely_ _worried_
Two words describing main character

3. _Camp_ _Green_ _Lake_
Three words describing setting

4. _chooses_ _camp_ _over_ _jail_
Four words stating problem

5. _boards_ _bus_ _bids_ _farewell_ _family_
Five words describing one event

6. _flashback_ _teacher_ _embarrasses_ _Stanley_ _about_ _weight_
Six words describing second event

7. _Stanley_ _is_ _handcuffed_ _to_ _armrest;_ _guard_ _watches_
Seven words describing third event

8. _Stanley_ _will_ _try_ _to_ _make_ _best_ _of_ _situation_
Eight words describing solution

BEFORE YOU READ

Remind students of the theme of this unit (Facing Adversity) and have a volunteer explain how that theme relates to the previous selection, "Life Doesn't Frighten Me." Then have students complete the prereading activity for "Stanley Yelnats," a **walk-through**. (Refer to the **Strategy Handbook** on page 40 for more help.)

Motivation Strategy

Ask students to think about a time they were faced with what seemed like an insurmountable problem. What was the problem and what did they do to solve it? What, if anything, did they learn from the experience? As students read the Sachar selection, they can think about what they would do if they were in Stanley's shoes. How would they face the problem that Stanley is up against?

Vocabulary Building

Help students use **context clues** as they read to figure out the meanings of difficult words, especially the key vocabulary for this lesson: *hammock*, *scorpions*, *stationery*, *stifling*, and *ratios*. Ask students to circle these words in the text. Although the footnotes define these words, students should try to use context clues to see if they can come up with meanings that are close to the ones in the footnotes. Remind them that synonyms and definitions in the form of appositives or explanatory phrases can function as context clues. For additional practice with these words, see page 182.

STRATEGY LESSON: COMPOUND WORDS Compound words that are spelled solid may look unfamiliar, but they can be easily decoded if students can see the separate words. Write some compound words, such as *wasteland, overweight,* and *daytime,* on the board, and tell students that compounds are formed by joining two or more words. Ask them to tell what the two words are in these three compounds.

For additional practice on this strategy, see the **Vocabulary** blackline master on page 182.

Prereading Strategies

A prereading **walk-through** encourages students to become actively engaged in what they're about to read. During a walk-through, the reader looks at the art and text, paying particular attention to words, phrases, ideas, or pictures that jump out at them. Ask a volunteer to read aloud the title and author and have students write the information on the diagram on page 137. Then model how to thumb through the selection, thinking aloud as you go. (In modeling the skill, you might comment on the length of the reading, memorable art, important-looking text, and so on.) Working with the class on this first walk-through will give them the confidence to use the strategy by themselves with future readings.

QUICKWRITE As an additional prereading strategy, have students do a quickwrite about the selection. Tell students that the story is about a boy named Stanley Yelnats who is sent to a juvenile detention facility. Ask students to write what they think he did wrong, what they think the facility might be like, and how they predict things will turn out. Remind the class that quickwriting can never be "right or wrong." Instead, students write whatever thoughts come to mind and then use those thoughts later to help them understand the selection.

Spanish-speaking Students

"Stanley Yelnats" viene de la novela *Holes* escrito por Louis Sachar. Se trata de un adolescente problemático que escoge ir a un campo para delincuentes juveniles en vez de ir a la cárcel. El campo, sin embargo, es parecido a una cárcel. Los jóvenes sufren condiciones ásperas para aprender la disciplina. No es claro lo que necesita Stanley Yelnats. Su vida ha sido marcada por la pobreza de su familia y el maltratamiento en la escuela.

II. READ

Students will naturally want to **react** to Stanley and his plight. Ask them to jot down their comments in the **Response Notes**. Also ask them to continue to think about what they would do if they were in his situation. This will help them **connect** to the literature on a personal level.

Response Strategy

As an alternate response strategy, ask students to **visualize** the setting of the story. Sachar offers some description, but readers have to "fill in the blanks" using their imagination. Have students make quick sketches of the camp, bus ride, and even the courtroom scene. They can refer to their sketches later when they are asked to write their thoughts and feelings about the characters and the scene.

Comprehension Strategies

Double-entry journals give students the chance to share their opinions and reactions about a selection. Instead of asking them to react to an entire story, which can be difficult to do, a double-entry journal has students share their thoughts and feelings about important lines or quotations. Their reactions to these quotes can give you an idea of how they feel about the selection as a whole and whether they are having trouble understanding the text. Notice that the journal entry on page 139 asks students to respond to a quotation that has been chosen for them and then respond to a quotation of their own choosing. The next journal entry asks students to choose two quotes. Have students choose phrases or sentences that they find interesting or important. They can check their **Response Notes** column to see if any of the comments they have made there lead them to a quotation to which they would like to respond.

For more help, see the **Comprehension** blackline master on page 183.

Discussion Questions

COMPREHENSION 1. Why is Stanley on the bus? *(He is on his way to Camp Green Lake.)*

2. What kind of camp is Camp Green Lake? *(It is a juvenile detention facility.)*

CRITICAL THINKING 3. Explain the quotation "If you take a bad boy and make him dig a hole every day in the hot sun, it will turn him into a good boy." *(Ask students to comment on the philosophy that hard and demoralizing work can "soften" criminals and make them see the error of their ways.)*

4. What examples of humor do you see in this story? *(Have students name funny, ironic, or sarcastic parts of the story. See the Literary Skill section for suggestions on how to teach this element.)*

5. What problems does Stanley have? *(Answers will vary. Possible: he's on his way to a juvenile detention camp, he's overweight, he's lacking in self-confidence, and says he has no friends.)*

Literary Skill

HUMOR Louis Sachar uses several different kinds of *humor* in his novel *Holes*. His puns and word plays (*Yelnats* is a palindrome for *Stanley*) make for lively reading, as does his use of understated humor that forces the reader to stop, think, and even reread ("Stanley was from a poor family. He had never been to camp before.") In addition, Sachar sprinkles ironic comments and situations throughout (a camp that has no lake is called Camp Green Lake). Invite students to discuss examples of humor in "Stanley Yelnats." What effect does the humor have on the tone and mood of the writing?

III. GATHER YOUR THOUGHTS

Prewriting Strategies

The prewriting activities on page 143 will help students make a bridge between text and personal experience. Students will begin by writing a few sentences about a time they were punished for doing something they didn't do, as Stanley is in *Holes*. Allow plenty of time for students to **choose a subject** about which they feel comfortable writing.

Next, students will complete a graphic organizer that helps them think carefully about the subject for their journal entries. The organizer asks that they list three details, but you may want to have them brainstorm a list of five or more and then choose the three details that they like best for the **journal entry**.

Have students use the **Prewriting** blackline master on page 184.

IV. WRITE

Students will write a **journal entry** about a time they were punished for something they didn't do. Remind them to consult their organizer on page 143 as needed. Also remind your writers to be as specific and detailed as possible. Encourage them to include sensory language and imagery to give readers a "you are there" feeling.

WRITING RUBRIC Use this rubric to evaluate students' writing.

Do students' journal entries

- explore a time they were wrongly punished?

- explain how they felt about it?

- include descriptive details about time and place?

- include a discussion of how the incident was resolved and how they felt once it was over?

Grammar, Usage, and Mechanics

After students have written a rough draft, have them read what they wrote, making any necessary corrections to the structure and form of their writing. Also encourage them to consult the **Writers' Checklist** for help with easily confused words. Remind them of the proper usage for *it's/its* and *their/there/they're*. For practice, have them correct these sentences:

Its going to be a great day at school. As soon as we get their, we'll find partners and help them practice there lines. Its almost time for the school play!

V. WRAP-UP

Take a moment at the end of the lesson for students to reflect on the **meaning** of "Stanley Yelnats." Ask them to read and respond to the questions on the **Readers' Checklist**. Remind students that these questions are the kind that critical readers ask themselves each time they finish a selection.

Assessment

To test students' comprehension, use the **Assessment** blackline master on page 185.

Name _____

VOCABULARY

Words from the Selection

DIRECTIONS Use context clues to help you decide which word from the box best completes each sentence.

> ◇ ratios   ◇ stifling   ◇ scorpions   ◇ hammock   ◇ stationery

1. A _____ for me to rest on was stretched between the two trees.

2. A rattlesnake and _____ were under a rock in the desert.

3. She pulled out some _____ to write a letter to her friend.

4. When the weather is _____, it can be very hard to work in the garden because it is so hot.

5. The _____ 3:1 and 2:1 were written on the board for all to see.

Strategy Lesson: Compound Words

DIRECTIONS Draw a line between the two separate words that make up each compound word.

6. armrest

7. handcuffs

8. backpack

9. pineapple

10. chopsticks

11. firearm

12. nickname

13. skyscraper

14. withhold

15. windowpane

Name _____

COMPREHENSION
Reciprocal Reading

DIRECTIONS Answer these questions about "Stanley Yelnats." They will help you think about the author's message.

SUMMARIZE: What is "Stanley Yelnats" about? Write three or four sentences explaining what happens in the story.

_____

_____

_____

_____

CLARIFY: What kind of person is Stanley?

_____

_____

_____

PREDICT: What do you think will happen once he gets to the camp? Name three problems you think he might have.

problem #1: _____

problem #2: _____

problem #3: _____

QUESTION: In what ways does "Stanley Yelnats" remind you of your own life?

_____

_____

_____

_____

Name _____

PREWRITING
Gathering Details

DIRECTIONS Use this organizer to show what happened when you were punished for something you didn't do. Give as many details as you can. Then use some of these details in your journal entry.

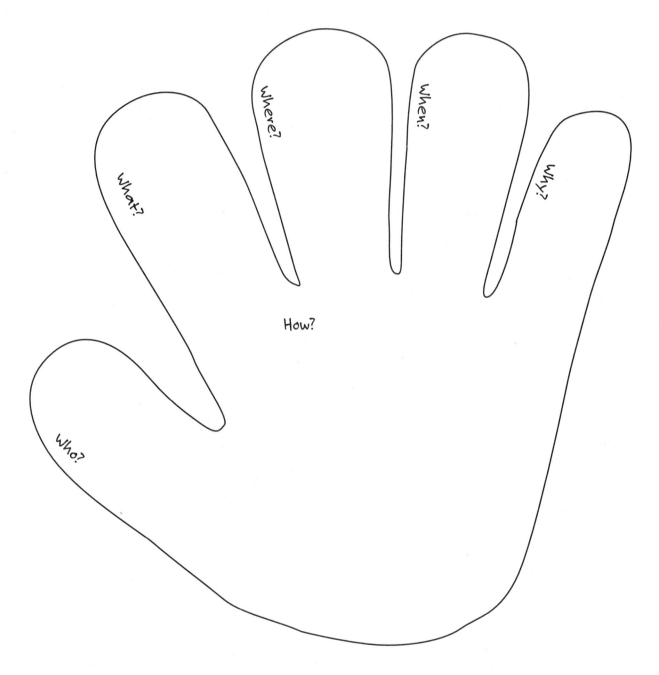

Name _____

ASSESSMENT

Multiple-choice Test

DIRECTIONS On the blanks provided, write the letter of the item that best answers each question.

_____ 1. What is missing from Camp Green Lake?
- A. campgrounds
- B. green trees
- C. a lake
- D. none of the above

_____ 2. How does Stanley feel about Camp Green Lake?
- A. happy
- B. anxious
- C. indifferent
- D. excited

_____ 3. What does the Warden own?
- A. a lake
- B. the shade
- C. a hammock
- D. B and C

_____ 4. What hides in the holes dug by the campers?
- A. turtles and frogs
- B. yellow-spotted lizards
- C. rattlesnakes and scorpions
- D. the campers

_____ 5. According to Stanley, what is the worst thing to be bitten by?
- A. a scorpion
- B. a yellow-spotted lizard
- C. a rattlesnake
- D. none of the above

_____ 6. Who goes to Camp Green Lake?
- A. Boy Scouts
- B. families
- C. summer vacationers
- D. "bad boys"

_____ 7. What is the alternative to camp for Stanley Yelnats?
- A. jail
- B. military school
- C. summer school
- D. getting a job

_____ 8. What does Stanley take with him to camp?
- A. a toothbrush
- B. stationery
- C. toothpaste
- D. all of the above

_____ 9. What problems does Stanley have?
- A. He is teased.
- B. He doesn't have any friends.
- C. He is overweight.
- D. all of the above

_____ 10. What is the tone of this selection?
- A. grim
- B. joyful
- C. humorous
- D. angry

Short-essay Test

Why do you think Stanley pretends he is going to Camp Fun and Games?

Unit Background   SLAVERY (pages 145–162)

Both selections in this unit are nonfiction. The first is an account of Denmark Vesey and his failed slave rebellion in South Carolina; the second is an excerpt from Frederick Douglass's autobiography.

Vesey and five of his co-conspirators were hanged outside Charleston, South Carolina, on July 2, 1822, for planning a slave rebellion. Vesey's grave has never been found, and no description or image of the man exists. For more background on Vesey, see the adult book *Denmark Vesey* by David Robertson (1999).

Lila Perl, author of "The Revolt of Denmark Vesey," was born in New York City and graduated from Brooklyn College. *Four Perfect Pebbles* (1996), written with Marion Blumenthal Lazan and telling Lazan's story of her Holocaust experience, is Perl's fiftieth book.

Frederick Douglass (c. 1817–1895) was born a slave in Maryland and escaped to New Bedford, Massachusetts, where he met and became an agent of the Massachusetts Anti-Slavery Society. Douglass's oratory was famous, and he spoke tirelessly for abolition. After spending two years in Britain speaking against slavery, he settled in Rochester, New York, where he started his anti-slavery paper, the *North Star*. During the Civil War, he assisted in recruiting African Americans for the Union Army, and he later served as U.S. consul general to Haiti. His autobiography was published in 1845.

Teaching the Introduction

Frederick Douglass and a business dealing in slaves are shown on page 145. The background depicts a diagram of a slave ship.

1. Tell students that the article about Denmark Vesey is about a failed slave rebellion. Ask students to speculate about why there were not many more attempts by slaves to revolt. *(Emphasize that in general slaves had no money, were carefully supervised, and were often beaten for insubordination. In light of these obstacles, it is remarkable that Vesey's attempts to assemble ammunition and gain participation from slaves were as successful as they were.)*

2. Frederick Douglass, as an escaped slave, was always in danger of being returned to his master until his freedom was purchased by friends. More-advanced students might like to research the Fugitive Slave Act, a federal law that provided for special commissioners to issue warrants for the arrest of fugitives. Citizens who prevented the arrest of a fugitive, concealed a fugitive, or aided in his rescue could be fined $1,000 and imprisoned.

Nevertheless, the so-called Underground Railroad was active, and some historians have estimated that 50,000 slaves escaped to freedom in the North through the secret routes and hiding places.

Opening Activity

Divide the class into small groups, and ask them to be ready to report on some aspect of Frederick Douglass's life. Assign various groups to look for an answer to one of these questions: What were his jobs as a slave? How did he learn to read and write? How did he manage to escape slavery? Did he marry and have children? Why did he have to flee to Canada at one time? Does his house still exist in Rochester, New York? Students whose research skills are weak will need help from you or from "experts" in the class.

The Revolt of Denmark Vesey

STUDENT PAGES 146–155

Skills and Strategies Overview

THEME	Slavery
READING LEVEL	average
VOCABULARY	◆bewildered ◆shackled ◆captives ◆humiliation ◆prosperous
PREREADING	picture walk
RESPONSE	question
COMPREHENSION	directed reading
PREWRITING	main idea and details
WRITING	summary / commas
ASSESSMENT	ease

BACKGROUND

Lila Perl tells the true story of a man named Denmark Vesey who gave his life in an attempt to end slavery forever. Vesey, who was born on a Caribbean island near St. Thomas, was captured and enslaved when he was 14 years old. Although his master treated him better than most slaves were treated, Vesey still knew that slavery was a violent, demoralizing, and inhumane practice.

After Vesey bought his freedom, he began thinking about ways he could help those who were still held as slaves. Perl tells the story of this quiet, unassuming hero who was eventually murdered for his role in planning an uprising.

UNIT THEME Lila Perl tells the story of one man's fight against the injustice of slavery.

GRAPHIC ORGANIZER The main idea/supporting details web students create on page 153 of their books might look something like this:

He was willing to give his life to end slavery.

Like so many others, Vesey was captured and sold into slavery at a young age.

He learned about successful slave revolts in America and abroad.

Denmark Vesey spent most of his life fighting the injustice of slavery.

He asked why slaves were still being imported when it was against the law.

For years he was a witness to the brutality and humiliation slaves had to endure.

BEFORE YOU READ

Read through the introduction to the lesson (page 146) with students. If you can, make a connection between this theme and what students are studying in their history classes. Then ask students to complete the prereading activity, a **picture walk**. (Refer to the **Strategy Handbook** on page 40 for more help.)

Motivation Strategy

In "The Revolt of Denmark Vesey," the author tells the true story of a man who was willing to sacrifice his life for what he believed in. Ask students to think about men and women in history who have done the same thing. Who are they and what did they do? What qualities do these people all have in common?

ENGAGING STUDENTS Slavery is often a difficult issue for students to talk about. Ask students to discuss stories (fiction or nonfiction) of slavery that have affected them in one way or another. Make a "Further Reading" list on the board that students can turn to later in the unit or perhaps use for a project in a history or government class. (See the bibliography for Lesson 16.)

Vocabulary Building

Help students use **context clues** as they read to figure out the meanings of difficult words, especially key vocabulary for this lesson: *bewildered, shackled, captives, humiliation,* and *prosperous.* Context clues can be found in the word's environment—that is, in surrounding words and phrases. Even though the footnotes define key vocabulary words for students, they still should try to define each word on their own. Ask students to circle the vocabulary words in the text. Once they understand how to search for clues, they'll get into the habit of doing it automatically. For additional practice with these words, see page 192.

STRATEGY LESSON: LATIN ROOTS Long or complex words can sometimes be broken down into smaller units that can give clues about their meaning. Since so many words in English contain Latin roots, it's important for students to become familiar with the more common roots. Use the **Vocabulary** blackline master for practice with the common root *port,* which means "carry." (The word *importation* appears on page 150.)

Prereading Strategies

Doing a **picture walk** before reading can help familiarize students with the topic of the selection. If you feel students would benefit, model the kinds of questions good readers ask themselves when they see a drawing or photograph. Such questions include these: What is this a picture of? Have I seen it before? If so, where? How does the picture make me feel? What is interesting or unique about it? What questions does the picture leave me with?

SKIM As an alternate prereading strategy, ask students to skim the selection. This strategy also offers a quick preview of the topic. Have students skim with one or two questions in mind. In this case, you might ask them to look for answers to these two questions: "Who was Denmark Vesey?" and "What kind of revolt did he lead?"

Spanish-speaking Students

"La rebelión de Denmark Vesey" es el cuento verdadero de un ex-esclavo en los últimos años del siglo diecisiete, y los principios del siglo dieciocho. Denmark Vesey fue dichoso porque compró su libertad después de ganar la lotería. Quería que la gente negra disfrutara de la misma fortuna que él, y por eso, planeó una gran rebelión para liberar a los esclavos. Desgraciadamente, la rebelión fracasó, y los esclvos tenían que esperar más de cuarenta años para conocer la libertad.

READ

As students are preparing to read, you might want to be sure they understand the response strategy of **questioning**. Have a volunteer review the types of questions students might ask themselves as they are reading. Remind the class that they should note every question in their **Response Notes**, even if they feel certain that it will be answered later on in the reading.

Response Strategy

VISUALIZE What mental images come to mind when students think about Denmark Vesey and the life he led? As an alternate response strategy, have students make sketches of what they "see" in the **Response Notes**. Their sketches will come in handy later, when they are trying to remember facts and detail for their summaries.

Comprehension Strategies

In a **directed reading**, the teacher or group leader guides a silent reading of the selection. Each time students come to a **stop and think** question, they should pause and spend a couple of minutes framing a careful response. Work through these questions as a class, if you like, or have students do them on their own. Be sure to keep track of any elements in the selection that seem to cause difficulty. Is the vocabulary a problem? If so, you might want to use some additional vocabulary strategies. Is the content a problem? If that's the case, you might provide some additional background information or lead a whole-class discussion about the article after everyone has finished.

GRAPHIC ORGANIZER As an alternate comprehension strategy, ask students to complete a word web for Denmark Vesey. Each spoke should tell something students have learned about the man.

For more help, see the **Comprehension** blackline master on page 193.

Discussion Questions

COMPREHENSION 1. When and where did Denmark Vesey live? *(He lived near Charleston, South Carolina, during the late 1700s and early 1800s.)*

2. How was he able to buy his freedom? *(He earned money from his master and then won the lottery.)*

3. How did Vesey feel about slavery? *(He despised it and decided to lead a revolt against it.)*

4. How did winning the lottery change Vesey's life? *(Remind students that it enabled him to buy his freedom. Then ask: "What other changes did Vesey make in his life as a result of winning the money?")*

CRITICAL THINKING 5. What words would you use to describe Denmark Vesey? *(Students might note that he was brave, determined, intelligent, and so on. Be sure they support what they say with evidence from the selection.)*

6. What do you think would have happened had Vesey's revolt succeeded? *(Answers will vary.)*

Literary Skill

FLASHBACK A *flashback* is an interruption in the action of a story to show an event or scene that happened earlier. Ask students to find the beginning and end of the flashback in "The Revolt of Denmark Vesey." (The flashback starts with the third paragraph on page 147 and runs to the end of the first full paragraph on page 149.) Then ask what the reader learns from this flashback.

III. GATHER YOUR THOUGHTS

Use the prewriting activities as a warm-up for the writing activity, a **summary**, which is assigned on page 154. Explain that before students can do any writing about Perl's article, they will need to decide on the **main idea** of the piece. Ask the class: "What was Perl's purpose in writing? What is Perl's most important idea?"

After students decide on the main idea, they'll need to see which facts and **details** directly support it. Ask them to use the web on page 153 as a way of keeping track of their notes.

Prewriting Strategies

GROUP DISCUSSION As an alternate prewriting strategy, ask students to discuss Perl's article in small groups. Have them decide as a group which parts are most important and which information they should include in their summaries. Group participants should keep their own set of notes to which they can refer as they're writing their summaries.

Have students use the **Prewriting** blackline master on page 194.

IV. WRITE

Be sure students understand that their assignment is to write a **summary** of Perl's article. Remind them that in a summary, the writer uses his or her own words and not the words of the author. Also be sure they know to include only the most important information in their writing, including names, dates, times, places, and similar facts.

WRITING RUBRIC When they've finished a rough draft, show students the writing rubric and have them read their work with these questions in mind. If they can answer "yes" to each question, they should go on to proofread their writing.

Do students' summaries

- clearly state Perl's main idea?

- explain how she supports her main idea?

- include a discussion of the most important details from the text?

Grammar, Usage, and Mechanics

When they are at the proofreading stage, refer students to the **Writers' Checklist** and teach a brief lesson on commas. Remind students to use a comma between coordinate adjectives not joined by *and*. For practice, write the following sentence on the board and have students insert commas.

Denmark Vesey recruited cool courageous well-organized supporters.

V. WRAP-UP

Take a moment at the end of the lesson for students to reflect on the **ease** or difficulty of the reading using the **Readers' Checklist**. If the article was difficult for students to read, the questions may help them figure out why. Use their responses to help you plan strategies for the next nonfiction selection they read.

Assessment

To test students' comprehension, use the **Assessment** blackline master on page 195.

Name _____

VOCABULARY

Words from the Selection

When you come to a difficult word, be sure to look at surrounding words and phrases. You might be able to pick up hints or clues about the word's meaning. This is called using context clues.

DIRECTIONS Choose a word from the box that could be substituted for each underlined word in the sentences below, and write that word on the line.

> ◆ bewildered　◆ shackled　◆ captives　◆ humiliation　◆ prosperous

1. When we came to a crossroads, we were <u>confused</u> about which direction to turn.

   _____

2. We stopped at a farmhouse where we saw two dogs <u>chained</u> to a fence.

   _____

3. Although the house had been recently painted, the farm itself did not look very <u>successful</u>. _____

4. When a little girl came to the door of the house, we said we felt sorry for the <u>prisoners</u> in the yard. _____

5. We thought we saw <u>shame</u> on the child's face when she said that she had been unable to untie the poor animals. _____

Strategy Lesson: Latin Roots

DIRECTIONS Study the prefixes in the box, all of which can be added to the Latin root *port*, which means "carry." Add one of the prefixes to *port* to answer each question.

PREFIXES

ex- = away　　*im-* = in　　*de-* = away　　*re-* = back　　*trans-* = across

6. What is the word for "carry in"? _____

7. What is one word for "carry away"? _____

8. What is another word for "carry away"? _____

9. What is the word for "carry back"? _____

10. What is the word for "carry across"? _____

Name _____

COMPREHENSION

Graphic Organizer

DIRECTIONS Use this graphic organizer to show the story of Denmark Vesey's life. Check your book for details.

As a boy, Denmark Vesey

When he was 14 years old, he

At this point, he felt

Over the next several years, Vesey

In 1799, he

His life changed in these ways:

In 1821, Vesey decided to

Here's what happened:

Name _____

PREWRITING

Writing a Summary

To write a good summary, you must select the most important ideas and combine them into clear, easy-to-understand sentences.

DIRECTIONS Follow these steps to write a summary for "The Revolt of Denmark Vesey."

STEP 1. REREAD. Go over the article carefully. Highlight key words and phrases.

STEP 2. LIST. Make a list of the most important events and quotations in the article.

Important events and quotes:

- _____
- _____
- _____
- _____

STEP 3. CHOOSE. Select the most important event or quote from your list and make this the main idea of your summary. Write a topic sentence that states the main idea.

Lila Perl's main idea in "The Revolt of Denmark Vesey":

_____

_____

STEP 4. FIND DETAILS. Gather important details from the article. Names, dates, times, and places are all examples of important details.

Perl's important details:

1. _____   6. _____
2. _____   7. _____
3. _____   8. _____
4. _____   9. _____
5. _____   10. _____

STEP 5. WRITE. Now write your summary on pages 154 and 155.

⇒ Begin with the topic sentence.

⇒ Then summarize Perl's most important details.

⇒ End with a concluding sentence that ties things together.

Name _____

ASSESSMENT

Multiple-Choice Test

DIRECTIONS On the blanks provided, write the letter of the item that best answers each question.

_____ 1. What is Denmark Vesey famous for?
    A. He was a white man who tried to free slaves.
    B. He was a freed slave who worked to free others.
    C. He was a slave who escaped to freedom.
    D. none of the above

_____ 2. How did Denmark Vesey come into money?
    A. He stole it from his master.
    B. He was given it by his master.
    C. He won it in the lottery.
    D. B and C

_____ 3. Why is it unusual for someone like Denmark Vesey to win the lottery?
    A. Most slaves didn't live near big towns.
    B. Most slaves didn't have much money.
    C. Slaves couldn't afford to buy a lottery ticket.
    D. all of the above

_____ 4. What job as a slave did Denmark Vesey not do?
    A. He didn't work on a plantation.
    B. He didn't work on a ship.
    C. He wasn't a carpenter.
    D. He wasn't a personal servant.

_____ 5. How did Denmark Vesey get his last name?
    A. He married into the Vesey family.
    B. He picked it out of a hat.
    C. He got it from his master.
    D. He got it from his father.

_____ 6. How much money did it take for Vesey to buy his freedom?
    A. six dollars
    B. sixty dollars
    C. six hundred dollars
    D. six thousand dollars

_____ 7. What was Vesey able to do with the remainder of his winnings?
    A. He bought his wife's freedom.
    B. He bought a house in Charleston.
    C. He bought a servant.
    D. He had no money left.

_____ 8. How did Vesey react to the Haitian slave revolt of 1804?
    A. This event meant very little to him.
    B. This event confused him.
    C. This event inspired him.
    D. all of the above

_____ 9. What did Vesey do to fight against slavery?
    A. He planned a revolt.
    B. He planned a peaceful protest.
    C. He talked to the President.
    D. He murdered his master.

_____ 10. Why was Denmark's plan unsuccessful?
    A. He couldn't find enough support.
    B. Word leaked out ahead of time.
    C. He decided not to risk his life.
    D. He was unable to get weapons.

Short-essay Test

What events in Denmark Vesey's life caused him to want to free other slaves?

Born into Slavery

Skills and Strategies Overview

THEME	Slavery
READING LEVEL	challenging
VOCABULARY	◇deprived ◇inquiries ◇complexion ◇hinder ◇affection
PREREADING	think-pair-and-share
RESPONSE	mark or highlight
COMPREHENSION	directed reading
PREWRITING	choosing a topic
WRITING	descriptive paragraph / adjectives and adverbs
ASSESSMENT	enjoyment

BACKGROUND

Frederick Douglass (c. 1817–1895) was an orator, journalist, and author of one of the most influential texts of his day, *Narrative of the Life of Frederick Douglass, an American Slave.* Douglass escaped from slavery in 1838 and rose through the ranks of the anti-slavery movement of the 1840s to become one of the most electrifying and persuasive speakers of the nineteenth century.

Published in 1845 and priced at 50 cents a copy, Douglass's *Narrative* sold briskly in the United States and abroad. In four years' time, more than 30,000 copies of the book had made their way into the public's hands—a remarkable accomplishment for a new author. The excerpt students will read in the *Sourcebook* is from an early part of his autobiography.

UNIT THEME Frederick Douglass, a man who was born into slavery, explores the injustice of slavery.

GRAPHIC ORGANIZER A word web can help students explore an important word (or concept) in some detail. This simple web for the word *slavery* can be started with what students learned in the previous selection.

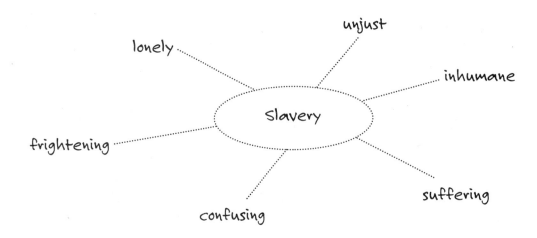

BIBLIOGRAPHY Students might benefit from reading these accounts of slavery in the United States: *Up from Slavery* (reissue, 1995) by Booker T. Washington; and *Remembering Slavery: African Americans Talk About Their Personal Experiences of Slavery and Emancipation* (2000), edited by Ira Berlin.

BEFORE YOU READ

Remind students of the theme of this unit and then have a volunteer read aloud the introduction to the lesson on page 156. To give some context for the literature, explain to students that the selection they're about to read is part of an autobiography. Then have them complete the prereading activity, a **think-pair-and-share**. (Refer to the **Strategy Handbook** on page 40 for more help.)

Motivation Strategy

Ask students to bring in one or two objects from home that they can use to tell a brief oral history of their lives. Limit each history to one or two minutes. What autobiographical story can they tell in that amount of time?

ENGAGING STUDENTS Make a quick **K-W-L** chart on the board. What do students know about Frederick Douglass? What knowledge gaps do they have? Many of these gaps will be filled by reading the selection.

Vocabulary Building

Help students pronounce words from the selection that are unfamiliar, especially key vocabulary words for this lesson: *deprived, inquiries, complexion, hinder,* and *affection*. Ask students to circle these words in the text. One or more of these words may be particularly difficult for low-level readers or for those who speak English as a second language. If this is the case, make an attempt to use the words in several different ways during the period. Or play a game with students, offering a star to a student each time he or she can use one of the words (in a way that makes sense) during the class period. Many times, repetition is the key to success when it comes to learning word pronunciations. For additional practice with these words, see page 200.

STRATEGY LESSON: NEGATIVE PREFIXES If you feel students will benefit, teach a brief lesson on negative prefixes. Remind the class that the prefixes *im-* and *in-* can change the meaning of a base word from positive to negative. Have students build word lists using these prefixes. Ask that they try to think of four or more words that contain each prefix.

For additional practice on this strategy, see the **Vocabulary** blackline master on page 200.

Prereading Strategies

A **think-pair-and-share** can arouse interest in the reading and help students begin thinking about the author's message. The quotations on page 156 have been chosen to give readers clues about the topic and tone of "Born into Slavery." Ask students to work together to number the five sentences. Then have them explain their reactions to the sentences. Finish by asking them what they think Douglass's main idea will be.

READ-ALOUD As an alternate prereading strategy, have a volunteer read aloud the first few paragraphs of "Born into Slavery." Be sure students notice that Douglass himself is the narrator. After the read-aloud, ask students to help you make a list of "Frederick Douglass Facts" on the board. Students can consult this list as they are reading the rest of the selection.

Spanish-speaking Students

Esta selección viene de la autobiografía famosa de Frederick Douglass. Describe con detalle vívido su vida como esclavo. Explica que no sabe con certidumbre cuántos años tiene, ni quién es su padre. Además, escribe que no se sentía nada al morirse su madre. Según Douglass, es raro que un esclavo sepa detalles personales y se sienta lazos familiares.

II. READ

Response Strategy

Remind the class that good readers take notes (or make notes if the book is consumable, as the *Sourcebook* is) as they read. Explain that as they read Douglass's memoir, they should highlight words and phrases that they think are important. To avoid the problem of having students highlight everything, tell them to use a highlighter each time they notice a name, date, place, emotion, or feeling.

Comprehension Strategies

Directed reading is a perfect comprehension strategy to use with this selection since students are likely to find it somewhat challenging. Ask students to read silently, perhaps one page at a time. At each **stop and think** question, have students pause and write an answer to the question. Then briefly discuss the question as a group. If there is time, ask students to read the selection a second time, at their own pace. If necessary, pull aside a small group of students who seem to be struggling and do an oral reading in one corner of the classroom.

Discussion Questions

COMPREHENSION 1. Who was Frederick Douglass? *(He was born a slave in Maryland. He went on to become a great orator and to fight against the injustice of slavery.)*

2. What was his relationship with his mother? *(He didn't know her well because she was sold from the plantation when he was an infant.)*

3. Who was Douglass's father? *(Douglass is not sure, although he heard stories that his father might have been the plantation owner.)*

CRITICAL THINKING 4. Why do you think it bothered Douglass not to know the date of his birth? *(Possible: Not knowing his birth date made it difficult for Douglass to have a strong sense of his own identity.)*

5. How did Douglass feel when he learned his mother had died? *(Answers will vary. Students might suggest that he felt sad or lonely or even angry. Have them support what they say with evidence from the text.)*

Literary Skill

WORD CHOICE To introduce a literary skill with this lesson, you might teach a brief lesson on *word choice*. Explain that an author's word choices can reveal a great deal of information about the writer. Douglass's formal language and sophisticated sentence structures show him to be a thoughtful, well-educated, and contemplative man. His word choices help reinforce the importance of his message. He has something serious and important to say, and he says it with serious and formal words, such as: *deprived, inquiries, impertinent, hinder,* and *affection.* Ask the class what these five words tell about Douglass. What "feel" do they give to the writing? Students might also note that Douglass does not use contractions, another characteristic of formal language.

III. GATHER YOUR THOUGHTS

Prewriting Strategies

Use the prewriting activities on page 161 to prepare students to write a **descriptive paragraph** of what it was like to be born a slave in America. (Invite students to call on prior knowledge and what they learned from reading "The Revolt of Denmark Vesey" to help them in their writing.) Students will begin by reflecting on Douglass's writing. In particular, they should note how Douglass felt about his situation.

Next, students will **choose a topic** for their paragraphs. Clearly they won't be able to cover everything they want to say about slavery in just one paragraph. They will need to narrow the focus of their topics and concentrate on just one aspect of what it was like. Ask them to brainstorm a list of words that describe how it might have felt to be a slave. Then have them draft a topic sentence and begin thinking about the kinds of details they'll want to use.

Have students use the **Prewriting** blackline master on page 202.

IV. WRITE

Read aloud the directions on page 162 to be sure that students understand the assignment. Remind them to feel free to use outside information in their writing, but they must limit their writing to just one paragraph. Also remind them that their **descriptive paragraphs** should begin with a topic sentence that tells the topic of the paragraph and their thoughts and feelings about the topic.

WRITING RUBRIC After students have written a first draft, have them stop and think carefully about what they've written. Encourage them to read their topic sentence to be sure it makes sense and to check to see that they've used adequate details as support. Show them this writing rubric and have them use it as a way of self-assessing their writing.

Do students' descriptive paragraphs

- begin with a topic sentence that states the topic to be discussed and the writer's thoughts and feelings about the topic?

- include descriptive details about time, place, and events?

- use sensory words that give readers a "you are there" feeling?

Grammar, Usage, and Mechanics

When they are ready to proofread their work, refer students to the **Writers' Checklist.** Since students often have trouble deciding when to use *good* and *well* and when to use *better* and *best,* you might have them practice by correcting these sentences.

Douglass felt ~~well~~ about his decision. He would escape and make a ~~best~~ life for himself.
           good   *better*

V. WRAP-UP

Take a moment at the end of the lesson for students to consider their **enjoyment** of the reading. Have them answer the questions on the **Readers' Checklist** and then explain their answers. Encourage them to use these questions whenever they are asked to evaluate a piece of writing. Help them make this process automatic by asking the same questions each time.

Assessment

To test students' comprehension, use the **Assessment** blackline master on page 203.

Name _____

VOCABULARY

Words from the Selection

DIRECTIONS Each sentence below contains the pronunciation of a word in parentheses. From the box, choose the word that matches the pronunciation. Write that word on the blank. You will not use one word.

> ✧recollect   ✧complexion   ✧affection   ✧deprived   ✧inquiries   ✧hinder

1. The child was (dee PRIVD) _____ of seeing his friends when he moved to another state.

2. A young boy came over earlier making (in KWI reez) _____ about who moved into this house.

3. His (kom PLEK shun) _____ was dark and his hair was curly.

4. The tall tree by the window may (HIN der) _____ your view, but you may be able to catch a glimpse of the visitor.

5. I (rek uh LEKT) _____ the young boy said he lived down the street.

Strategy Lesson: Negative Prefixes

Prefixes come at the beginning of a word. A prefix can give you clues about the meaning of a word. Negative prefixes can give the base word the opposite meaning. For example, if you add the prefix *in-* (meaning "not") to the adjective *direct*, you get the adjective *indirect*, which means "not straight."

DIRECTIONS On the blanks provided, write the underlined word from each sentence. Then add the prefix *im-* or *in-* (both mean "not") to the words and write the meaning of the new words.

6. The master felt <u>decisive</u> about allowing the family their freedom.

_____

7. Many of the slaves had <u>accurate</u> knowledge about their date of birth.

_____

8. Most felt it was <u>possible</u> to buy their freedom.

_____

9. After a long day's work, the horse was too <u>active</u> to be used for a journey.

_____

10. Many felt the boy was too <u>mature</u> to attend the funeral of his loved one.

_____

Name _____

COMPREHENSION
Graphic Organizer

DIRECTIONS Use this web to show what slavery was like. Consult your book as needed.

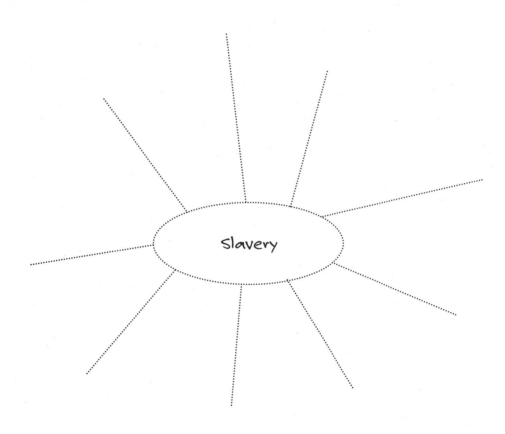

Name _____

PREWRITING

Narrowing a Topic

When you narrow the focus of your writing, you take a big topic (My Life) and divide it into smaller topics (Childhood Memories; School Days; Friends; Family). Narrowing your focus is like cutting a pie into pieces.

DIRECTIONS Use this diagram to help you narrow the focus of a topic about slavery.

1. Think of four small topics that relate to the larger topic. Write them in the four "slices" of pie.

2. Then list several words related to each of the smaller topics.

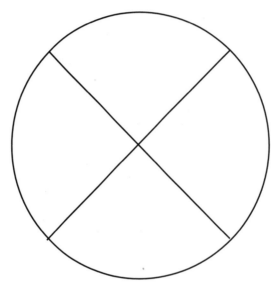

Writing a Topic Sentence and Details

Your descriptive paragraph must have a topic sentence. A topic sentence tells the subject of the paragraph and how you feel about the subject. You can use this formula to help you write a topic sentence.

(A specific topic) + (a specific feeling) = a good topic sentence.

DIRECTIONS Follow these steps to write a topic sentence and supporting details.

1. Write a topic sentence about one of the slices of the pie.

_____ + _____ =
(specific topic)   (thoughts and feelings)

_____
(your topic sentence)

detail #1: _____

detail #2: _____

detail #3: _____

Name _____

ASSESSMENT

Multiple-Choice Test

DIRECTIONS On the blanks provided, write the letter of the item that best answers each question or completes each statement.

_____ 1. What information did Douglass *not* know about himself?
A. He didn't know who his mother was.
B. He didn't know where he lived.
C. He didn't know his master's name.
D. He didn't know his birthday.

_____ 2. Why did masters keep the knowledge of a slave's birth a secret?
A. They wanted to keep the slaves ignorant.
B. They could get them to work at an earlier age.
C. They paid taxes on older slaves.
D. none of the above

_____ 3. How did Douglass feel about not knowing his birthday?
A. confused
B. excited
C. unhappy
D. He didn't care.

_____ 4. How old did Douglass think he was at the time he wrote this?
A. 17 or 18
B. 27 or 28
C. 37 or 38
D. 47 or 48

_____ 5. Why didn't Douglass know much about his family history?
A. His mother was taken away early on.
B. His father was taken away early on.
C. He had a blow to the head.
D. none of the above

_____ 6. How often was Douglass able to see his mother?
A. never
B. once or twice
C. four or five times
D. very often

_____ 7. Douglass only saw his mother at night because . . .
A. she worked during the day.
B. she was ashamed of him.
C. she didn't love him.
D. she was in his dreams.

_____ 8. Why did Douglass stop seeing his mother?
A. She was punished for visiting him.
B. She didn't like walking far.
C. They got into an argument.
D. She died.

_____ 9. Why wasn't Douglass present at his mother's death?
A. He was too young.
B. He didn't care about her.
C. He didn't know about it.
D. She didn't want him there.

_____ 10. What is the main idea of this selection?
A. The slave business made whites poor.
B. The feelings of slaves were ignored.
C. Slaves didn't live long lives.
D. The bond between mother and child was not strong.

Short-essay Test

Tell three or more ways Frederick Douglass and his family were treated unfairly.

Victor Martinez

Unit Background **VICTOR MARTINEZ** (pages 163–182)

This unit contains two excerpts from the novel *Parrot in the Oven: Mi Vida* by Victor Martinez.

Martinez was born in Fresno in 1954 and attended California State University in Fresno and Stanford University. He has worked as a field laborer, truck driver, and firefighter and is a poet and novelist. Partly autobiographical, *Parrot in the Oven* has been praised for its insight into Chicano culture.

Teaching the Introduction

Images on page 163 depict the cover of Martinez's book, a large family (not Martinez's family, however), a young boy working in a field, and a map of Mexico and California.

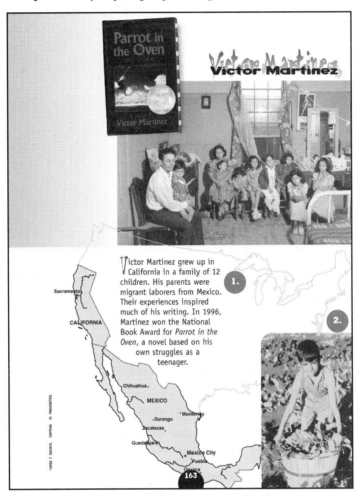

1. Read the introduction on page 163 with students. Ask how many students have no brothers or sisters, have older siblings, or have younger siblings. Then ask students to talk about the worst and the best things about having brothers and sisters. Do students who have no siblings feel that to be an ideal situation or not?

2. Tell students that in these two novel excerpts, Manny, the narrator, and his brother Nardo have to work hard for what they have, although Nardo runs through a series of jobs for various reasons. Ask how many students have brothers or sisters who have jobs. Do they complain about the work, or do they like it? Have students or anyone in their family ever worked on farms or in fields? If so, ask them to tell about their experiences.

Opening Activity

The unit introduction says that Martinez's parents were "migrant laborers." Ask students what this term means to them.

Skills and Strategies Overview

THEME Victor Martinez

READING LEVEL easy

VOCABULARY ✧busboy ✧stereos ✧fogies ✧pledge ✧blotches

PREREADING one-minute quickwrite

RESPONSE clarify

COMPREHENSION prediction

PREWRITING character map

WRITING autobiographical paragraph / capitalization

ASSESSMENT style

BACKGROUND

Victor Martinez's *Parrot in the Oven,* winner of the 1996 National Book Award for Young People's Fiction, is in many ways a coming-of-age story. The protagonist, Manuel Hernandez, experiences the same emotional aches and pains that all adolescents feel at one time or another. Manny awakens one morning with a yearning for something that he cannot name. He also longs for a family that doesn't shame him and feels the pain of a kind of passion that is always slightly out of reach.

Through his protagonist, Martinez shows readers the universality of their emotions and offers promise to those who feel despair. Using a dryly humorous tone, Martinez captures exactly the all-encompassing joys and desperate lows that are an inevitable part of growing up.

UNIT THEME Victor Martinez explains how hard it is to be "normal" when everyone around you—especially your family—is a little on the strange side.

GRAPHIC ORGANIZER The character map students create on page 169 of their books may look something like this.

1. daring
challenges other busboy to ask a girl to dance

2. impulsive
Rather than wasting time double-daring the boy, he decides to do it himself.

3. self-confident
He is "smooth" and never sees anything wrong with his behavior.

Nardo

4. intuitive
has a "sixth sense"

5. smart
He knows exactly how long he can stay somewhere before punishment comes "through the door."

BIBLIOGRAPHY Students might enjoy the Spanish-language version of Martinez's book: *El Lorno en el Horno, Mi Vida* (1997)

BEFORE YOU READ

Offer background information about Victor Martinez as you see fit. Then explain that the excerpt students are about to read is taken from his book, *Parrot in the Oven*, which is a series of stories about his own struggles as a teenager. Finish by asking students to complete the prewriting activity, a **one-minute quickwrite**. (Refer to the **Strategy Handbook** on page 40 for more help.)

Motivation Strategy

Nardo, or Bernardo, is the narrator's brother. Explain that the narrator is sometimes embarrassed by Nardo and at other times in awe of his abilities. Ask students to think of a family member they would enjoy writing about. Have them jot down the person's name in the margins of the text and then make a brief note about why this person would be interesting to describe.

ENGAGING STUDENTS Borrow a copy of *Parrot in the Oven* and read aloud a few passages to students as a warm-up to Martinez's style. Look for parts that are funny or that offer information about Manny, the narrator of the story.

Vocabulary Building

Help students use **context clues** as they read to figure out the meanings of difficult words, especially the key vocabulary for this lesson: *busboy, stereos, fogies, pledge,* and *blotches.* (*Pledge* on page 166 is not footnoted.) Ask students to circle these words in the text. Remind the class that context clues can be supplied through synonyms, comparisons and contrasts, and through definitions and descriptions. For additional practice with these words, see page 210.

STRATEGY LESSON: WORD ANALYSIS By now students have learned a number of strategies for defining new words, analyzing word parts, and understanding word origins. To help students review some of these strategies, assign the **Vocabulary** blackline master on page 210.

Prereading Strategies

The purpose of a **quickwrite** is to get students writing almost before they know it. To make the strategy meaningful, always ask students to quickwrite with a particular topic in mind. In this case, students should read the introductory paragraph at the top of page 164 and then write about something they did recently that seems funny or unusual. When they have finished, ask them to circle words or phrases in their writing that they like and may want to use in future writing.

WORD WEB As an alternate prereading strategy, think of a word related to the selection for which students might find synonyms. For example, one word that comes to mind when describing Nardo is *impulsive*. Have students list two or more synonyms for the word and then write a sentence that shows they understand the word's meaning. Use a chart like this one:

word	synonym	sentence

Spanish-speaking Students

"Nardo" viene de la novela *El lorno en el horno*, escrito por Victor Martinez. En esta selección, el narrador describe un verano en que su hermano, Nardo, fue despedido de muchos trabajos. Nardo lavó platos, limpió mesas en un restaurante, y hizo hamburguesas durante poco tiempo. El único trabajo que echa de menos es el en un club exclusivo, donde fue un ayudante de camarero. A Nardo le gustó el trabajo mucho. No se arrepienta, sin embargo, haberse sido despedido.

 **II. READ**

Be sure students understand that they are to make notes that help **clarify** why Nardo (and perhaps Manny) say the things they do and act the way they do. Tell them that their comments will help them develop a stronger understanding of the characters and what motivates them. As you know, understanding character is an important part of understanding the text as a whole.

Response Strategy

VISUALIZE   Before they begin reading, tell students to watch for the scene at the country club and then draw a couple of quick sketches of everything they "see." This will give students a purpose for reading and guarantee a close reading of at least one part of the text.

Comprehension Strategies

Predicting outcomes can enhance a reader's enjoyment. Students should stop every once in a while and ask: "What do I think will happen next?" or "What's he going to say now?" Good readers ask these kinds of questions without even thinking about them. Your goal is to get students to the point that they automatically make predictions as they are reading.

RETELLING   As an alternate prereading strategy, ask students to retell one or two different parts of the story. This will help students who are struggling a bit with the selection, but a whole-class retelling can benefit everyone, not just those in need of extra help. When a reader listens to a retelling, he or she is likely to hear words or phrases that provoke new ideas about the selection. If you like, encourage students to take notes during the retelling just as they do when they are listening to a story read aloud.

For more help, see the **Comprehension** blackline master on page 211.

Discussion Questions

COMPREHENSION   1. Who is the narrator of the story? *(Manny)*

2. What is the narrator's relationship to Nardo? *(They are brothers.)*

3. What do Nardo and Randy dare each other to do? *(They dare each other to get a ticket and ask a guest at the club to dance.)*

CRITICAL THINKING   4. How does Manny feel about his brother? *(Students will need to make inferences, or read between the lines, to answer this question. Encourage them to support what they say by pointing to the place in the text that gave them the idea.)*

5. What type of person do you think Nardo is? *(Answers will vary. Possible: He is impulsive, brash, and self-confident. Remind students to provide evidence for their responses.)*

Literary Skill

ANECDOTE   To introduce a literary skill with this lesson, you might teach a brief lesson on anecdotes. Explain that an *anecdote* is a very short account told to make a point or clarify an idea. Manny tells the anecdote about Nardo and the dare in order to give readers a strong sense of what his brother is like. Ask students to skim the selection, searching for other anecdotes that provide clues about Nardo's character. What do these stories reveal about Nardo?

III. GATHER YOUR THOUGHTS

Prewriting Strategies

The prewriting activities on pages 169 and 170 are meant to help students reflect on what they've read in "Nardo" and then build a bridge between the reading and their own lives. Students will begin by creating a **character map** that shows their inferences about Nardo. They will need to come up with four adjectives that describe him and then write a supporting example underneath each adjective.

Once they finish the character map about Nardo, students will be ready to make a character map about themselves. As they're working on this activity, they should be thinking about little anecdotes that they could tell to help readers understand the adjective or adjectives they have listed.

On page 170, students will prepare to write an **autobiographical paragraph** about one of the events they listed on their character maps. They will write an opening sentence and then fill out a graphic organizer that helps explore the event.

Have students use the **Prewriting** blackline master on page 212.

IV. WRITE

Remind students that their assignment is to write an **autobiographical paragraph** about an event in their life that was important or interesting or funny. If they like, they can use "Nardo" as a model for their own writing style. Students should begin with a topic sentence and then tell about the event using chronological order. Remind them that sensory words can add vibrancy and immediacy to a piece of writing.

WRITING RUBRIC   Use this writing rubric to help students focus on the assignment requirements and for assistance with a quick assessment of their writing.

Do students' autobiographical paragraphs

- open with a sentence that indicates the event to be described?

- include descriptive details about time and place?

- stay focused on this one event throughout?

Grammar, Usage, and Mechanics

After students have written a first draft, have them proofread their writing, looking carefully for grammatical, mechanical, and usage errors. (Draw their attention to the **Writers' Checklist** if they haven't noticed it already.) Remind students that a title before a proper noun is always capitalized, as are titles that describe family relationships. For practice, have them proofread this sentence and make any necessary corrections.

My aunt Helga has an interesting friend named mrs. stein.

V. WRAP-UP

Ask students to reflect on Martinez's **style** by reading and responding to the questions on the **Reader's Checklist.** Explain that they won't always like a writer's style but that good readers always make an attempt to identify and understand the style.

Assessment

To test students' comprehension, use the **Assessment** blackline master on page 213.

Name _____

VOCABULARY

Words from the Selection

DIRECTIONS Using context clues, fill in each blank with the most appropriate word from the list.

> ◆ busboy ◆ stereos ◆ fogies ◆ pledge ◆ blotches

1. The _____ on his face, which looked like tiny red spots, were caused by an allergic reaction to a bee sting.

2. The _____ cleared the table and took the dishes into the kitchen.

3. People who have old-fashioned views are sometimes referred to as "old _____."

4. The _____ were at the audio repair shop because they were all broken.

5. After I gave my _____ to support the local kids' club, I promised to ask my friends to help too.

Strategy Lesson: Word Analysis

DIRECTIONS Write the word from the box that correctly answers each question.

> ◆ sufficient ◆ unoccupied ◆ permit ◆ novice ◆ steamed

6. Which word means both "angry" and "how you cooked a vegetable"?

_____

7. Which word means both "allow" and "a license that gives permission to do something"?

_____

8. Which word is a synonym for "enough"? _____

9. *Nov* is a Latin root that means "new." Which word comes from this Latin root?

_____

10. Which word has a prefix meaning "not"? _____

Name _____

COMPREHENSION

Directed Reading

DIRECTIONS Answer these questions about "Nardo." Your answers can help you understand Victor Martinez's story.

1. Who is the narrator and what is his relationship to Nardo?

_____

_____

_____

2. How does the narrator feel about Nardo?

_____

_____

_____

3. What does the incident at the country club reveal about Nardo?

_____

_____

_____

4. Why do you think Nardo says, "Don't you ever get braces, Manny?" What does the comment show about him?

_____

_____

_____

5. What advice would you give the narrator if he came to you for help with Nardo?

_____

_____

_____

Name _____

PREWRITING
Writing an Autobiographical Paragraph

DIRECTIONS Follow these steps to write an autobiographical paragraph.

A. Choose a topic. Before you can write a paragraph about yourself, you need to decide what you want to say. First think of a topic. Tell about an event or experience that you thought was interesting or important or funny. (Your book asks you to write about an event that tells the reader a little something about you.)

My topic: _____

B. Gather details. Then gather details about the event. These questions can help you consider the most important details.

What happened?

Where were you?

Who else was there?

When did it happen?

Why did it happen?

How did it end?

How did you feel once the whole thing was over?

What did you learn about yourself from the experience?

C. Write a topic sentence. Write a topic sentence that tells about the event and what it shows about you. Use this formula:

(The event) + (what it shows about me) = my topic sentence.

My topic sentence: _____

Name _____

ASSESSMENT

Multiple-Choice Test

DIRECTIONS On the blanks provided, write the letter of the item that best answers each question or completes each statement.

_____ 1. What job or jobs does Nardo lose during the summer?
- A. dishwasher
- B. busboy
- C. parking attendant
- D. all of the above

_____ 2. Why is Nardo unable to work at the hamburger stand?
- A. The stand closes unexpectedly.
- B. The owner doesn't like him.
- C. He shows up too late.
- D. all of the above

_____ 3. Why does Nardo miss working as a busboy?
- A. He enjoyed watching others dance.
- B. He liked being around rich people.
- C. He got a lot of tips.
- D. His boss respected him.

_____ 4. Nardo takes off his busboy jacket because . . .
- A. he gets fired.
- B. he has a stain on it.
- C. he is pretending to be a guest.
- D. he is hot while dancing.

_____ 5. Randy and Nardo dare each other to . . .
- A. get a ticket and ask a girl to dance.
- B. pretend they are performers.
- C. steal a drink.
- D. run around and yell.

_____ 6. Why does Nardo take the dare?
- A. He needs the money.
- B. He is afraid of Randy.
- C. He hopes to get fired.
- D. He enjoys doing these stunts.

_____ 7. What does the girl with the freckles and braces say to Nardo?
- A. "I would never dance with you!"
- B. "You dance real nice."
- C. "You hurt my feelings."
- D. "You are a liar!"

_____ 8. According to Martinez, what is Nardo's sixth sense?
- A. He has a photographic memory.
- B. He knows what people are thinking.
- C. He can avoid trouble.
- D. He can see ghosts.

_____ 9. What does Nardo learn from this experience?
- A. Always show up to work on time.
- B. Rich girls don't date busboys.
- C. Always have a lookout.
- D. nothing

_____ 10. What is the best word to describe Nardo?
- A. angry
- B. hard-working
- C. easy-going
- D. cruel

Short-essay Test

In your opinion, is Nardo a likable character? Why or why not?

STUDENT PAGES 173–182

Skills and Strategies Overview

THEME	Victor Martinez
READING LEVEL	easy
VOCABULARY	◇sockets ◇hustled ◇hobble ◇blossomed ◇foreman
PREREADING	preview
RESPONSE	prediction
COMPREHENSION	reciprocal reading
PREWRITING	using anecdotes
WRITING	autobiographical essay / commas
ASSESSMENT	depth

BACKGROUND

For Manny Hernandez, the major challenge in life is stopping himself from succumbing to the negativity and prejudice that surround him. His life in the projects of the Central Valley of California is little more than a series of troubles, worries, and dangers that Manny tries to resist, no matter what the cost.

Although *Parrot in the Oven* is largely autobiographical, it is a novel. It is made up of a series of vignettes about growing up, each one told in the matter-of-fact and dryly humorous tone that is a hallmark of Martinez's style. In every episode of his life, the protagonist battles discrimination from the outside world and crisis within the family itself.

In this second excerpt from the novel, reprinted on pages 174–179 of the *Sourcebook,* Manny offers more information about Nardo and his work habits. In so doing, Manny gives readers a revealing glimpse of himself and what is important to him.

UNIT THEME Victor Martinez writes of the ups and downs of being a brother to someone as unique and interesting as Nardo.

GRAPHIC ORGANIZER A Venn diagram like this one can help readers explore the similarities and differences between Manny and Nardo.

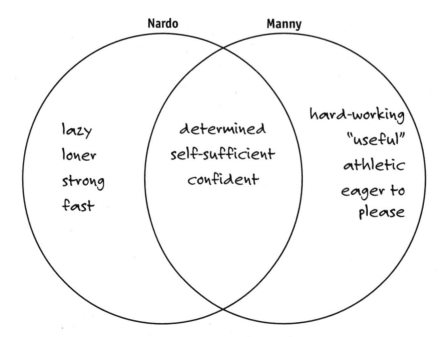

Nardo   Manny

lazy
loner
strong
fast

determined
self-sufficient
confident

hard-working
"useful"
athletic
eager to
please

I. BEFORE YOU READ

Remind students that this unit concerns writer Victor Martinez and that both selections in the unit are excerpts from *Parrot in the Oven*. Read aloud another excerpt or two from the book to help motivate and focus students. Then ask them to complete the prereading activity, a **preview**. (Refer to the **Strategy Handbook** on page 40 for more help.)

Motivation Strategy

Ask students whether they have read works by Walter Dean Myers, Patrice Kindl, Gary Soto, or John Marsden. Ask students to comment on characteristics of the narrator or protagonist. What "learning" did this character endure? What was the outcome?

ENGAGING STUDENTS Ask students: "What's the hardest job you've ever done? What did it involve? What made it so difficult?" Have volunteers discuss their experiences. A brief discussion on this topic will help students make a connection between the topic of the selection they're about to read and their own lives.

Vocabulary Building

Draw attention to the key vocabulary words for this lesson: *sockets, hustled, hobble, blossomed,* and *foreman*. Have students circle these words in the text. Ask students to volunteer pronunciations and definitions for the words. Also have them use the words in sentences of their own. A series of quick vocabulary exercises can help students become more comfortable with any words that are new to them. For more practice, have students complete the **Vocabulary** blackline master on page 218.

STRATEGY LESSON: WORD ANALYSIS Students have learned a number of strategies for defining new words, analyzing word parts (prefixes, suffixes, and roots), and understanding word origins (Greek and Latin roots plus word families). To help students review some of these strategies, assign the **Vocabulary** blackline master, page 218.

Prereading Strategies

During a **preview**, the reader looks carefully at the first and perhaps last paragraph of the selection and then glances through the rest of the text, paying particular attention to headlines, questions, vocabulary words, art, and captions. A preview can familiarize the reader with the topic of the selection and provide valuable clues about the main idea. Encourage students to make notes after they finish their previews. The chart on page 173 is an example of how they might record their notes. Have them add to this chart any ideas or information they noticed on their previews.

QUICKWRITE As an alternate prereading strategy, ask students to complete a one-minute quickwrite about Nardo. Have them write everything they know about him and their opinion of what he's like. This quick activity will help prepare students to see and understand a slightly different side of his character—one that they'll meet in "Picking."

Spanish-speaking Students

Esta selección también viene de la novela *El lorno en el horno*. El narrador explica que a diferencia de su hermano, a él le gusta trabajar. Se siente inútil si no trabaja. Por eso suigiere a Nardo que los dos trabajen en un campo de guindillas para ganar dinero. El narrador está preparado para el día laborioso aunque sabe que va a ser difícial ganar el dinero que necesite.

II. READ

By this time, students should be fairly familiar with the process of responding as they read. Remind them that their job as reader will be to make **predictions** about characters and outcomes. Each time they make a new prediction, they should make a note of it in the **Response Notes**.

Response Strategy

REACT AND CONNECT Many students will want to share their work experiences. As an alternate response strategy, have students make react and connect comments such as "Something like this happened to me once!" or "I would have said. . . ." Their observations will help them stay interested and involved in the story.

Comprehension Strategies

In a **reciprocal reading**, readers share the process of reading and responding to a text. This can make the activity easier and more enjoyable for students, as well as help refine their cooperative skills. Ask students to work together in a group to read "Picking." Have them switch readers every page or so. Each time a reader comes to an interrupter question, he or she should direct the question to the group and lead the others in brainstorming a response. In some cases (with the **clarify** question, for example), the group may come up with several different answers. These can be noted in the book and shared with the rest of the class later.

STORY FRAME As an alternate comprehension strategy, ask students to complete a story frame as they are reading. Write these words on the board: "*First, Next, Then, Later,* and *Finally.*" Ask students to plot the sequence of events in the story using these words.

For more help, see the **Comprehension** blackline master on page 219.

Discussion Questions

COMPREHENSION 1. Why is Manny so desperate for a job? *(He feels empty without one. Also, he wants to buy a baseball mitt he saw in the window of a store.)*

2. What job does he ask Nardo to help him with? *(picking chili peppers)*

3. Why does the foreman at first refuse to give the boys a row to pick? *(He says Manny is too young and that all the rows are taken.)*

CRITICAL THINKING 4. What do you think Manny means when he says, "I was of my grandpa Ignacio's line of useful blood"? *(He means that he is a hard worker, in contrast to Nardo, whom Manny implies is lazy.)*

5. What would you say Manny learns in the chili field? *(Answers will vary. Encourage students to discuss how the experience makes Manny feel about himself and his brother. Remind them to support what they say with evidence from the selection.)*

Literary Skill

SIMILE You may want to reteach *simile* with this lesson. Read the following simile from page 175, and ask students to tell what two words suggest a relationship between the two things being compared: ". . . his ankles swelled up blue and tender as a ripened plum." Then ask students to find the simile in the first line of paragraph two on page 175 and the two similes in the penultimate paragraph on page 179 and discuss their effectiveness.

III. GATHER YOUR THOUGHTS

Prewriting Strategies

The purpose of the prewriting activities on page 180 is to help students write an **autobiographical essay** about a time they worked hard. Students will begin by reflecting on the **anecdote** Martinez tells about the chili field. Remind the class that anecdotes (brief stories) are used to make a point or shed some light on an idea or emotion. Then have them explain what the anecdote about the chili field reveals about Nardo and Manny. What information does it give about their personalities?

Students will use a graphic organizer to plan a three-paragraph **autobiographical essay**. Remind the class that the first paragraph will set the scene by giving details about time, place, and who was involved. The next paragraph should describe the event. (Encourage students to use chronological order.) The final paragraph will be a discussion of what the writer learned about himself or herself from the event.

Have students use the **Prewriting** blackline master on page 220.

IV. WRITE

If you feel students will benefit, have them reread the autobiographical paragraphs that they wrote on pages 171 and 172 of their books. Explain that you'd like them to use this same style when writing their **autobiographical essays.** Remind them to consult their planners on page 180 as they write.

WRITING RUBRIC You might use this rubric to help students focus on the assignment requirements and for assistance with a quick assessment of their writing.

Do students' autobiographical essays

- open with a paragraph that sets the scene and explains the experience to be described?
- include plenty of descriptive details in the body?
- end with a discussion of what the writer learned from the experience?

Grammar, Usage, and Mechanics

Next have students proofread their work. Refer them to the **Writers' Checklist** and ask that they check carefully for problems with comma usage. You might want to teach a brief lesson on this topic, since commas usually cause problems for young writers. (They often use too many or too few.) Explain that commas are always used to set off explanatory and introductory phrases. In addition, they are used to separate interruptions from the rest of the sentence. For example:

Incorrect: In August Teresa my neighbor went to Canada.

Correct: In August, Teresa, my neighbor, went to Canada.

V. WRAP-UP

Invite students to talk about the **depth** of their understanding. As a starting point, have them answer the questions on the **Readers' Checklist**. Its intent is to help students think about the bridge they've created between the literature and their own lives.

Assessment

To test students' comprehension, use the **Assessment** blackline master on page 221.

Name _____

VOCABULARY

Words from the Selection

DIRECTIONS Read these sentences. Write the words from the box that best fit each of the following descriptions.

> ✧sockets ✧hobble ✧hustled ✧blossomed ✧foreman

1. These are electrical fixtures. _____

2. This is slang for "sold." _____

3. This is another word for walking awkwardly. _____

4. This is a person in charge of a work crew. _____

5. This word means "to become developed." _____

Strategy Lesson: Word Analysis

DIRECTIONS Write the word from the list below that correctly answers each question.

> ✧spunky ✧scalding ✧enthusiastically ✧scrawny ✧suspicious

6. Which word is a synonym for *excitedly*? _____

7. Which word has a suffix meaning "state or quality of"? _____

8. Which word means both "spirited" and "lively"? _____

9. Which word is an antonym for *fat*? _____

10. Which word means "burning"? _____

Name _____

COMPREHENSION
Story Frame

DIRECTIONS Fill in this story frame about "Picking." Add lines if you need to.

The story takes place _____

_____

_____ is a character in the story who _____

_____ .

_____ is another character in the story who _____

_____

_____ . A problem occurs when _____

_____

_____ . After that, _____

_____

_____ .

And _____

_____

_____ .

The problem is solved when _____

_____

_____ .

The story ends with _____

_____

_____ .

Name _____

PREWRITING
Writing an Autobiographical Essay

DIRECTIONS Use this organizer to plan the details of your essay.

1. Answer each question as thoroughly as you can.

2. Then include the information from the organizer in your essay.

Introduction

PARAGRAPH 1   Who was there   Where we were   When the event occurred

_____   _____   _____

_____   _____   _____

_____   _____   _____

_____   _____   _____

_____   _____   _____

Body

PARAGRAPH 2   What happened first   What happened next   What happened after that

_____   _____   _____

_____   _____   _____

_____   _____   _____

_____   _____   _____

Conclusion

PARAGRAPH 3   What I learned about myself   What I learned about others   How I felt once the whole thing was over

_____   _____   _____

_____   _____   _____

_____   _____   _____

_____   _____   _____

Name _____

ASSESSMENT

Multiple-Choice Test

DIRECTIONS On the blanks provided, write the letter of the item that best answers each question or completes each statement.

_____ 1. Who in his family is Manny most like?
   A. his brother Nardo   C. his grandfather
   B. his father   D. his mother

_____ 2. How would Manny describe his grandfather?
   A. He was a hard worker.   C. He could never find a job.
   B. He was lazy.   D. all of the above

_____ 3. What does Manny do with his cousins Rio and Pete?
   A. They hang out on the street.   C. They lift weights.
   B. They play baseball.   D. They sell fruit.

_____ 4. Why does Manny want to go to work?
   A. His father requires him to do so.   C. He needs to pay tuition.
   B. He wants to buy things.   D. He has debts to pay off.

_____ 5. Why does Manny ask Nardo to work with him?
   A. He wants to get closer to his brother.   C. He needs a ride.
   B. His father asks him to.   D. all of the above

_____ 6. How does Manny's father feel about the boys picking chili peppers?
   A. He is thrilled.   C. He is skeptical.
   B. He is nervous.   D. He is angry.

_____ 7. The man at the field says "no" at first to the boys because . . .
   A. Manny looks too young.   C. all the rows had been taken.
   B. it was too late to start.   D. all of the above

_____ 8. What kind of work were the brothers finally given?
   A. They picked from a scrawny row.   C. They dug ditches.
   B. They filled the soda machine.   D. They were given no work.

_____ 9. How long did the brothers work?
   A. 1 hour   C. 3 hours
   B. 2 hours   D. 30 minutes

_____ 10. What is the author's purpose in writing "Picking"?
   A. to entertain   C. to persuade
   B. to tell the steps in a process   D. none of the above

Short-essay Test

How do you think Manny feels about his brother?

Fitting In

Unit Background   FITTING IN (pages 183–200)

This unit contains an essay by Judith Ortiz Cofer and a poem by Aurora Levins Morales.

Judith Ortiz Cofer was born in 1952 in Hormigueros, Puerto Rico, and immigrated with her family to the United States in 1956. She received a B.A. from Augusta College in 1974 and an M.A. from Florida Atlantic University in 1977. She also attended Oxford University. She has been a public school bilingual teacher, an instructor in English at the University of Georgia and Macon College, and a member of the literature panel of the Fine Arts Council of Florida. She received a grant from the Witter Bynner Foundation for Poetry in 1988 for *Letters from a Caribbean Island* and a National Endowment for the Arts Fellowship in poetry in 1989. In addition to poetry, her published works include essays and a novel, *The Line of the Sun* (1989).

Aurora Levins Morales was born in Indiera, Puerto Rico in 1954. The daughter of a Puerto Rican mother and Jewish father, Levins Morales immigrated to the United States in 1967. She is known for her introspective writing, which focuses primarily on her experiences living in urban Chicago, rural New Hampshire, and radical San Francisco. *Getting Home Alive* (1986), a collection of short stories, essays, and poems, is her most famous work.

Teaching the Introduction

Images on page 183 show the hands of two different people, a tropical landscape, and a young woman.

1. Read the unit introduction, and ask students whether "fitting in" is a hard thing to do. Why do people "try to erase the traits that set them apart from others"?

2. Ask: "Do some people try too hard to fit in? Do other people not care whether they fit in or not? What makes the difference between these two types of people?"

3. Do students think that it is difficult to just be themselves?

Opening Activity

Ask students to write one or two sentences in their journals about what they think sets them apart from others and how they feel about this "apartness."

Skills and Strategies Overview

THEME	Fitting In
READING LEVEL	average
VOCABULARY	◇ stature ◇ la gringa ◇ covet ◇ repertoire ◇ naively
PREREADING	anticipation guide
RESPONSE	question
COMPREHENSION	directed reading
PREWRITING	support an opinion
WRITING	paragraph of opinion / comma splices
ASSESSMENT	meaning

BACKGROUND

When she was a little girl, Judith Ortiz Cofer sat spellbound while her grandmother told fabulous stories about people and places. Quite often these stories served as a distraction from the taunts of neighborhood children and classmates who told Ortiz Cofer that her skin was not the "right" color and that she would never fit in.

What Judith-the-child never realized was that "fitting in" is a worry shared by all children, no matter what their skin color, nationality, or personality. Unfortunately, Judith felt completely alone in her misery. In her autobiographical essay "The Story of My Body," Ortiz Cofer explains her feelings of isolation. She also shows readers that feeling good about yourself is the best way—or perhaps the only way—to combat these miserable feelings.

UNIT THEME Young Judith worries that she will never fit in. One quick moment in a supermarket teaches her that the world she is trying to fit into is a place she wants to have nothing to do with.

GRAPHIC ORGANIZER A graphic organizer like this one can help readers keep track of individual episodes in a work of fiction or nonfiction.

Episode Analysis: "The Story of My Body"

episode	problem	response	outcome
#1	scars from chicken pox	embarrassment	learns to be "invisible"
#2	blanca in some worlds; brown in others	proud at times; ashamed at others	fixates on how she looks, rather than who she is
#3	yelled at in the grocery store	flees	decides she is no "dirtier" than anyone else
etc. ↓			

BIBLIOGRAPHY Students might enjoy these works by Judith Ortiz Cofer: *An Island Like You: Stories from the Barrio* (1996); and *The Latin Deli: Prose and Poetry* (1995).

I. BEFORE YOU READ

Explain that "The Story of My Body" is an autobiographical essay. Although the essay describes only one woman's experiences, students will likely find that the feelings the author describes are some of the same ones they've experienced in their own lives. Then ask the class to complete the prereading activity, an **anticipation guide**. (For help with this activity, see the **Strategy Handbook**, page 40.)

Motivation Strategy

"The Story of My Body" is an interesting title for an autobiographical essay. Ask students to make predictions about Ortiz Cofer's writing using just the title for clues. Students' predictions may serve to pique their interest in the selection.

ENGAGING STUDENTS Tell students that in this essay, the author describes a painful childhood experience. Have the class think about a childhood experience of their own that still causes them pain some years later. Ask them to make a note of it in their books, along with a description of how they felt. Students might be surprised to discover later that the feelings they jot down are also experienced by the author of this piece.

Vocabulary Building

Help students use **context clues** as they read to figure out the meanings of difficult words, especially the key vocabulary for this lesson: *stature, la gringa, covet, repertoire,* and *naively.* Have students circle these words in the text. Model using context and then checking your idea against the footnote: "I don't know the word *stature.* I see, however, that it appears in a paragraph in which the author is describing her height. I can safely assume that *stature* means 'height.' I'll check the footnote to see if my guess is correct." For additional practice with these words, see page 228.

STRATEGY LESSON: WORD FAMILIES As you know, words that share a common root are said to belong to the same "family." Explain to students that if they know and understand the root, they will have an easy time understanding other words in the family. Ask students to practice with *vis,* from *visere,* "to see." Have the class build word families that use this root. Then ask volunteers to define each word in the family.

For additional practice on this strategy, see the **Vocabulary** blackline master on page 228.

Prereading Strategies

Anticipation guides are easy to create and interesting for students to do. They work especially well with longer or more complex selections because they give students a head start on topic and theme work. As a part of the anticipation guide, students will make predictions about the selection. In most cases they will rely on their own ideas and experiences to form their predictions. Almost without thinking about it, students will activate prior knowledge and make personal connections to the people, places, and themes the author explores in the essay.

QUICKWRITE Ask students to quickwrite for one or two minutes about the theme of "fitting in." When they've finished, have them highlight words or phrases in their writing that they'd like to remember. This activity will serve as an excellent warm-up to theme. In addition, it will show students that writing is not always something that has to be *labored* over. It can be quick and fun.

Spanish-speaking Students

En "El cuento de mi cuerpo" Judith Ortiz Cofer describe cómo le afectaba su raza durante su juventud. Ella fue considerada blanca en Puerto Rico debido al color pálido de la piel. Al trasladarse a los Estados Unidos, sin embargo, Ortiz Cofer fue considerada morena por cierta gente. Ella escribe de un momento en particular, cuando un hombre le insultó por ser puerto riqueña y sucia.

II. READ

Because "The Story of My Body" is one of the longer selections in the *Sourcebook*, be sure that students focus on making notes as they read. Their notes will help them keep track of the various events and ideas that Ortiz Cofer describes. In particular, they should make a note of any **questions** that occur to them. Point out the example on page 185 and explain that the reader may or may not find an answer to this question later in the selection. If the author does not provide an answer, it will be up to the reader to make inferences or reasonable guesses.

Response Strategy

VISUALIZE Ortiz Cofer uses sensory language in her essay, especially language that appeals to the sense of sight. As an alternate or additional response strategy, have students try to "see" what she saw as a girl. Have them make sketches of these images in their **Response Notes**.

Comprehension Strategies

Directed reading can help reluctant or low-level readers better comprehend what they are reading. During your directed reading of "The Story of My Body," students will need to stop every other page or so and answer a question that can help clarify the action or main idea. If you feel students might struggle with this selection, ask them to answer these questions aloud. This will help you keep track of any problems and cope with reading difficulties as they come up. Begin your directed reading by asking a question that calls for prediction. For example: "What might an essay called 'The Story of My Body' be about?"

For more help, see the **Comprehension** blackline master on page 229.

Discussion Questions

COMPREHENSION 1. Who is the narrator of "The Story of My Body"? *(Judith Ortiz Cofer)*

2. What happens to cause the narrator to become self-conscious about her face? *(She has a bad case of chicken pox that results in scarring.)*

3. What happens in the grocery store that causes the narrator so much pain? *(If necessary, have students reread this section before answering the question. Then ask: "Why is the narrator so upset by what the man says to her?")*

CRITICAL THINKING 4. What does the narrator means when she says she "learned to become invisible"? *(Answers will vary. Students might suggest that she tries to blend in and draw no attention to herself because she is ashamed of how she looks. They might also suggest that her bad feelings about herself make her assume that she is not worth noticing.)*

5. What would you say the narrator learns about herself as a result of the incident in the grocery store? *(Have students support their opinions. One idea is that she decides that she is in fact just as good as anyone else—that there's nothing dirty or ugly about her.)*

Literary Skill

IMAGERY Ask students to notice how important visual *imagery* is in this essay. Judith Ortiz Cofer shows a poet's love for language when she describes the colors that she associates with her childhood. For practice with this strategy, ask students to find places in which the author names a color and then describes it in a unique way. For example, white is *paloma blanca* and the brown in her skin is *leche con café*.

III. GATHER YOUR THOUGHTS

Prewriting Strategies

The prewriting activities will help prepare students to write a **paragraph of opinion** that relates to the theme of Ortiz Cofer's writing. As a first step, students will complete a **Venn diagram** that helps them see that one's perception of oneself is sometimes quite different from the perceptions of others. Remind students that when they are completing the diagram, they should look at all the different episodes that Ortiz Cofer describes. In what ways do her feelings about herself change?

As a final prewriting activity, students will think of facts, details, and reasons that **support their opinions**. Encourage them to think of an anecdote from their own lives that illuminates their point of view.

Have students use the **Prewriting** blackline master on page 230.

IV. WRITE

If you feel it would help, have students review the point of view writing they did on pages 129 and 130 of their *Sourcebook*. The writing they do in response to the Ortiz Cofer piece will be similar to this. Then be sure students understand that they are to write a **paragraph of opinion** that clarifies how they feel about the statement on page 193. They should open their paragraphs with a strong agree/disagree opinion statement and then follow that up with support for their ideas.

WRITING RUBRIC In their paragraphs of opinion, do students

- open with a clear statement of disagreement or agreement?

- explain why they feel this way?

- use ideas and events from their own life as support?

- include an anecdote that relates to the topic and helps support the opinion statement?

Grammar, Usage, and Mechanics

When they are ready to proofread their work, refer students to the **Writers' Checklist.** Explain that a comma is not strong enough to join two simple sentences (independent clauses). To fix a comma splice, you either add a conjunction and a comma, insert a semicolon, or divide the two clauses into two separate sentences.

Incorrect: The man at the supermarket was an idiot I was angry and upset.

Correct: The man at the supermarket was an idiot, so I was angry and upset.

Correct: The man at the supermarket was an idiot; I was angry and upset.

V. WRAP-UP

Take a moment at the end of the lesson for students to explain what "The Story of My Body" **meant** to them personally. (Have them use the **Reader's Checklist** as a starting point for discussion.) Explain that it is always important to stop and think about what a reading taught you or made you think about.

Assessment

To test students' comprehension, use the **Assessment** blackline master on page 231.

Name _____

VOCABULARY

Words from the Selection

DIRECTIONS To build vocabulary, fill in each blank with one of the words from the box.

> ◇ stature   ◇ *la gringa*   ◇ covet   ◇ repertoire   ◇ naively

1. I stretched myself up to my full _____, which was five feet.

2. I assumed, _____ I guess, that everyone would like me.

3. I was called _____ by many of the natives because my skin color was lighter than theirs.

4. I did _____ several things in the store.

5. My sister's _____ of English sentences was impressive.

Strategy Lesson: Word Families

DIRECTIONS Look at the definition of the root word *vis*. Then look at the words in Column 1 and their possible definitions in Column 2. Circle the correct meaning for each word in Column 1.

> *vis* = see

Column 1

6. invisible

7. television

8. supervise

9. visit

10. vision

Column 2

A. something that cannot be seen
B. something that can be seen easily

A. an invention used for seeing pictures
B. an invention used for listening to music

A. to ignore
B. to watch over

A. to go to see someone or something
B. to avoid someone or someplace

A. the act of hearing
B. the act of seeing

Name _____

COMPREHENSION

Word Bank

DIRECTIONS With a partner, make a bank of transition words and phrases that you can use when writing a paragraph of opinion. (Transitions help readers move along from one sentence to the next in a piece of writing.) Try to think of at least ten.

Word Bank

therefore

to begin with

Reflect

DIRECTIONS Complete these statements. Then explain how you feel.

I see myself as someone who _____

_____

because: _____

_____

Others see me as someone who _____

_____

because: _____

_____

PREWRITING

Writing a Paragraph of Opinion

DIRECTIONS Follow these steps to write a paragraph of opinion.

STEP 1. WRITE AN ANECDOTE. An anecdote is a very brief story that helps you make a point. Write an anecdote about a time that made you think about your self-image.

My anecdote: _____

_____

_____

STEP 2. WRITE AN OPINION STATEMENT. Next, write your opinion statement. Use this formula:

(A specific topic) + (a specific opinion) = a good opinion statement.

my topic sentence: (How others see you is not as important as how you see yourself) + ___

(_____) =

_____

STEP 3. GATHER FACTS. Now, gather details to support your opinion. These details come from your own experiences and observations.

fact #1: _____

fact #2: _____

fact #3: _____

STEP 4. WRITE. Write your paragraph of opinion.

    1. Open with your anecdote.

    2. Then give your opinion statement and support.

    3. End with a closing sentence that says your opinion statement in a slightly different way.

Name _____

ASSESSMENT

Multiple-choice Test

DIRECTIONS On the blanks provided, write the letter of the item that best answers each question or completes each statement.

_____ 1. Where was the narrator born?
   A. the United States   C. Puerto Rico
   B. Mexico   D. Canada

_____ 2. What caused the narrator to have scars on her face?
   A. sunburn   C. chicken pox
   B. poison ivy   D. a fight

_____ 3. The narrator says "color" in mainstream U.S. society is . . .
   A. an embarrassing topic.   C. a common topic.
   B. a touchy subject.   D. A and B

_____ 4. Where was the narrator when she first experienced color prejudice?
   A. a supermarket   C. Puerto Rico
   B. her neighborhood   D. at school

_____ 5. What did the narrator enjoy as a child?
   A. being trusted with money C. a secret
   B. going to the supermarket D. A and B

_____ 6. In what way does the supermarket help the narrator learn English?
   A. She reads the magazines in the store. C. She buys books there.
   B. She reads the labels on the products. D. One of the storekeepers teaches her to read.

_____ 7. Who first referred to the narrator as "colored"?
   A. her teacher   C. the butcher
   B. the mean brother at the store D. the school nurse

_____ 8. How did the narrator feel when she was yelled at in the store?
   A. humiliated   C. angry
   B. sad   D. scared

_____ 9. What did the narrator want when she was in the store?
   A. to talk to someone   C. to read
   B. candy   D. the Susie doll

_____ 10. Which theme or themes does Ortiz Cofer explore in "The Story of My Body"?
   A. prejudice   C. self-esteem
   B. growing up   D. all of the above

Short-essay Test

Why does the narrator wash her hands when she gets home? How does she feel after she has done this?

Child of the Americas

Skills and Strategies Overview

THEME	Fitting in
READING LEVEL	easy
VOCABULARY	◇ghettos ◇passion ◇ripples ◇mangoes ◇Spanglish
PREREADING	word web
RESPONSE	react and connect
COMPREHENSION	double-entry journal
PREWRITING	using sensory language
WRITING	poem / plural nouns
ASSESSMENT	understanding

BACKGROUND

Aurora Levins Morales is a poet best known for her book *Getting Home Alive* (1986), a collection of stories, essays, and poems written in collaboration with her mother, Rosario. In this collection, Levins Morales celebrates the lives of mothers, daughters, grandmothers, sisters, friends, and family who live worlds apart, yet are able to stay connected in spite of language barriers, differing cultural identities, and generation gaps.

In "Child of the Americas" (a poem included in *Getting Home Alive),* Morales uses simple language and repetition to create a rhythmic celebration of her own heritage. Thanks to her poetic style, Levins Morales's enthusiasm and positive self-esteem—so clearly displayed in this poem—are infectious. The reader can't help but be gathered up in the identity "dance" that the poet so clearly enjoys performing.

UNIT THEME Aurora Levins Morales celebrates her multicultural heritage in a short poem of identity.

GRAPHIC ORGANIZER A word study chart like the one below can help students explore important words and ideas in a piece of literature.

"Child of the Americas"

WORD STUDY	
Word	**Definition**
Spanglish	mix of Spanish and English
	What the Word Reminds Me of
	migration
	two cultures
	blending cultures
Example sentence:	
I learned to speak Spanglish.	

BEFORE YOU READ

Remind students of the theme of the unit ("Fitting in") and ask them to think how this theme applies to their own lives. (They may want to skim the **Response Notes** they made while reading "The Story of My Body.") Then ask the class to complete the prereading activity, a **word web**. See page 40 of the **Strategy Handbook** for help with this activity.

Motivation Strategy

In "Child of the Americas," Aurora Levins Morales explores her feelings of identity and wonders how and where she "fits in." Discuss with students this issue of cultural identity. How does their family's heritage impact their feelings about self? Does it seem to make any difference in how others treat them? If so, how?

CONNECTING WITH STUDENTS Ask students to complete this sentence: "I am a child of _____." They should fill in the blank with a word or words that best reflect how they see themselves. For example: "I am a child of the library; or I am a child of the video store." It's possible that students will want to use the sentence later in a poem of their own.

Vocabulary Building

Word analogies help students sharpen their higher-level thinking skills. Any practice you can give students with this skill will be helpful to them, since analogies are an important part of most standardized tests. To understand a word analogy, students need to first know a short definition of the word and then be able to think of a synonym and antonym. Show students this list of key vocabulary words from the selection: *ghettos, passion, ripples, mangoes,* and *Spanglish*. (*Passion, ripples,* and *gestures* are not footnoted.) Then have students circle the words in the text. Help them pronounce and then define each of the words. Then have them complete the word analogy exercise on the **Vocabulary** blackline master. See page 236.

STRATEGY LESSON: HOMOGRAPHS Remind the class that a homograph is a word that has the same pronunciation (and often the same spelling) as another word, but a different origin and meaning. For example, *pike* (a turnpike) and *pike* (a fish) are homographs. Tell students that the meaning of such words is usually made clear by context.

For additional practice on this strategy, see the **Vocabulary** blackline master on page 236.

Prereading Strategies

Word webs and word studies are helpful exercises for three reasons: 1. they can improve a reader's vocabulary; 2. they can deepen a reader's understanding of the selection; and 3. they can help forge a link between the reader's prior knowledge of a topic and the topic or theme of the work. When you create a word web for students, try to choose words that are thematically important.

K-W-L Tell students that Puerto Rico (line 5 in the poem) is an island in the West Indies, a chain of islands, and that the West Indies are in the Caribbean Sea. Ask students what they know and would like to know about Puerto Rico and its people. Have them make some notes on a K-W-L chart like the one on page 43. After they have read the poem, they should have some new ideas or impressions to add to the L column.

Spanish-speaking Students

"Hija de las américas" retrata vívidamente lo que significa ser mutlicultural. El poeta describe los múltiples ingredientes de sí misma, la sangre caribeña, la africanidad, la raíz española. Estas partes se han mezclado y formado su propia ser. Explica que no se puede separar el contenido de su carácter ni definir quién es. Es suficiente saber que está completa.

II. READ

Remind students that even the shortest selections should be read slowly and carefully. Ask them to pay particular attention to lines in Levins Morales's poem that they can **react** and **connect** to. How do her ideas make them feel? What do her words or images remind them of in their own lives? Their reactions will help them in their task of decoding the poet's message.

Response Strategy

QUESTION Questions about word choice or topic may come up as students are reading this poem. As an additional response strategy, ask students to make a note each time a question occurs to them. When the class is finished, divide them into quick discussion groups and ask them to think about possible answers to group members' questions.

Comprehension Strategies

In a **double-entry journal,** students note their individual responses to specific words, phrases, and lines from the selection. Have students comment on lines from the poem that they find interesting, confusing, or relevant to their own lives. A double-entry journal can help readers by giving them the chance to do a line-by-line analysis of the text and by showing them that their own personal responses to a text assist them in a search for the author's or poet's meaning.

GRAPHIC ORGANIZER As an alternate strategy, have students work on a graphic organizer related to the poet's message. Your more-advanced readers can do a stylistic analysis of the poem on a chart that has entries for rhythm, word choice, imagery, tone, and form. Other readers can create a simple chart that explores Levins Morales's message. How does it compare with Ortiz Cofer's message in "The Story of My Body"?

For more help, see the **Comprehension** blackline master on page 237.

Discussion Questions

COMPREHENSION 1. What does the speaker mean when she says she was born at a "crossroads"? *(She is a product of many cultures.)*

2. What is the speaker's "tool" and "craft"? *(the English language)*

CRITICAL THINKING 3. With which nationality do you think the speaker identifies most? Or does she feel that all these nationalities are equally a part of her? *(Remind students to support what they say with evidence from the selection. Many students will say that the author feels as if she is many nationalities rolled into one and that no single nationality is more important than another.)*

4. Which words and phrases are repeated most often in the poem? *(I and I am)*

5. What is the effect of this repetition? *(Levins Morales's repetition helps to unify the lines, add rhythm, and strengthen the message that this is a poem about identity.)*

6. What does the last line, "and I am whole," mean to you? *(Ask students to first explain what the line means in the context of the rest of the poem and then discuss the connection they can make to it. How is it possible to be of so many different cultures and still feel "whole"?)*

Literary Skill

REPETITION To introduce a literary skill with this lesson, you might teach a brief lesson on repetition. *Repetition* of a word or phrase in a piece of writing helps draw attention to or place special emphasis on a thought or idea. Ask students to find repeated words, phrases, and ideas in Levins Morales's poem. Make a list of them on the board. Then ask them to tell you the message the author wants to get across. How does repetition help her reveal this message?

III. GATHER YOUR THOUGHTS

Prewriting Strategies

The goal of the prewriting activities on page 199 is to prepare students to write a **poem** of their own about an object of importance. To begin, students will brainstorm a list of **sensory details** from "Child of the Americas." With a partner, they will find three or more words or phrases that appeal to the five senses. The chart students complete at the top of the page might also be used later, when they are thinking about imagery for their own poems.

Next, students will think about an object of importance and then make a list of words that describe how the object looks, smells, and/or feels. They'll finish by saying what the object means to them or says about their personalities.

To help students brainstorm topics, suggest that they try to think about objects that provoke strong emotional responses—laughter, tears, surprise, anger, and so on. This will make it easier for them to adopt a consistent tone in their verse.

Have students use the **Prewriting and Writing** blackline master on page 238.

IV. WRITE

The directions on page 200 ask students to write a poem of at least four lines. To help, offer the class a variety of choices for their poetic form, including these:

- blank verse: unrhymed poetry with a regular rhythm; each line should have 10 syllables

- free verse: no pattern of rhyme or rhythm

- limerick: funny verse in five lines: lines one, two, and five rhyme, as do lines three and four

WRITING RUBRIC Use this writing rubric to help students focus on the assignment requirements and for assistance with a quick assessment of their writing.

Do students' poems

- describe a single object?

- include two or more examples of sensory language?

- demonstrate knowledge of at least one poetic technique, such as rhyme, rhythm, or repetition?

Grammar, Usage, and Mechanics

When they are ready to proofread their work, refer them to the **Writers' Checklist.** At this point, you might want to introduce a brief lesson on plural nouns. For practice, show students these words. Ask them to rewrite each correctly.

| sockes | rockses | citys | noisess | birchs |

V. WRAP-UP

Take a moment at the end of the lesson for students to talk about their **understanding** of "Child of the Americas." Ask them to read and then respond to the questions on the **Readers' Checklist.** Remind the class that many times the theme of a poem is whatever the reader can take. It is not important to reach consensus on what a literary work means.

Assessment

To test students' comprehension, use the **Assessment** blackline master on page 239.

Name _____

VOCABULARY
Words from the Selection

ANALOGIES An analogy is a comparison between two things that are similar. In the following example, the two parts are similar because they are both opposites.

rich : poor :: happy : sad. (Rich is to poor as happy is to sad.)

DIRECTIONS Use the vocabulary words in the word box to finish the analogies. First, figure out the relationship between the first pair of words. Then add a word to the second pair that expresses the same relationship.

> ◇ mangoes ◇ ghettos ◇ passion ◇ ripples ◇ Spanglish

1. carrots : vegetables :: _____ : tropical fruits

2. fail : pass :: indifference : _____

3. man : boy :: waves : _____

4. country : farms :: city : _____

5. algebra : mathematics :: _____ : language

Strategy Lesson: Homographs

A *homograph* is a word that has the same pronunciation (and the same spelling) as another word but a different origin and meaning. For example, *sole* can mean "the bottom or undersurface," "one and only," or "a flat fish." Context can tell you which meaning is intended.

DIRECTIONS Use the clues in each sentence to tell you the meaning of the underlined words. Draw a line matching each word to its correct definition.

Column A

6. Her hair was <u>light</u> from the sun.

7. The boxes we carried were <u>light</u>.

8. When she arrived, she hung her <u>cape</u> on a hook.

9. The wind swept in from the <u>cape</u>.

10. We found a <u>cricket</u> on the windowsill

11. Several of the boys were playing <u>cricket</u>.

12. The parrot pecked us with his sharp <u>bill</u>.

13. Exchange the torn <u>bill</u> at the bank.

14. The price of gasoline was <u>steep</u>.

15. Let the tea bag <u>steep</u> for a few minutes.

Column B

A. outer garment without sleeves

B. insect

C. pale in color

D. outdoor game

E. not heavy

F. beak

G. point of land extending into the water

H. too high

I. soak

J. piece of paper money

Name _____

COMPREHENSION

Sketch

DIRECTIONS Sometimes making a sketch of a piece of writing can help you "see" the author's message. Reread "Child of the Americas." Then draw a picture of what the poem reminds you of.

Reflect

DIRECTIONS Now answer these questions about your sketch. They can help you decide on the main idea of Levins Morales's poem.

1. Did I draw a sad scene or a happy scene? _____

2. Who or what is the most important part of my scene?

   _____

3. If a person from my sketch could talk, what would he or she say?

   _____

4. I think Levins Morales's main idea has something to do with

   _____ and _____ .

Name _____

PREWRITING AND WRITING
Writing a Free-Verse Poem

Follow these steps to write a free-verse poem. Remember that free-verse poetry does not follow a specific form, and it usually does not rhyme.

STEP 1. SELECT A SUBJECT. Think of an object that is important to you.

Object: _____

Why it is important: _____

STEP 2. COLLECT YOUR THOUGHTS. Write freely for a few minutes about this object. Use words that describe how it looks, smells, feels, and sounds.

My freewrite:

_____

_____

_____

STEP 3. WRITE A FIRST DRAFT. Now take your freewrite and insert some line breaks so that you end with a poem of four or five lines. Try to put breaks where you hear natural pauses in the sentences.

My freewrite with line breaks:

_____

_____

_____

_____

STEP 4. SHAPE YOUR POEM. Pay special attention to your first line. It should give your readers an idea of the subject of the poem. (Levins Morales opens with "I am a child of the Americas. . . .")

My first line: _____

_____

Name _____

ASSESSMENT

Multiple-Choice Test

DIRECTIONS On the blanks provided, write the letter of the item that best answers each question or completes each statement.

_____ 1. The speaker says she is a child of . . .
- A. the islands.
- B. the world.
- C. the Americas.
- D. none of the above

_____ 2. The speaker makes it clear that . . .
- A. she is multicultural.
- B. she is proud of her heritage.
- C. she wants to fit in.
- D. A and B

_____ 3. If you are taína, your ancestors are . . .
- A. Native American.
- B. African.
- C. European.
- D. Spanish.

_____ 4. When you buy mangoes, you are buying . . .
- A. jewelry.
- B. books.
- C. clothes.
- D. fruit.

_____ 5. The speaker says that the Spanish language . . .
- A. rolls off your tongue.
- B. sings like poetry.
- C. invites you to use your hands.
- D. all of the above

_____ 6. The speaker feels a connection to . . .
- A. her heritage.
- B. her friends.
- C. her government.
- D. her religion.

_____ 7. The speaker says she cannot go back to . . .
- A. Africa.
- B. Europe.
- C. the taína.
- D. A and C

_____ 8. The speaker says Europe lives within her, but cannot provide . . .
- A. a history.
- B. a family.
- C. a home.
- D. love.

_____ 9. What has made the speaker who she is?
- A. her children
- B. her history
- C. her job
- D. all of the above

_____ 10. What is the tone at the end of the poem?
- A. triumphant
- B. depressed
- C. confused
- D. nervous

Short-essay Test

What does the speaker mean by the line, "I am whole"?

Unit Background WORLD WAR II (pages 201–218)

A novel excerpt from *The Upstairs Room* by Johanna Reiss and a nonfiction excerpt from *John F. Kennedy and the PT-109* by Richard Tregaskis make up this unit.

Johanna (de Leeuw) Reiss was born in Holland and was just a child at the beginning of World War II when the Nazis invaded. *The Upstairs Room* (1972) is the story of the almost three years she and her sister spent in hiding in the attic of a Christian family who risked their lives to protect the two Jewish girls. The book received many awards, including the Jewish Book Council Juvenile Book Award and was chosen a Notable Children's Book by the American Library Association. The sequel to her book is *The Journey Back* (1976), which tells of her family's reunion and their attempt to make a new life after the war. The excerpts in the *Sourcebook* are from Chapter 1 of *The Upstairs Room*. The excerpt mentions the narrator's mother's headaches. After students have read the excerpt, you might want to tell them that Sophie (the mother) died in a hospital.

Richard Tregaskis (1916–1973) was born in Elizabeth, New Jersey. He was a journalist, screenwriter, and war correspondent during World War II; flew on many combat missions; and received a Purple Heart. His books include *Guadacanal Diary* (1943), *Invasion Diary* (1944), *Vietnam Diary* (1963), and *The Warrior King: Hawaii's Kamehameha the Great* (1973).

Teaching the Introduction

Pictures on page 201 show the cockpit of a plane and its pilot, a young John F. Kennedy, and Adolf Hitler reviewing his troops.

World War II

John F. Kennedy

World War II (1939–1945) was one of the most destructive wars in history. It began when, under Adolf Hitler's command, Germany invaded Poland and then took over much of Western Europe. The situation only worsened when Italy joined Germany in an effort to control the continent. Then Japan and Russia joined in the fighting, and war raged on nearly every ocean and continent.

201

Hitler reviewing his troops

1. Read the unit introduction with students. Ask whether they have or have had grandparents, great aunts, or great uncles who fought or participated in World War II. (If you think that the relatives of some of your students may have been on opposing sides during the war, omit this suggestion.)

2. Some students may be familiar with Anne Frank's diary or the play based on the diary. Tell them that they will be reading about another young girl in Holland whose family was threatened by the Nazis.

3. Ask students to tell what they know about John F. Kennedy.

Opening Activity

Define or have students define *stereotype* (a simplified notion about a person or group held by another person or group). Ask students how stereotyping can cause conflict between people within nations and between nations. How do stereotypes affect one's reactions to people of various ethnic or religious groups? How can people avoid making assumptions about others based on stereotypes?

The War Arrives

Skills and Strategies Overview

THEME World War II

READING LEVEL average

VOCABULARY

◇remained ◇capable ◇refuse ◇furious ◇mumbled

PREREADING picture walk

RESPONSE mark or highlight

COMPREHENSION prediction

PREWRITING graphic organizer

WRITING character sketch / adjectives

ASSESSMENT style

BACKGROUND

In her book *The Upstairs Room,* Johanna Reiss describes the anguish and hardship her Dutch-Jewish family was forced to endure during World War II. The fictional narrator of the story, Annie, explains the events leading up to the war, her parents' decision to send the girls into hiding, and the two-and-a-half years Annie and one of her sisters spent tucked away in the upstairs room of a farmhouse in the country.

Although a fictional child narrates the story, *The Upstairs Room* is essentially Reiss's own story. The anxiety, boredom, and grief Annie experiences are exactly what young Johanna experienced some 60 years ago.

UNIT THEME Johanna Reiss reveals the horror and confusion surrounding the Nazi invasion of Holland at the beginning of World War II.

GRAPHIC ORGANIZER

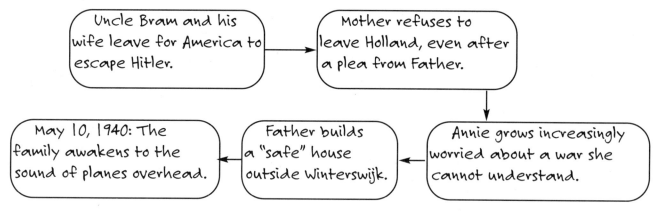

BIBLIOGRAPHY If students are interested in this period of history, you might suggest these books: *The Journey Back* by Johanna Reiss; *Freidrich* (1987) by Hans Peter Rickter; and *Shadow of the Wall* (1997) by Christa Laird.

BEFORE YOU READ

Explain that the theme of this unit is World War II, which some of your students may be studying in their history or social studies classes. Tell the class that they're about to read an excerpt from a novel that was written by a woman who was forced into hiding for more than two years during the war. Then ask them to complete the prereading activity, a **picture walk**. (Refer to the **Strategy Handbook** on page 40 for more help.)

Motivation Strategy

In "The War Arrives," Johanna Reiss gives readers a quick glimpse of how European civilians felt during World War II. Work with students to create a "fact" list about this war. When was it fought? Who was involved? What was the outcome? Keep the list on the board for students to refer to as they write.

Vocabulary Building

As students read, point out key vocabulary words such as *remained, capable, refuse, furious,* and *mumbled.* Ask students to circle these words in the text, and then ask for volunteers to pronounce and offer definitions. Then ask for sample sentences that use the words correctly. Help students become accustomed to hearing the words in many different contexts. For an additional activity with these words, turn to the **Vocabulary** blackline master on page 246.

STRATEGY LESSON: HOMOGRAPHS/HETERONYMS A homograph is a word that has the same spelling as another word but a different origin and meaning. Explain to students that some homographs are also heteronyms, which means that they have different pronunciations. For example, *lead* (a metal) and *lead* (to conduct) are homographs. They are pronounced differently, so they are heteronyms as well. Tell students that the meaning of such words is usually made clear by context. They'll need to look carefully at words and phrases surrounding the word in question.

For additional practice on this strategy, see the **Vocabulary** blackline master on page 246.

Prereading Strategies

PICTURE WALK For their prereading activity, students will do a picture walk of "The War Arrives." Have them tell you which pictures capture their attention and why. What do the pictures reveal about the topic and tone of the selection? Have them pay particular attention to the photo of the girl on page 202. How does this picture make them feel? Also be sure that students read the captions for the art. What questions do they have about the captions? Students can make notes about the art and their predictions on page 202.

Spanish-speaking Students

"La Guerra llega" se trata de la realidad brutal de la Segunda Guerra Mundial. El cuento se enfoca en una familia judía que está en peligro de perderse la vida. Los Nazis están conquistando al oeste de Europa y acercándose a holanda, donde vive la familia. La madre cree que los Nazis no van a dañarles y insiste en quedarse en holanda. Con disgusto, el padre se pone de acuerdo, y la familia no huye. Desgraciadamente, sin embargo, la guerra llega.

II. READ

Before they begin reading, remind students that you'd like them to **mark** or **highlight** details about the characters. Have them make a note of anything that strikes them as interesting, important, confusing, or puzzling.

If students need to do a second reading, have them use a different-colored pen to mark their second set of notes. This will help them see that doing an additional reading can enhance their understanding of the plot, characters, and setting. It is not necessary that they always read an assignment twice, but it's a good idea if they know the assignment is important or challenging.

Response Strategy

REACT AND CONNECT As an alternate response strategy, ask students to write their reactions and connections to Reiss's story in the **Response Notes**. In particular, students should note connections between what Annie, the narrator, describes and what they themselves have heard about war. Does any part of Reiss's story seem familiar on a personal level? Have students heard stories about battles or war-related events that they'd like to share or write about later?

Comprehension Strategies

Making **predictions** keeps readers involved and interested in the story. As they read the selection, students will make guesses about what they think will happen next to the characters. Many of their predictions will be far off the mark, but that is irrelevant. What is important is that students take a moment to think carefully about what has happened so far in the story and what they think is likely to happen in the pages to come.

For more help, see the **Comprehension** blackline master on page 247.

Discussion Questions

COMPREHENSION 1. What war is "arriving" near Annie's home? *(World War II, in the form of a German invasion)*

2. Why is Annie's father afraid? *(He senses danger and predicts that Holland will be invaded.)*

3. What does he want Annie's mother to do? *(Leave for America with the uncle and aunt)*

CRITICAL THINKING 4. Why, in addition to having headaches, do you think Annie's mother refuses to go anywhere or even think about the war? *(Answers will vary. Students might suggest that it's too upsetting to think about, so she just blocks it out.)*

5. What three words would you use to describe Annie? Why? *(Accept reasonable responses. Be sure students support what they say with evidence from the selection.)*

Literary Skill

POINT OF VIEW You might take this opportunity to discuss point of view with students. Remind the class that *point of view* is the vantage point from which an author presents the events of a story. Ask students to think about the point of view in "The War Arrives." Although Reiss could have narrated the story in the third person, she chose the first person and used a fictional narrator. Ask students to consider why an author might choose to create a fictional narrator. Students might conclude that a fictional character allowed Reiss to maintain distance from memories that were still too fresh or painful.

III. GATHER YOUR THOUGHTS

Prewriting Strategies

The goal of these prewriting activities is first to help students collect what they learned from "The War Arrives" and then use that knowledge to write a **character sketch** about a person they know well. Students will begin by reflecting on the three main characters in "The War Arrives": Annie, Ies, and Sophie. Have them write their thoughts and ideas on the **graphic organizer** at the top of page 207.

Next, students will fill in a similar organizer, although in this one, they will concentrate on describing a person from their own lives. Ask students to answer the seven questions on the organizer as carefully as they can. Students will finish their preparations by planning a topic sentence and supporting details.

Have students use the **Prewriting** blackline master on page 248.

IV. WRITE

Read aloud the directions on page 208. Remind students that a **character sketch** is a short piece of writing that reveals or shows something about a person or a fictional character. For this assignment, students are to write their impressions of a real person and then support those impressions with strong, compelling details.

WRITING RUBRIC If you like, show this writing rubric to students before they begin writing, or post it on the board for them to refer to as they are working on their first drafts.

Do students' character sketches

- begin with a topic sentence?

- contain three or more vivid details that support the topic sentence?

- conclude with a closing sentence that ties things together?

Grammar, Usage, and Mechanics

After students have written a first draft, have them stop and think carefully about what they've written. They should ask themselves: Have I used adequate details to describe the person? Is there something I could add that would make my writing stronger?

When students are ready to proofread their work, refer them to the **Writers' Checklist.** Many inexperienced writers (and speakers) confuse the comparative and superlative form of adjectives, so you might want to teach a brief lesson on this subject. For example:

Incorrect: Annie was the younger of the three sisters.

Correct: Annie was the youngest of the three sisters.

V. WRAP-UP

Take time at the end of the lesson to talk about Reiss's writing **style**. Ask the class: "Why do you think the author included dialogue? How does the author convey that the narrator is quite young? What words does the author use to indicate how people are feeling?" Then refer students to the **Readers' Checklist**, and ask them to answer each question.

Assessment

To test students' comprehension, use the **Assessment** blackline master on page 249.

Name _____

VOCABULARY

Words from the Selection

DIRECTIONS To build vocabulary, answer these questions about five words from the selection.

1. If your family <u>remained</u> at home, did they stay or leave? _____

2. If you feel you are <u>capable</u>, are you able or not able to do a job?

   _____

3. If you <u>refuse</u> to do your homework, are you deciding not to do it?

   _____

4. Is someone who is <u>furious</u> very angry or very happy? _____

5. Are <u>mumbled</u> words said clearly or are they hard to understand?

   _____

Strategy Lesson: Homographs/Heteronyms

A *homograph* is a word that has the same spelling as another word, but a different origin and meaning. Some homographs are also *heteronyms*, which means that they have a different pronunciation. For example, *content* ("all things inside") and *content* ("satisfied") are homographs. They are pronounced differently, so they are heteronyms as well.

DIRECTIONS Circle the correct meaning for the homographs/heteronyms in each sentence.

6. The soldiers were waiting at the <u>entrance</u> of the old church. (place to go in; to delight or charm)

7. We watched Father <u>lead</u> the way to the train station. (conduct; metal)

8. All my worries about school seemed <u>minute</u> when we heard the German planes fly by. (sixty seconds; very small)

9. I wondered why Mom would <u>object</u> to traveling to America. (a thing; protest)

10. I could see a <u>tear</u> running down my sister's face. (drop of liquid from the eye; pull apart)

Name _____

COMPREHENSION
Graphic Organizers

DIRECTIONS Think about what Annie, Sophie, and Ies are like. What do their words and actions tell you about them? Look over the story again and record some details on this chart.

Character name	says . . .	What this tells me about him or her
Annie	"I was often glad when Mother told me that it was time for me to go to bed."	She's afraid.
Sophie		
Ies		

DIRECTIONS Now look over the chart you just completed. Write 5–10 words that describe one of the characters on the web below.

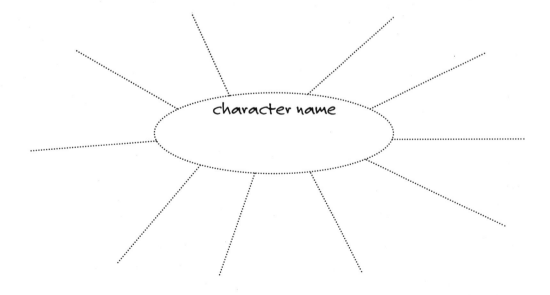

character name

Name _____

PREWRITING
Writing a Character Sketch

DIRECTIONS Follow these steps to write a character sketch about someone you know.

STEP 1. WRITE A TOPIC SENTENCE. A topic sentence sets the stage for what you want to tell readers.

+   =

_____   _____

(person's name)   +   (my impression of him/her)   =

_____

a good topic sentence

STEP 2. List three characteristics of the person you've named. Don't worry about writing complete sentences—just list words that you think describe the person. Then give examples that support these characteristics.

characteristic #1: _____

proof: _____

_____

characteristic #2: _____

proof: _____

_____

characteristic #3: _____

proof: _____

_____

STEP 3. Finish by writing a concluding sentence that sums up your impression of this person. Then write your sketch on page 209 and 210.

My concluding sentence: _____

_____

Name _____

ASSESSMENT

Multiple-Choice Test

DIRECTIONS On the blanks provided, write the letter of the item that best answers each question.

_____ 1. Where did Uncle Bram and his wife go?
- A. to Poland
- B. to America
- C. to Germany
- D. to Holland

_____ 2. Why did Uncle Bram and his wife leave their own country?
- A. They were looking for adventure.
- B. They were moving away from Hitler and the Nazis.
- C. He was mad at his brother.
- D. He had a new job.

_____ 3. Why didn't Father and his family leave too?
- A. Mother didn't want to leave.
- B. Father didn't want to leave.
- C. They had nowhere to go.
- D. none of the above

_____ 4. Why is nobody interested in Mother's stories about her girls?
- A. They thought she bragged too much.
- B. They were worried about war.
- C. They thought she was lying.
- D. She was exaggerating.

_____ 5. Who is the narrator of "The War Arrives"?
- A. Annie, the youngest daughter
- B. Rachel, the teacher
- C. Sini, who works on a farm
- D. Sophie, the mother

_____ 6. Why did the Gans family spend a lot of time over at Sophie's house?
- A. They listened to the radio.
- B. They hid in their house.
- C. They watched TV.
- D. They danced to records.

_____ 7. Why did Annie like to go to bed?
- A. She wanted to talk to her sisters.
- B. She wanted to play with her toys.
- C. She wanted to read her books.
- D. She couldn't hear the radio.

_____ 8. Why did Father build another house?
- A. His house was too small.
- B. His house was falling apart.
- C. His new house was "safe."
- D. all of the above

_____ 9. What woke the family on May 10, 1940?
- A. a car crash
- B. children crying
- C. the sound of planes
- D. the sound of soldiers

_____ 10. How did Father feel at the end of the passage?
- A. angry
- B. frustrated
- C. scared
- D. all of the above

Short-essay Test

What do you think Sophie, the mother, would have done differently if she had to relive the whole experience over again? Why?

Skills and Strategies Overview

THEME	World War II
READING LEVEL	challenging
VOCABULARY	◇destroyers ◇destination ◇looming ◇valiantly ◇severed
PREREADING	K-W-L
RESPONSE	question
COMPREHENSION	storyboard
PREWRITING	brainstorm
WRITING	narrative paragraph / plurals
ASSESSMENT	depth

BACKGROUND

Early in 1943, John F. Kennedy became commander of the patrol boat PT-109 in the South Pacific. In August of 1943, his boat was in the area of the Solomon Islands when it was rammed by a Japanese destroyer. The boat was sliced in half upon impact, and 2 of the 12 men aboard were killed instantly. Kennedy and the rest of his crew abandoned ship and stayed afloat by holding onto wreckage from the ship. Rather than wait for a rescue team, Kennedy directed his men to swim to a small island three miles away. Kennedy towed a wounded crew member by clenching the strap of the man's life jacket between his teeth.

For the next four days, Kennedy swam back and forth along a water route that he knew American ships often used. Eventually, a group of natives found him and carried his message for help (written on a coconut shell) to a U.S. infantry patrol. The crew was finally rescued. Later, Kennedy was awarded a medal for his "courage, endurance, and excellent leadership." "Disaster at Sea" tells the story of Kennedy and the PT-109 at the moment of impact.

UNIT THEME John F. Kennedy and his crew show bravery in the face of a Japanese attack during World War II.

GRAPHIC ORGANIZER This web shows the most important details in Tregaskis's account.

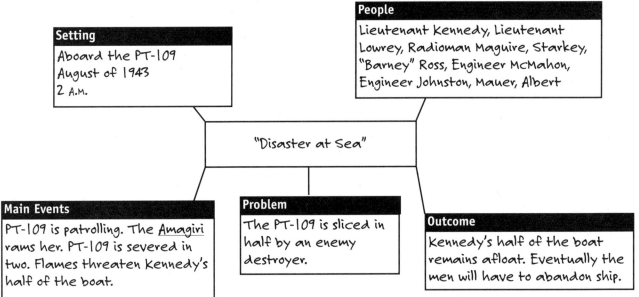

Setting
Aboard the PT-109
August of 1943
2 A.M.

People
Lieutenant Kennedy, Lieutenant Lowrey, Radioman Maguire, Starkey, "Barney" Ross, Engineer McMahon, Engineer Johnston, Mauer, Albert

"Disaster at Sea"

Main Events
PT-109 is patrolling. The Amagiri rams her. PT-109 is severed in two. Flames threaten Kennedy's half of the boat.

Problem
The PT-109 is sliced in half by an enemy destroyer.

Outcome
Kennedy's half of the boat remains afloat. Eventually the men will have to abandon ship.

I. BEFORE YOU READ

Remind students that the theme of the unit is World War II. Then explain that they are about to read an excerpt from a biography of John F. Kennedy that describes his adventures on a navy ship in the Pacific during the war. Tell them that *PT* stands for "patrol torpedo." Before they begin reading, have them complete the prereading activity, a **K-W-L**. (Refer to the **Strategy Handbook** on page 40 for more help.)

Motivation Strategy

Students should be able to talk knowledgeably about John F. Kennedy since he is such an important historical figure. Ask the class to interview an older friend or relative about Kennedy. (They might ask what the person knows about Kennedy's youth and naval career.) What does this person remember most about him? Then have them report to the class what the interviewee said. How many people interviewed remembered something about the PT-109 disaster?

ENGAGING STUDENTS Ask students to read and respond to the questions in the introductory paragraph at the top of page 211. Which of your students stays calm in a crisis? What kind of qualities does a calm person have versus a panicky person? Which type of person do they think Kennedy was?

Vocabulary Building

Help students use **context clues** as they read to figure out the meanings of difficult words, especially the key vocabulary for this lesson: *destroyers, destination, looming, valiantly,* and *severed.* Ask students to circle these words in the text. The footnotes offer definitions for these and other words from the article, but encourage students to try to define on their own before checking the footnote. For more practice defining in context, see page 254.

STRATEGY LESSON: ROOT WORDS The Latin word *navis,* meaning "ship," is the root of several English words. Ask students to think of words containing *nav* or *navi.* (For example, *navy, navigate,* and *navigation.*) Write these words on the board, and underline the root. Then write the prefix *circum-* ("around") and ask students to add the prefix to *navigate* and tell what *circumnavigate* means.

For additional practice with this strategy, see the **Vocabulary** blackline master on page 254.

Prereading Strategies

The purpose of a **K-W-L** is to activate prior knowledge and allow students to take responsibility for their own knowledge gaps. In the K column, students will make notes about John F. Kennedy. Later, they will chart what they learned about him in the L column. A K-W-L can show students that ultimately they are responsible for their own learning.

SKIM As an alternate prereading strategy, ask students to skim "Disaster at Sea." (You might tell them to skim for an answer to this question: "What is the 'disaster' referred to in the title?") Have them make notes about words, phrases, or ideas that pop out at them. Also have them look carefully at the footnoted material and the interrupter questions. A quick skim beforehand will make the article seem like familiar territory when it comes time to do a close reading.

Spanish-speaking Students

"Desastre en el mar" pinta un retrato vívido del combate naval durante la Segunda Guerra Mundial. Marineros Kennedy y Maguire se enfrentan con el enemigo japonés, que acaba de destruir parte de su nave. Los Estados Unidos está en peligro de perder la batalla y ahogar en el mar hondo.

READ

As students begin to read, walk through the process of responding to literature. Introduce the strategy of **questioning**, and point out the example given on page 212. If you feel students would benefit, read the first and second paragraphs aloud and then describe the kinds of questions you would write in the **Response Notes** if you were reading the article for the first time.

Response Strategy

VISUALIZE Tregaskis uses sensory detail to describe the moment of impact between the *Amagiri* and PT-109. Ask students to visualize the scene, making sketches in their **Response Notes** as they go along. These sketches will help them complete the storyboards that interrupt the selection.

Comprehension Strategies

Students are asked to fill in **storyboards** as they are reading "Disaster at Sea." Storyboards can help students understand the sequence of events in a narrative and can show them which events are of primary importance. Rather than simply asking students to "tell what happens," a storyboard gives a framework for response that prods the reader into thinking carefully about elements of setting, character, and plot. Encourage students to review their storyboard notes once they've finished the selection. The nine frames can offer an instant summary of the main events, problem, and outcome.

For more help, see the **Comprehension** blackline master on page 255.

Discussion Questions

COMPREHENSION 1. What was PT-109's "mission" on that day in August? *(to patrol)*

2. Why did Kennedy turn toward the *Amagiri* instead of away from it? *(He wanted to line up for a torpedo shot.)*

3. What happened when the *Amagiri* rammed Kennedy's boat? *(The patrol boat was sliced in two.)*

CRITICAL THINKING 4. Do you think Kennedy was frightened when he discovered that his boat was so badly damaged? *(Answers will vary. Students might suggest that Kennedy might have been afraid, although Tregaskis gives no indication of this. Kennedy's actions show him to be calm and level-headed.)*

5. What kind of commander would you say Kennedy was? *(Answers will vary. Ask students to support what they say with evidence from the selection and perhaps evidence from their own reading.)*

Literary Skill

IMPRESSIONISM To introduce a literary skill with this selection, you might teach a brief lesson on impressionism as a literary element. *Impressionism* is the recording of events or situations as they have been impressed upon the mind. Tregaskis interviewed survivors of the PT-109 disaster and used their impressions of the event to tell his story. To make the telling vivid, the author included details that help the reader see and hear the events described. For example, he tells of the "babble" of the short-wave radio, the "white flashes" of two ships engaged in battle, and the "orange flash" that illuminates the sky after the impact. When taken together, these images create a scene of chaos. For practice, ask students to find other words and phrases that contribute to the impression of chaos on the boat.

III. GATHER YOUR THOUGHTS

Prewriting Strategies

Use the prewriting activities on page 217 to help students plan a **narrative paragraph** that describes an exciting or surprising incident from students' own lives. Before they begin, you might ask the class to review the prewriting work they did on pages 29 and 30 of the *Sourcebook*. (The **Prewriting** blackline master on page 256 asks students to complete a story frame similar to the one that follows "Thank You, Ma'am.")

As a first activity, students will **brainstorm** a topic for their paragraphs. Ask them to list three events that come to mind. (Students work in pairs on this activity.) Then ask them to choose which of the three events they would most like to write about.

Next, students will fill out a **storyboard** about the event that is similar to the storyboards they completed while reading "Disaster at Sea." Since there are only four cells on the storyboard, students will need to decide beforehand which details are most important.

Have students use the **Prewriting** blackline master on page 256.

IV. WRITE

The directions at the top of page 218 ask students to write a **narrative paragraph** that tells about an exciting or surprising incident. Tell them that they should feel free to model their writing style on Tregaskis's.

WRITING RUBRIC You might want to show students this writing rubric to give them a strong sense of what you expect to see in their narrative paragraphs:

Do students' narrative paragraphs

- tell about an exciting or surprising event from the writer's life?

- show a clear progression—a beginning, a middle, and an end?

- include adequate details to describe the event?

- contain sensory language that helps the reader see, hear, and feel the event described?

Grammar, Usage, and Mechanics

When students are ready to proofread their work, have them look carefully at the questions on the **Writers' Checklist** and apply those questions to their own writing. Ask students to pay particular attention to the spelling of any plural words. For practice, ask students to proofread these sentences that relate to the selection:

Incorrect: The *Amagiri* chopped the PT-109 into two halfs that were fairly equal in size. Kennedy called down to the ship's headquarter and ordered all the man to the deck.

Correct: The Amagiri chopped the PT-109 into two <u>halves</u> that were fairly equal in size. Kennedy called down to the ship's headquarter<u>s</u> and ordered all the <u>men</u> to the deck.

V. WRAP-UP

Take a moment at the end of the lesson for students to reflect on the **depth** of their understanding using the **Readers' Checklist**. Help them express what this article made them think about or reminded them of in their own lives. Give students the chance to tell any stories that come to mind that relate to the two World War II selections they just read.

Assessment

To test students' comprehension, use the **Assessment** blackline master on page 257.

Name _____

VOCABULARY

Words from the Selection

DIRECTIONS To build vocabulary, answer these questions about five words from the selection.

1. Are <u>destroyers</u> huge warships or little sailing boats? _____

2. Is a <u>destination</u> a place you are coming from or going to?

   _____

3. If there is a plane <u>looming</u> above you, is it close or far away?

   _____

4. If soldiers act <u>valiantly,</u> are they brave or cowardly? _____

5. If a boat is <u>severed</u> in an attack, is it split in half or sunk?

   _____

Strategy Lesson: Root Words

DIRECTIONS Study the root word. Then answer each question below by choosing the correct word from the box and writing it in the blank.

nav, navi = ship

◇naval   ◇navigation   ◇navy   ◇circumnavigate   ◇navigate

6. Ferdinand Magellan planned to _____ the globe.

7. John F. Kennedy was a lieutenant in the _____.

8. The captain tried to _____ the ship through dangerous waters.

9. Cadets learn a lot about _____ before they go to sea.

10. The _____ officer would like a full report of the incident by morning.

Name _____

COMPREHENSION
Retell

DIRECTIONS Use your book to help you retell the incident PT-109 accident.

1. Use your own words, not the author's words.

2. Be sure to include all important details.

Beginning

Middle

End

Name _____

PREWRITING

DIRECTIONS Complete this story frame with information from the surprising or exciting incident that happened to you.

The incident took place

_____ (where)

_____ (when)

_____
was there when it happened.

was also there.

I was _____ while the incident was happening.

The main problem was

Another problem was

The problems were solved when

The whole thing ended when

Name _____

ASSESSMENT

Multiple-Choice Test

....

DIRECTIONS On the blanks provided, write the letter of the item that best answers each question or completes each statement.

_____ 1. At the beginning of his account, Tregaskis says Kennedy and Lowrey feel . . .
A. sad because they miss their families.
B. upset because they've missed the excitement.
C. happy to be going home.
D. sick because of the flu.

_____ 2. What are Kennedy's and Lowrey's boats ordered to do?
A. patrol
B. fire
C. perform a rescue
D. none of the above

_____ 3. Why does each boat use only one engine?
A. They are saving fuel.
B. They are trying to be quiet.
C. They are trying to be less visible.
D. Only one engine works.

_____ 4. What does a lookout from Kennedy's boat notice at 2:30 A.M.?
A. an enemy ship
B. a U.S. navy boat
C. an enemy plane
D. an iceberg

_____ 5. The _Amagiri_ was . . .
A. a Chinese aircraft carrier.
B. a German destroyer.
C. a Japanese destroyer.
D. a British troop ship.

_____ 6. Why does Kennedy try to line up PT-109 with the enemy destroyer?
A. He wants to fire a torpedo.
B. He wants to get out of enemy range.
C. He wants to ride their waves.
D. He's on a suicide mission.

_____ 7. What does the destroyer do?
A. It puts up a peace flag.
B. It sends a radio message.
C. It fires back at PT-109.
D. It crashes into PT-109.

_____ 8. What happens to Kennedy when the boats crash?
A. He gets shot in the foot.
B. He suffers a concussion.
C. He breaks his hand.
D. He is knocked flat.

_____ 9. What happened to Kennedy's half of the boat after impact?
A. It started sinking immediately.
B. It stayed afloat.
C. It exploded.
D. It turned upside-down.

_____ 10. Why did Kennedy order the crewmen into the water?
A. He didn't want them to be captured.
B. He wanted them to be away from the fire.
C. The boat was sinking.
D. He was angry with them.

Short-essay Test

....

Would you call Kennedy a hero? Why or why not? Use examples from the selection to defend your answer.

Christopher Paul Curtis

Unit Background   **CHRISTOPHER PAUL CURTIS** (pages 219–238)

The last unit contains two excerpts from *The Watsons Go to Birmingham—1963* by Christopher Paul Curtis.

Christopher Paul Curtis was born in 1954 in Flint, Michigan. He received a B.A. degree from the University of Michigan in 1996. He has worked in the Fisher Body Plant in Flint and been assistant to Senator Don Riegle in Lansing. *The Watsons Go to Birmingham—1963* was a Newbery honor book in 1996. Four years later, he won the Newbery Medal and the Coretta Scott King award for *Bud, Not Buddy*.

Teaching the Introduction

The pictures on page 219 show the cover of Curtis's novel and contrasting photos of the cold North and the warm South, the latter in an earlier time than the novel's setting.

1. After you read the unit introduction with students, tell them that the two novel excerpts take place in two different places—Michigan and Alabama—but that they involve the same family. The family moves, and the narrator, who becomes the new kid in school, is looking for some help.

2. Ask students to talk about how it feels to be the new kid in school.

Opening Activity

Divide students into small groups, and ask each group to compile a five-item list of how to adjust to being a new kid in school and a five-item list of how to treat a new kid in school.

Combine the lists to come up with two final lists, and post them on the bulletin board.

Super-duper-cold Saturdays

STUDENT PAGES 220–228

Skills and Strategies Overview

THEME	Christopher Paul Curtis
READING LEVEL	easy
VOCABULARY	◇ automatically ◇ thermostat ◇ generate ◇ cushion ◇ respectable
PREREADING	story impression
RESPONSE	visualize
COMPREHENSION	double-entry journal
PREWRITING	brainstorm
WRITING	descriptive paragraph / confusing words
ASSESSMENT	enjoyment

BACKGROUND

Christopher Paul Curtis, a Newbery-award-winning novelist, wrote his first novel, *The Watsons Go to Birmingham—1963,* in 1995. The book was well received by critics and won a series of prestigious awards the following year.

In some ways, *The Watsons Go to Birmingham—1963* is two stories rolled into one. The first part of the book is mainly a family story, narrated by a ten-year-old boy named Kenny Watson. In the early part of the novel, most of Kenny's problems have to do with his brother Byron, who is "officially a juvenile delinquent." Later in the novel, Kenny and his family head for Birmingham, Alabama. Unfortunately, they choose 1963 as the year to make their trip. On the journey from Michigan to Alabama, the Watsons witness a degree of racial prejudice that none of them will soon forget.

"Super-duper-cold Saturdays" is an excerpt from the opening chapter of Curtis's book. In these first pages, Curtis introduces his characters and offers readers hints of some of the conflicts to come.

UNIT THEME Christopher Paul Curtis describes a close-knit family that would rather laugh than complain when trouble comes their way.

GRAPHIC ORGANIZER An organizer similar to this one will help students understand Curtis's story-within-a-story narrative style.

MAIN STORY

It's a terribly cold winter day. The Watson family huddles together on a couch underneath a blanket. The family tries to watch a little TV, but it ends up reminding them all how cold they are.

FLASHBACK
Dad tells about Hambone Henderson, his wife's old boyfriend. Mom says it's simply the story of "a young girl who made a bad choice," and there's nothing funny about it.

Dad switches off the TV and decides to tell a story to distract everyone from the cold. . . .

BEFORE YOU READ

Explain that this last unit in the *Sourcebook* explores the literature of author Christopher Paul Curtis and his writing style. Offer background information on Curtis as you see fit. Then assign the prereading activity, a **story impression**.

Motivation Strategy

Ask a small group of computer-savvy students to check the Internet for information about Christopher Paul Curtis. (There are several Web sites, including those created by many middle-school students.) Have them research what he's written, what awards he's won, what book he's working on now, and how others feel about his writing.

Once they have found this information, have them give a brief oral report to the rest of the class. Tell them to present their information in such a way that it makes the class feel motivated to read the selections in the *Sourcebook*.

Vocabulary Building

The most efficient way to uncover the meaning of an unfamiliar word is to examine the word in **context.** Good readers know that writers often leave clues about a word somewhere in the word's environment. Sometimes these words appear in the same sentence; other times they can be found in the preceding or following sentences. Ask students to circle these words in the text and practice defining them in context: *automatically, thermostat, generate, cushion,* and *respectable.* Although each word is footnoted at the bottom of the page, students should check the footnote only as a last resort. First they should try to define on their own. For more help with **Vocabulary**, see page 264.

STRATEGY LESSON: PREFIXES Tell students that in the story, a man on television *forecasts* the weather. Teach students the definition of the prefix *fore-* ("front, in front" or "before"). Then ask them to think of some words with this prefix.

For additional practice on this strategy, see the **Vocabulary** blackline master on page 264.

Prereading Strategies

The purpose of a **story impression** is to help students get a feel for a work of literature even before they begin reading. They can do this by reading a list of words (or sometimes a list of phrases or sentences) that relate to the setting and tone of the story. In this case, students should be able to infer that "Super-duper-cold Saturdays" takes place in cold weather and that it concerns at least one child. Encourage students to write as many guesses as they have about the story. When they finish reading, they may want to return to the notes and make adjustments to their ideas.

Spanish-speaking Students

"Los sábados fríos" viene de la novela *The Watsons Go to Birmingham—1963*, escrito por Christopher Paul Curtis. En esta selección, la familia Watson lucha calentarse en su casa, donde hace tanto frío como afuera. Los inviernos son amargos en Flint, Michigan, pero el padre no quiere que su familia desespere. Bien abrigados, todos se juntan y escuchan al padre intentar convencerles de lo bueno de la situación.

II. READ

As they read the selection, students should try to **visualize** the people and places. Ask them to make sketches in the **Response Notes** of everything they "see." Tell them to keep a sharp eye out for clues to character.

Response Strategy

PREDICT As an additional or alternate response strategy, ask students to make some during-reading predictions about the characters. Have them save their predictions until after they read "New Kids" (pages 230–235), which is another excerpt from the same novel. At that point, they may want to review what they wrote and see how many of their predictions came true.

Comprehension Strategies

A **double-entry journal** gives students the chance to think about parts of a reading that are interesting, puzzling, or thematically important. In the left side of each of the double-entry journal boxes, there is either a quotation from the text or space for students to write a quotation of their own choice. Students should write their thoughts and feelings about the author's words in the right-hand box. If you would like to make suggestions for quotations to respond to, you might suggest these:

"Byron had just turned thirteen, so he was officially a teenage juvenile delinquent and didn't think it was 'cool' to touch anybody or let anybody touch him, . . ."

"We all huddled as close as we could get because we knew Dad was going to try to make us forget about being cold by cutting up."

For more help, see the **Comprehension** blackline master on page 265.

Discussion Questions

COMPREHENSION 1. Why are the Watsons all huddled on the couch? *(It is freezing in the house.)*

2. What does the narrator tell you about Byron? *(He is a teenager who doesn't want to have much to do with his family.)*

CRITICAL THINKING 3. What inferences can you make about the other characters? *(Be sure students support their inferences with evidence from the text. Also be sure that they make inferences about the narrator himself. What clues can they find about this boy?)*

4. What is the tone of Curtis's writing? *(Accept reasonable responses. Help students see that Curtis's tone is humorous. Just like the father in the story, Curtis makes light of this family's situation without making fun or generating pity for the characters.)*

5. What word or words would you use to describe Curtis's writing style? *(Answers will vary. Students might suggest that his style is loose and casual. Many of his descriptions imitate the sound of conversation, which makes for a smooth, natural-sounding style.)*

Literary Skill

FLASHBACK "Super-duper-cold Saturdays" provides an opportunity to review the characteristics of—and purpose for—a flashback. Explain that a *flashback* is an interruption in the narrative that shows an episode that happened before the "interrupted" point in a story. Sometimes a flashback will shed light on a story's events. Other times, as in this story, the flashback is meant to shed light on a character or characters. Curtis's flashback, which begins on page 224, gives the reader clues about the father and mother of the Watson family.

GATHER YOUR THOUGHTS

Prewriting Strategies

Students will complete a series of prewriting activities designed to help them understand the setting of Curtis's story. Their goal is to write a paragraph describing a setting for a story that they will begin on page 237.

Ask students to complete the chart at the top of page 226. First, they will search through the selection, looking for words that describe sounds, sights, feelings, tastes, and touch. Explain that these words help create mood and establish setting.

Next, students will **brainstorm** words for a setting of their own. Remind them that the setting tells the time and place and often helps establish mood. (For help teaching mood, see page 118 of this book.)

Have students use the **Prewriting** blackline master on page 266.

IV. WRITE

Be sure students understand they will be creating a setting for a story that they will begin writing for Lesson 24, "New Kids." If needed, remind them of the definition for the word *setting*. Then ask them to write a **descriptive paragraph** about the setting for their story, paying special attention to words that help readers "see" and "feel" the time and place they describe.

WRITING RUBRIC Use this writing rubric to help students focus on the assignment requirements and for assistance with a quick assessment of their writing.

Do students' descriptive paragraphs

- begin with a topic sentence?
- include sensory details about time and place?
- stay focused on the setting of the story throughout?

Grammar, Usage, and Mechanics

After students have written a first draft, have them exchange papers and proofread each other's work. Ask them to refer to the **Writers' Checklist** as needed during the proofreading process.

At this point, you may want to teach a grammar and usage mini-lesson on confusing words. Ask a volunteer to explain the difference between *affect* and *effect*. Have another volunteer explain the difference between *accept* and *except*. Then ask students to use the words in four sentences of their own.

V. WRAP-UP

Take a moment at the end of the lesson for students to reflect on their **enjoyment** of Curtis's writing. Ask students to read and respond to the questions on the **Readers' Checklist**. Then tell them that Curtis is one of the most popular writers today. What do students think kids like about him? What do they think adults like about him? Was there anything about his writing that students did *not* enjoy?

Assessment

To test students' comprehension, use the **Assessment** blackline master on page 267.

Name _____

VOCABULARY

Words from the Selection

DIRECTIONS To build vocabulary, answer these questions about words from the selection.

> ✦automatically   ✦thermostat   ✦generate   ✦cushion   ✦respectable

1. Sitting on the soft _____ helped me fall asleep in front of the television.

2. When I came inside from the cold, I decided to adjust the _____ to make the house warm.

3. By having us all sit close together, Dad was hoping to _____ some extra heat.

4. The heat kicked on _____.

5. Mom thought Moses Henderson was a _____ boy, not a clown at all.

Strategy Lesson: Prefixes

Prefixes are "word parts" that come before a root word (*pre-* = before).

DIRECTIONS Look at the prefix and its meaning. Then add the prefix to each of the words in the box to answer each question. Write the complete word in the blank.

fore- = front, in front, before

> ✦caster   ✦head   ✦see   ✦shadowing   ✦man

6. Who predicts the weather? _____

7. What is the part of the body above the eyes? _____

8. What do you do when you know something beforehand?

    _____

9. Who is in charge of a group of workers? _____

10. What is the technique of giving the reader a hint of what is to come?

    _____

Name _____

COMPREHENSION

Quickwrite

DIRECTIONS Do a one- or two-minute quickwrite about "Super-duper-cold Saturdays." Write whatever comes to mind. Begin your quickwrite with this sentence:

The Watson family reminds me of

_____

_____

_____

_____

_____

_____

_____

_____

_____

_____

_____

_____

_____

_____

_____

_____

_____

_____

Name _____

PREWRITING
Creating a Setting

DIRECTIONS Sometimes it helps to draw a picture before you write. In the frame below, sketch the setting you will describe in your descriptive paragraph.

1. Use colored pencils or crayons to help create the mood.

2. Then answer a question about the mood.

What is the mood of your setting? List words that describe the mood here:

_____   _____   _____

_____   _____   _____

_____   _____   _____

Name _____

ASSESSMENT

Multiple-Choice Test

DIRECTIONS On the blanks provided, write the letter of the item that best answers each question or completes each statement.

_____ 1. The narrator compares his breath to . . .

A. a storm cloud. C. a big marshmallow.

B. puffs of train smoke. D. all of the above

_____ 2. The narrator says that it was so cold outside, people had to . . .

A. blink a thousand times. C. cover their eyes.

B. close their eyes. D. run.

_____ 3. What does the narrator say would be an ice cube before it hit the ground?

A. spit C. a tear

B. water D. raindrops

_____ 4. What is the family wearing inside the house?

A. hats and scarves C. sweaters

B. three pairs of socks D. all of the above

_____ 5. What is the family doing?

A. They are huddled up on the couch. C. They are watching television.

B. They are playing a game. D. A and C

_____ 6. Why doesn't Byron want to sit too close to anyone?

A. He is sick. C. He feels hot.

B. It's not "cool." D. all of the above

_____ 7. Where is Momma from?

A. Michigan C. Alabama

B. Ohio D. Georgia

_____ 8. What does the weather report tell the family?

A. It will warm up. C. The weather will stay the same.

B. It will snow. D. It will be getting colder.

_____ 9. What does Dad do to take everyone's mind off the cold?

A. He makes a warm snack. C. He begins a fun game.

B. He tells a funny story. D. He sings a song.

_____ 10. Of whom does the dad make fun?

A. Hambone Henderson C. Wilona

B. Daniel Watson D. A and C

Short-essay Test

Why do you think Dad makes fun of the man from Momma's past?

Skills and Strategies Overview

THEME	Christopher Paul Curtis
READING LEVEL	average
VOCABULARY	✦thugs ✦regards ✦punctual ✦miracle ✦panning
PREREADING	think-pair-and-share
RESPONSE	predict
COMPREHENSION	reciprocal reading
PREWRITING	story map
WRITING	story beginning / easily confused words
ASSESSMENT	ease

BACKGROUND

What distinguishes Christopher Paul Curtis's *The Watsons Go to Birmingham—1963* from other books about family is the voice of the narrator, Kenny Watson (nicknamed Poindexter in this selection). Kenny is a good boy surrounded by "thugs" who resent him for his intelligence and his ability to get along well with adults. Kenny, who longs to be cool, finds himself lumped together with the good kids, day in and day out. Instead of appreciating this, he tries to think up ways to rebel against it.

Kenny's voice is as authentic as it is touching, which is why Curtis's novel appeals to young and old alike. In this excerpt from the novel, Kenny is overjoyed to discover a personal "saver"—a boy who is even nicer and more "uncool" than Kenny.

UNIT THEME   Christopher Paul Curtis explores the anguish of being the kid who is always "picked on."

GRAPHIC ORGANIZER   A story map for "New Kids" might look something like this one:

> **The situation:**
> Kenny (Poindexter) and others watch as two new kids board the school bus.

> **A problem occurs:**
> The boys draw attention to themselves by being extra polite.

> **Things get worse:**
> The bus driver suggests one of the new boys sit next to Kenny.

> **A possible answer appears**
> Could this be the "saver" Kenny has been waiting for?

> **The problem is solved:**
> Kenny decides that he really is saved!

> **The end:**
> Kenny is surprised that God would send a "saver" in raggedy clothes.

BIBLIOGRAPHY   If students enjoyed these selections by Christopher Paul Curtis, ask them to read the rest of the *Watsons Go to Birmingham—1963* or *Bud, Not Buddy* (1999), which won the Newbery and Coretta Scott King awards in 2000.

BEFORE YOU READ

Explain that "New Kids" is another story written by Christopher Paul Curtis. Ask volunteers to quickly review what they know of Curtis's style. Then have them complete the prereading activity, a **think-pair-and-share**. (Refer to the **Strategy Handbook** on page 40 for more help.)

Motivation Strategy

ENGAGING STUDENTS Tell the class that "New Kids" is a story about being new to school. Many of your students will be able to relate to this topic. Ask volunteers to complete this statement: "I think being the new kid is _____." Hold a group discussion to talk about students' answers. Your discussion will serve as a warm-up to the story's topic.

Vocabulary Building

Help students use **context clues** as they read to figure out the meanings of difficult words, especially the key vocabulary for this lesson: *thug, regards, punctual, miracle,* and *panning.* *Regards* and *miracle* are not footnoted. Model using context clues and then checking your ideas against the footnote: "I don't know the meaning of the word *thugs.* I see, though, that the word is used to describe a group of boys who cause trouble on the bus. I also see that it is positioned as the opposite of 'regular kids.' Could *thugs* mean 'bad kids'? I'll use the footnote to help refine my own definition." Ask students to circle these words in the text. For additional practice with these words, see page 272.

STRATEGY LESSON: SUFFIXES Word games can improve students' vocabulary and make them feel more confident about their language skills. Show how easy it is to attach suffixes to words. Give students a group of common suffixes such as *-ed, -able, -al,* and *-ant* and have them think of words that use the suffixes. Make a list on the board of the words and then ask for volunteers to define each one. You might incorporate these words that relate to the selection: *punctual, defiant, interrupted,* and *reliable.*

For additional practice on this strategy, see the **Vocabulary** blackline master on page 272.

Prereading Strategies

Students are asked to complete a **think-pair-and-share** before they begin reading "New Kids." This strategy will help them become actively involved in the selection. In addition, the think-pair-and-share will refine their ability to work cooperatively in a group. During the "pair" exercise, students should build upon each other's ideas and help the group reach consensus on what the five statements mean. Students can work together to answer the questions at the bottom of the page.

QUICKWRITE As an alternate prereading strategy, ask students to do a quickwrite. Read the first paragraph of "New Kids" aloud while students follow along in their books. Then have them do a one-minute quickwrite about a topic that is somehow related to the selection. For example, you might have them write about being the new kid, feeling left out, or dealing with bullies. This type of writing is meant to help readers make a bridge between their own ideas and the piece of literature they're about to read.

Spanish-speaking Students

"Niños nuevos" también viene de la novela de Christopher Paul Curtis, *The Watsons Go to Birmingham—1963.* En esta selección, el narrador, Poindexter, describe cómo fue salvado de los abusadores de su clase. Cada mañana en al autobús de la escuela ha sido molestado por los niños más grandes. Con la llegada de dos estudiantes nuevos, sin embargo, Poindexter sabe inmediatamente que no más va a ser víctima.

READ

Before students begin reading, remind them that the directions at the top of page 230 ask them to **predict** as they are reading. Each time they make a new prediction, students should jot it down in the **Response Notes**. Making predictions can keep readers actively involved in the story line.

Response Strategy

MARK OR HIGHLIGHT As an alternate or additional response strategy, ask students to mark or highlight anything they think is interesting or important in the story. In particular, have them watch for clues about Kenny, whom the boys call Poindexter. What kind of person is he? Why is he in need of a personal "saver"?

Comprehension Strategies

In a **reciprocal reading**, readers share the process of reading and responding to a text. This simple strategy can make the reading process easier and more enjoyable for students. Divide the class into small groups, and ask the groups to read the selection cooperatively. Each time students come to an interrupter question, they should first note their own answer in the book and then discuss what they've written with the rest of the group. Remind the class that it is not important to reach consensus on an answer. Part of the fun of interpreting and discussing a story is listening to other people's ideas about a character, an event, or a topic.

For more help, see the **Comprehension** blackline master on page 273.

Discussion Questions

COMPREHENSION 1. What does Byron mean when he says, "Give my regards to Clark, Poindexter." *(He is skipping school and wants to be sure Kenny knows it.)*

2. What problems does Kenny have with the other kids? *(They tease him, and he worries about what they think.)*

3. Why doesn't the bus driver usually allow the late kids on the bus? *(He wants to teach them to be punctual.)*

CRITICAL THINKING 4. What kind of miracle is Kenny looking for? *(Answers will vary. Possible: He wants someone else to draw attention away from him so that the kids stop teasing him.)*

5. What is the mood of "New Kids"? *(Remind students that* mood *is the overall feeling, or effect, of a work. Students might note that the mood is tense in places and suspenseful. There is humor as well.)*

Literary Skill

LOCAL COLOR In fiction, the use of of dialect, physical setting, customs, and dress of a particular region is called *local color*. Since the selection does not specifically identify the setting (except as an excerpt from a book with *Birmingham* in the title), ask students to suggest some clues to the regional setting. The use of *y'all* (for *you all*) is the only instance of dialect in this selection, but it should provide a strong clue. Students can also infer that the setting is rural from the references to "country" and "down-home," the latter an adjective usually associated with the southern United States.

III. GATHER YOUR THOUGHTS

Prewriting Strategies

The prewriting activities on page 236 (and also the graphic organizer on page 235) will help students reflect on the story they've just read and prepare them to write.

Students should begin by rereading the descriptive paragraphs that they wrote on page 227 of their books. This is the setting for the story they'll write on page 237. As an opening activity, have students make a list of characters they want to include in their stories.

Next, students will plan their stories. Remind the class that every story has a conflict or problem to be resolved by the end. Have them make notes on the **story map** at the bottom of page 236.

Have students use the **Prewriting** blackline master on page 274.

IV. WRITE

Set aside plenty of time for students to write their **story beginnings.** Remind them that their stories must incorporate the setting they have already created. Show them this plan for their stories. If you want them to write a complete story, have them write all four paragraphs. Otherwise, ask them to write just the first two.

- **paragraph 1:** Describe the setting and introduce the characters.

- **paragraph 2:** Establish the conflict.

- **paragraph 3:** Resolve the conflict.

- **paragraph 4:** Tie up any loose ends and perhaps show what the characters have learned or are feeling.

WRITING RUBRIC Use this writing rubric to help students focus on the assignment requirements and for assistance with a quick assessment of their writing.

Do students' story beginnings

- open with a description of the setting?

- give information about the characters, including how they look and act, and how others feel about them?

- establish a conflict that involves one or more of the central characters?

Grammar, Usage, and Mechanics

After students have written a first draft, they should read through their story beginnings twice to be sure that the narrative flows well. Then they will need to proofread their writing. Have them read the **Writers' Checklist** before they begin. For practice, ask students to edit this sentence that relates to the text.

~~Than~~ Poindexter said, "I want ~~too~~ move ~~two~~ a new seat ~~to.~~"
Then   to   to   too

V. WRAP-UP

Take a moment at the end of the lesson for students to say whether or not Curtis's writing was **easy** for them to read. To get your discussion started, have them read and respond to the questions on the **Readers' Checklist**.

Assessment

To test students' comprehension, use the **Assessment** blackline master on page 275.

Name _____

VOCABULARY

Words from the Selection

DIRECTIONS To build vocabulary, answer these questions about five words from the selection.

1. If a group of kids are referred to as <u>thugs</u>, are they well behaved or troublemakers?

   _____

2. When you give your <u>regards</u> to a group, are you insulting them or greeting them?

   _____

3. If you are <u>punctual</u>, are you on time? _____

4. Is a <u>miracle</u> an everyday occurrence? _____

5. When you are <u>panning</u> someone, are you complimenting or criticizing?

   _____

Strategy Lesson: Suffixes

Suffixes are word parts that come at the end of a root word. Suffixes can give you clues about the meaning of a word and how it should be used in a sentence. For example, if you add the suffix *-ous* to the noun *grace*, you get the adjective *gracious*, which means "full of grace."

DIRECTIONS Circle the suffix in the word. Then use each word in a sentence that shows you know what it means.

```
-al = of, like; having the nature of

-ant = inclined to promote or cause; being in a certain state
```

Example: serv(ant) (one who serves) The *servant* brought me my drink.

6. signal

sentence: _____

7. defiant

sentence: _____

8. factual

sentence: _____

9. pleasant

sentence: _____

10. personal

sentence: _____

Name _____

COMPREHENSION
Graphic Organizer ....

DIRECTIONS Use this chart to plan the characters for your story beginning. Give as many details as you can.

	Name	Words describing appearance	Words describing personality	Sketch of character
character #1				
character #2				
character #3				
character #4				

Name _____

PREWRITING

Plan a Story Opening

DIRECTIONS Use this story pie to plan what you will write in the first two paragraphs of your story.

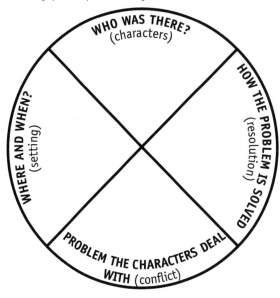

Write Dialogue

DIRECTIONS Next write some dialogue for your story opening. When writing dialogue, you need to consider these three questions:

- Who is there?
- What are they saying? (What topic are they discussing?)
- How are they saying it? (Are they angry? tired? excited?)

STEP 1. Which characters will be in your story opening?

_____

STEP 2. What are the characters talking about?

_____

STEP 3. What do they say?

character #1 says: _____

character #2 responds: _____

character #1 says: _____

character #2 responds: _____

STEP 4. How do they say it? (Are they *muttering, laughing, murmuring, questioning, shouting, whispering, replying, giggling,* or *crying?*)

character #1 talks in a _____ voice.

character #2 talks in a _____ voice.

Name _____

ASSESSMENT

Multiple-Choice Test

DIRECTIONS On the blanks provided, write the letter of the item that best answers each question or completes each statement.

_____ 1. Who is often standing by himself at the bus stop?
   A. Byron   C. Poindexter
   B. Banky   D. Clark

_____ 2. If Byron doesn't ride the bus, where does Kenny (Poindexter) sit?
   A. in the middle   C. in the back
   B. behind the driver   D. with his friends

_____ 3. What does the bus driver do that he doesn't usually do?
   A. drives by kids who are late   C. stops the bus for late kids
   B. falls asleep   D. laughs at the students

_____ 4. Kenny believes that the boys who got on the bus are . . .
   A. part of his miracle.   C. unkind.
   B. troublemakers.   D. stupid.

_____ 5. What does Kenny believe being saved means?
   A. Someone has been sent to   C. Someone can take away your problems.
       protect you.
   B. You can feel better.   D. all of the above

_____ 6. Why does Kenny believe he has been sent a "saver"?
   A. because he has no friends   C. because he is teased and picked on
   B. because he asked for one   D. because he is the youngest

_____ 7. What words are *not* used to describe Kenny's "saver"?
   A. jacket with holes   C. torn-up jeans
   B. scary frown   D. raggedy tennis shoes

_____ 8. What do the new boys do on the bus?
   A. wave at everyone   C. grin at everyone
   B. say hello to everyone D. all of the above

_____ 9. What do the kids on the bus do to the new boys?
   A. greet them politely   C. tease them
   B. ask them questions   D. ignore them

_____ 10. What is Kenny's concern at the end of the story?
   A. His "saver" is not what   C. The new boys may not like him.
       he expected.
   B. He may be teased more.   D. The new boys may get hurt.

Short-essay Test

Explain why Kenny thinks the new boy is his "saver."

THE TURTLE

I. Before You Read

Who is the story about?
(The story is about an eight-year-old boy, Dennis, and his turtle, Oscar.)
What do you know about the main characters?
(Dennis is sad about his turtle dying, and his mother and father try to comfort him.)
Where does the story take place?
(The story takes place in Dennis's house.)
When does it take place?
(It takes place during the day, after Dennis gets home from school.)
What do you predict will be the problem in the story?
(The problem of the story revolves around the death of Oscar.)

II. Read

(Students' answers will vary.)
Why is Dennis crying?
(He is upset because he believes Oscar is dead.)
Is Dennis's father a caring or uncaring person? Explain your opinion.
(Some students may believe he is caring, because he tries to comfort Dennis and he suggests having a funeral service for Oscar in order to help him deal with his grief. Others may say Dennis's father is uncaring, because he is irritable when Dennis's mother calls him and he behaves as though he's in a rush.)
Why is the ending of "The Turtle" such a surprise?
(Throughout the story, the reader believes that Oscar is dead. At the end, he flips over and swims. He has been alive the whole time, and therefore the action of the story has been centered around a mistake. Also, at the end Dennis says, "Let's kill him," which is a far cry from the grieving he was doing earlier.)

Vocabulary

1 cry
2 easily annoyed
3 persistently; repeatedly
4 small coffin
5 carve
6–10 Sentences will vary.
6 visual + ize
7 sincere + ity
8 public + ity or + ize
9 native + ity
10 mobil + ity or + ize

Assessment

1	D	6	B
2	B	7	C
3	A	8	B
4	C	9	C
5	A	10	D

THANK YOU, MA'AM

II. Read

1. The boy tries to snatch the woman's purse as she walks down the street late one night. He loses his balance and falls down.
2. The woman picks him up and starts to talk to him, making him give back the pocketbook.
3. The woman tells the boy her name, Mrs. Jones, and drags him to her home.
4. Mrs. Jones lets go of Roger so he can wash his face at the sink. He doesn't run away and he goes to wash up.
5. Roger tells Mrs. Jones that the reason he tried to steal her pocketbook is that he wanted a pair of blue suede shoes.
6. Mrs. Jones tells Roger that she was young once too, and wanted things she couldn't have. She tells him that she has also done things that were wrong.

The story takes place in (a city street and in the home of Mrs. Jones.)
(Mrs. Jones) **is a character in the story who** (Answers will vary.)
(Roger) **is another character who** (Answers will vary.)

Vocabulary

1 permit
2 presentable
3 snatch
4 frail
5 frowned
6 scolded him
7 had no defense
8 meet trouble bravely
9 remain where he was
10 be careful

Assessment

1	D	6	A
2	C	7	C
3	A	8	D
4	D	9	A
5	B	10	D

CARING FOR THE WOUNDED
I. Before You Read

Who was Clara Barton?
(She was a nurse on the battlefield during the Civil War.)
When did she live?
(She was alive at the time of the Civil War, in the 1860s.)
What did she do?
(She cared for soldiers who were injured fighting in the Civil War.)
Why was her work so important?
(Her work was important because she provided the much-needed medical care. As women were rarely on the battlefields, their presence, and hers in particular, boosted the soldiers' spirits.)

II. Read

What has happened so far?
(A surgeon has told Clara Barton about a soldier who is dying on the battlefield and crying for his sister, Mary. Clara has gone with the surgeon to see the soldier.)
What does Barton do to calm the wounded soldier?
(She pretends to be his sister in order to calm him. She then holds him in her lap.)
What have you learned about Clara Barton? Explain.
(She is a caring person who is willing to sacrifice her own time and comfort in order to make the soldiers' last moments less agonizing. She is unselfish, patient, and brave.)
What have you learned about medical treatment during the Civil War?
(Medical treatment was primitive. Many dying soldiers could not be saved, so surgeons often just focused on easing their pain before they died.)

Vocabulary
1 careful
2 in pain
3 stomach ache
4 gloomy
5 help out
6 audiovisual
7 auditorium
8 audience
9 audible
10 audition

Assessment
1 B   6 A
2 A   7 B
3 C   8 C
4 D   9 B
5 D   10 A

THE PRESIDENT'S BEEN SHOT
II. Read

(Students' answers will vary.)
Who was Mr. Hawk, and what was he doing at the time Lincoln was shot?
(Mr. Hawk was an actor in the play that Lincoln and his wife were watching at the theater. He was looking at Mrs. Lincoln's smiling face when he heard the shot.)
What happened immediately after Lincoln was shot?
(Quiet bewilderment was followed by pandemonium.)

Vocabulary
1 strengthen
2 crazed
3 hole
4 bony
5 confusion
6 admirer
7 prevent from carrying out
8 lift with force
9 made a hole
10 dramatic performance

Assessment
1 D   6 A
2 C   7 B
3 B   8 B
4 D   9 C
5 C   10 A

TOBY BOYCE AND GIDEON ADAMS

I. Before You Read

Who is the author? (Paul Fleischman)
What character names did you notice? (Toby Boyce, the recruiter, Gideon Adams)
What place names did you notice? (Georgia, the South)
What do you think these selections will be about? (the Civil War)

III. Gather Your Thoughts

HOW HE ACTS
eager to fight for the South in the Civil War; bold because he is willing to play the fife for the recruiter even though he doesn't know how

HOW HE SOUNDS
excited at the chance to be involved in the Civil War, perhaps nervous when he's talking to the recruiter

HOW HE FEELS
scared, brave, proud

Toby Boyce

WHAT HE LOOKS LIKE
white, young and boyish

HOW HE DRESSES
clothes are probably dirty, as he walked 15 miles to the courthouse

HOW HE FEELS
worried that he won't be able to fight, upset that he isn't allowed to fight because he is black, determined to fight anyway

WHAT HE LOOKS LIKE
black, probably light-skinned because he is able to pass as a white man; probably relatively young because he is going to be an infantry soldier

HOW HE SOUNDS
self-assured, firm

Gideon Adams

HOW HE ACTS
proud, nervous

HOW HE DRESSES
large cap with chin strap to cover his hair so the recruiter won't know he's black

Vocabulary

1 North
2 amazing thing
3 wrinkled
4 a group of people
5 confused
6 scowled
7 limp
8 commenced
9 infantry
10 impolite

Assessment

1	D	6	A
2	A	7	A
3	B	8	D
4	B	9	D
5	C	10	B

SHEM SUGGS AND JUDAH JENKINS

II. Read

How does this story begin?
(The soldiers who are headed off to war are waiting in camp for the battle to begin. They are restless, anxious, and nervous.)

What does Shem hear about Gulliver?
(Shem hears that, in the book *Gulliver's Travels*, Gulliver goes to a country where horses are in charge. The horses are shocked to hear that men have wars, pay soldiers to kill other men, and have so many inventions designed to increase the numbers of men that can be killed in wars.)

In your own words, what promise does Shem make to himself?
(Shem promises that if he survives his time on the battlefields of the Civil War, he will learn how to read and will read the rest of *Gulliver's Travels*.)

What problem is Judah having with his horse?
(He is riding through a battlefield to deliver a message to Colonel Evans. He and his horse get close to the fighting, and the horse becomes scared. It is confused and doesn't know what to do.)

How did Judah do at "showing his worth"?
(He reaches Colonel Evans and can therefore deliver the message as he was ordered. However, as his horse has run away, he cannot continue to serve as a courier.)

Vocabulary

1 galloped
2 courier
3 legions
4 hooves
5 muskets
6 C
7 F
8 E
9 B
10 A
11 D
12 G

Assessment

1	A	6	C
2	D	7	B
3	A	8	D
4	C	9	B
5	B	10	A

A MOMENT IN THE SUN FIELD

I. Before You Read

What will this story be about?

(The story will be about the way that Bobby feels as he plays 500 with his father and his friend Mike. He will describe the events of the game and why it is special to him.)

Vocabulary

1–5 Sentences will vary.
6 to put in a proper place
7 to place for safekeeping
8 to form by placing together
9 placed at risk of a harmful action or condition
10 the positioning or bearing of the body

Assessment

1	C	6	A
2	B	7	C
3	B	8	B
4	B	9	C
5	C	10	A

THE ONE SITTING THERE

II. Read

What's the narrator doing? Why?

(The narrator is throwing away all of the food that was in her refrigerator and freezer. The power has gone out, so the food must be disposed of before it spoils.)

What is the theme of Woś's story?

(The theme of Woś's story is the idea that memories and experiences from childhood have lasting effects. The narrator remembers her childhood and imagines how it would have been different had her sister survived. The simple act of throwing away food stirs a complex mix of emotions and triggers old memories.)

Vocabulary

1 destroying
2 sick
3 slowly
4 outside
5 department store
6 prosper + ity = state of having wealth or plenty
7 scarce + ity = state of being hard to get; shortage
8 care + less = without care; not cautious
9 form + less = without form; shapeless
10 timid + ity = state of being shy

Assessment

1	D	6	D
2	B	7	B
3	A	8	C
4	C	9	A
5	C	10	D

PANDORA

I. Before You Read

Vocabulary

WHAT ARE SOME KEY NAMES AND PLACES?	WHAT REPEATED WORDS DID YOU FIND?
Names: Zeus, Pandora, Epimetheus, Hermes. Places: Mount Olympus, the home of Pandora and Epimetheus, the dusty storeroom, the garden	garden, dance, golden box, promise, hope

1 torment
2 scheme
3 grieves
4 scorch
5 rustling
6 dis + appear; not appear; not arrive
7 un + grateful; not grateful; not thankful
8 un + shackled; untied
9 in + sane; not sane
10 mis + fortune; bad fortune; bad luck

WHAT ARE SOME KEY EVENTS?

Zeus creates Pandora, the gods give Pandora their gifts, Hermes gives her the golden box, Epimetheus marries Pandora, Pandora shows curiosity about the contents of the golden box. She first hides the box in the storeroom and then buries the box. She later digs up the box, opens it, and releases creatures. Pandora keeps the most dangerous creature, the foreboding one, inside the box.

III. Gather Your Thoughts

Assessment

1. Zeus creates Pandora to punish man.	2. Hermes gives her a beautiful golden box, and Hera gives her curiosity.

3. Pandora wonders what's in the box and thinks Hermes really wants her to open it.

4. She is so consumed by curiosity about the box that she puts it in a heavy chest and buries it in the garden.	5. She digs up the box and opens it.

6. The creatures representing the ills of man's existence fly out of the box. She manages to keep the creature that represents foreboding inside the box.

1	C	6	C
2	B	7	C
3	D	8	B
4	A	9	D
5	B	10	C

HERA

I. Before You Read

Vocabulary

Number which sentence appears first, which second, and so on.
(1. d 2. b 3. c 4. a)

II. Read

1 pain
2 receive
3 rage; anger
4 delicate
5 sad
6 geology
7 monorail
8 immortality
9 mortal
10 monologue

Example: He created a storm and then turned himself into a cuckoo so that Hera would pity and hold the wet bird. Then he turned himself back into Zeus and she was holding the god in her arms. By this means he won Hera to be his wife after she had initially refused.

deceitful — Zeus — fearful of Hera's wrath

Example: He secretly goes to Earth to marry other women.

Example: The story says that "Even Zeus, who was afraid of nothing, feared her fits of temper." When Hera catches Zeus with Io and he has to turn Io into a cow, he is afraid to change her back into a human because of the reaction it would provoke in Hera.

Assessment

1	C	6	C
2	B	7	C
3	D	8	C
4	A	9	A
5	B	10	A

Example: She compels Argus to guard Io so Zeus can't turn her back into a human. She is very determined to ensure that Zeus and Io are apart. When she finally lets Zeus turn Io back into a human, he has to promise never to look at her again.

Example: Zeus, who is all powerful, is afraid of Hera's temper. She is furious when she learns that Hermes has bored Argus to death and that Io has escaped his surveillance.

strong-willed — Hera — temperamental — jealous

Example: Hera does not want Zeus to have any other wives. She goes to great lengths to intervene in his relationships with mortals.

ARRIVAL

III. Gather Your Thoughts

A. Reflect on Character

Laurie is . . .

1. (upset with Andy for stranding them for the night at the farm. He volunteered them for an orienteering expedition and led them on the wrong path.)
2. (very observant of the way that the machine moves and behaves.)
3. (sickened by the way the machine picks up the people and kills the dog.)

Summary Sentence:

(Laurie is dealing with the situation of being stuck in the woods and sleeping in an unfamiliar area when he is awakened by a strange machine. He watches it destroy a farmhouse and take away the inhabitants.)

Andy is . . .

1. (initially not worried about the sounds they hear at night, and urges Laurie to go back to sleep.)
2. (focused on attempting to convince himself that the machine is only part of a science-fiction movie.)
3. (very scared once he sees the machine kill the dog and take the farmer inside; he says he wants to run away quickly so the machine won't see them.)

Summary Sentence:

(Andy is at first unconcerned by the strange sounds that he and Laurie hear outside the shed they're sleeping in, but when he sees the machine he becomes terrified and attempts to figure out how to escape.)

B. Compare and Contrast Characters

LAURIE

(blames Andy for their situation. He reacts logically to the noise they first hear, realizing it couldn't be from the artillery range. He doesn't believe Andy's theory that the machine is part of a science-fiction movie and feels sick when the machine kills the dog.)

LAURIE AND ANDY

(are very sleepy because of the long day of hiking. They are terrified when they see the machine's destructive power. They sit silently watching the machine because they have no other options. They feel close to each other because they're in a dangerous situation together.)

ANDY

(dismisses the noise they first hear as just stray fire from an artillery range. He awakens Laurie when the noise starts again and he realizes it's being produced by something big. He says that the machine is probably part of a science-fiction movie but later says they should run for cover.)

Vocabulary

1. old
2. offering to do something
3. over time
4. just eaten
5. destroyed
6. three
7. a group of four
8. three
9. a four-footed animal
10. play in which three base runners are put out

Assessment

1	B	6	C
2	A	7	A
3	A	8	C
4	D	9	B
5	B	10	D

ARRIVAL continued

II. Read

What 3 things did the army try to do?

1. Fighter planes flew by twice and a helicopter circled around taking pictures.

2. The army attempted unsuccessfully to make radio contact with the machine.

3. A single tank went underneath the machine, displayed a white flag, and played classical music.

How did the machine respond? Fill in 2 things it did.

4. It waved one of its tentacles above the tank in time with the music.

5. It brushed a second tentacle against the turret of the tank.

What were the next 3 things that happened in the story? Write them below.

6. The machine raised the tank in the air. The tank fired at the machine. The machine crushed and then dropped the tank.

7. The fighter-bomber planes flew in and fired at the machine. They destroyed it.

8. School started for Andy and Laurie three weeks later. Laurie talked a lot about the experience, both to his friends and to the media.

Who are the main characters in "Arrival"?
Andy, Laurie, the machine, Wild Bill

Where does the action take place?
The action takes place in a field in England. Andy and Laurie are spending the night in a shed there after becoming lost on an orienteering trip.

What is the problem or conflict?
The problem revolves around how humans should react to the machines that have landed on Earth. People don't know why they have come, what their intentions are, or how to communicate with them. They fear they may be dangerous threats to Earth.

How is the conflict solved or resolved?
The humans use force to destroy the machines in Russia and Britain, and the one in the United States simply self-destructs. Nobody was able to communicate with the machines or discover their intentions on Earth. The problem is not entirely resolved because although the machines are gone, there was knowledge gained from their presence on Earth.

Vocabulary

1–5 Student answers will vary.
6. reluctantly—willingly
7. civilized—wild
8. emerged—disappeared
9. pulverizing—building
10. sarcastic—sincere
11. pushover—strong
12. Sentences will vary.

Assessment

1	D	6	C
2	C	7	A
3	B	8	C
4	A	9	B
5	D	10	C

LIFE DOESN'T FRIGHTEN ME

II. Read

(Students' answers will vary.)

Why does the speaker name things like Mother Goose from nursery rhymes?
(The poem has the feel of a nursery rhyme, with its short, rhythmic lines and quick beats.)

Why do you think the speaker names all the things she's *not* afraid of?
(The speaker may actually mean the opposite of what she says, and these are all things that actually do scare her or make her uncomfortable. By saying she's not afraid of them, she reassures herself of her own security.)

III. Gather Your Thoughts

(Students' answers will vary.)

Poem title: **Poet's name:**
(Life Doesn't Frighten Me)   (Maya Angelou)

Is there rhyme? (yes)
examples:
(wall/hall/all, Goose/loose, cry/fly, and sleeve/breathe)

Are there repeated words or phrases? (yes)
examples: (The line "Life doesn't frighten me at all" appears six times in the poem. "They don't frighten me at all" also appears numerous times.)

Are there words that appeal to the 5 senses? (yes)
examples: (There are many sensory images in the poem. Some are "shadows" [sight], "barking" [sound], and "Dragons breathing flame" [touch].)

Brief summary of what the poem is about:
(The poem may be the speaker's attempt to deal with fears by acknowledging their existence.)

The poet's main idea is: (The main idea is that one doesn't have to give in to fear.)

Vocabulary

1 shade
2 bedspread
3 people not known before
4 not tied
5 something that has magical powers
6 self-centered
7 self-control
8 self-assured
9 self-respect
10 Sentences will vary.

Assessment

1	B	6	D
2	A	7	A
3	D	8	B
4	B	9	C
5	C	10	D

STANLEY YELNATS

I. Before You Read

SETTING:
Texas; flat wasteland; no shade; very hot

CHARACTERS:
Stanley; campers; guard; Mrs. Bell

PICTURES:
barracks; boy

Stanley Yelnats

BEGINNING AND ENDING:
Camp Green Lake; arrested; overweight; embarrassed

REPEATED WORDS:
shade; rattlesnakes; scorpions; Usually; bitten; hot

Vocabulary

1 hammock
2 scorpions
3 stationery
4 stifling
5 ratios
6 arm / rest
7 hand / cuffs
8 back / pack
9 pine / apple
10 chop / sticks
11 fire / arm
12 nick / name
13 sky / scraper
14 with / hold
15 window / pane

Assessment

1	C	6	D
2	B	7	A
3	D	8	D
4	C	9	D
5	B	10	C

THE REVOLT OF DENMARK VESEY

II. Read

(Students' answers will vary.)

What have you learned so far about Denmark Vesey?
(He is a former slave who had been a personal servant to a sea captain named Joseph Vesey. He was born in the Caribbean and became Vesey's servant at age 14. As the story begins, Vesey has won $1,500 in the lottery in Charleston, South Carolina.)

How does Vesey plan to buy his freedom?
(He plans to use some of the money from his lottery winnings to buy his freedom from Captain Vesey. This will cost him $600.)

What leads Vesey to plan a revolt?
(He had been a servant on Captain Vesey's slave ship and had witnessed firsthand the brutality and cruelty that the slave trade inspired. Newly free, he now feels obligated to help the slaves who are less fortunate.)

What happens to Vesey's revolt?
(A house slave, who has found out about Vesey's plans, becomes scared and tells the master. The authorities are alerted, and though they fail to catch most of Vesey's 9,000 followers, they catch Vesey and kill him.)

III. Gather Your Thoughts

(Students' answers will vary.)

Subject: (Denmark Vesey)
What the author says about the subject:
(He is a former slave of a sea captain who specializes in the importation of slaves from Africa to the United States. He is more wealthy and fortunate than the typical slave. He pays for his own freedom. He opposes the system of slavery in the United States and works to overthrow it.)

List Details:
(Vesey was upset that the slave trade continued despite the fact that it had been made illegal in 1807. Vesey had contact with, and read and discussed the writings of, various abolitionists. Vesey began to enlist the help of other blacks in order to execute a rebellion that would free slaves throughout the United States. Vesey believed that it was his duty as a black man who had gained his freedom, and who had both education and money, to help other blacks overcome their oppression.)

Vocabulary

1 bewildered
2 shackled
3 prosperous
4 captives
5 humiliation
6 import
7 export
8 deport
9 report
10 transport

Assessment

1	B	6	C
2	D	7	B
3	D	8	C
4	A	9	A
5	C	10	B

BORN INTO SLAVERY

I. Before You Read

5. "I do not recollect of ever seeing my mother by the light of day."
4. "Frequently, before the child has reached its twelfth month, its mother is taken from it, and hired out on some farm a considerable distance off. . . ."
3. "My mother and I were separated when I was but an infant—before I knew her as my mother."
2. "The opinion was also whispered that my master was my father; but of the correctness of this opinion, I know nothing. . . ."
1. "I do not remember to have ever met a slave who could tell of his birthday."

II. Read

(Students' answers will vary.)

Why do you think slave masters refused to give a slave's age?
(Masters didn't tell slaves their age because they wanted to dehumanize them.)

From what you've read, how does Douglass feel about his mother?
(He hardly knows her because they were separated when he was very young. He understands the reason for their separation is to keep the child and the mother from developing a natural human attachment.)

How does Douglass feel when he hears his mother has died?
(He says that it affected him no more than would the news of a stranger's death.)

III. Gather Your Thoughts

1. Why were slave children separated from their mothers?
(Douglass infers that the separation is imposed to keep the slaves from feeling human and from developing natural relationships and affections.)

2. What effect did the separation have?
(Douglass never got to know his mother and saw her only 4 or 5 times in his life. When she died, he says he was emotionally unaffected.)

Vocabulary

1 deprived
2 inquiries
3 complexion
4 hinder
5 recollect
6 indecisive; not decisive, in the habit of putting off decisions
7 inaccurate; not accurate, not exact
8 impossible; not possible, not able to happen
9 inactive; not active, showing inability to act
10 immature; not mature, undeveloped

Assessment

1	D	6	C
2	A	7	A
3	C	8	D
4	B	9	C
5	A	10	B

NARDO

III. Gather Your Thoughts

(Students' answers will vary.)

A. REFLECT ON CHARACTER

> 2. unlucky
> He goes through many jobs in one summer and loses them for various reasons.

> 3. condescending
> He talks condescendingly about the rich people at the parties he caters. He calls them "old fogies" and says they would drink and then make fools of themselves when they danced.

> 4. smooth-talking
> He is able to buy a prize ticket and ask a girl to dance at a party where he is working.

> 5. crafty
> The narrator says Nardo could "duck trouble better than a champion boxer could duck a right cross." He says he is almost always able to sense when some sort of punishment is coming.

Vocabulary

1 blotches
2 busboy
3 fogies
4 stereos
5 pledge
6 steamed
7 permit
8 sufficient
9 novice
10 unoccupied

Assessment

1	D	6	D
2	A	7	B
3	B	8	C
4	C	9	D
5	A	10	C

PICKING

I. Before You Read

WHO ARE THE CHARACTERS?
Nardo, the narrator, his grandfather Ignacio, their Dad, the foreman

WHAT ARE SOME KEY WORDS?
work, money, chili peppers, lazy, hot, sun

WHAT DOES THE ART REMIND YOU OF?
working, fields, farming, baseball, children, cars, immigrants

WHAT'S THE STORY ABOUT?
The narrator is hard-working and feels useless if he isn't doing some sort of work. He is younger than most workers, but he decides to pick chili peppers with his brother Nardo in order to make some money to buy the baseball glove he wants. The brothers are treated poorly at the field and are given the worst place to work.

Vocabulary

1 sockets
2 hustled
3 hobble
4 foreman
5 blossomed
6 enthusiastically
7 suspicious
8 spunky
9 scrawny
10 scalding

II. Read

(Students' answers will vary.)

What does the narrator mean when he says that he is of his grandfather's line of "useful blood"?
(He means that, like his grandfather, he feels that his time is wasted if he isn't being productive.)

What 3 things have you learned about the narrator?
(1. The narrator wants to earn money so he can buy a baseball glove, clothes, and papers for school. 2. The narrator's brother Nardo is suspicious and untrusting of the narrator's genuine desire to work. 3. The narrator is active and feels useless if he isn't working.)

What will happen when they go to the field to pick chilis?
(Nardo is not enthusiastic about going to the field, so students may think that he will not do a good job.)

How did the foreman react to their request for work?
(The foreman is very condescending toward them. He makes fun of them because they have a lunch bag, because they've arrived late, and because the narrator is young.)

What does the narrator learn about himself and his brother?
(He learns that Nardo is actually more hard-working than he once believed. He also learns that, though he is determined to do a good job, things don't always work out as planned.)

Assessment

1	C	6	A
2	A	7	D
3	D	8	A
4	B	9	B
5	C	10	A

THE STORY OF MY BODY

II. Read

Why does she make herself invisible?
(She is embarrassed and self-conscious about her appearance because she has scars on her face from a bad case of chicken pox.)

Why is skin color so important to her family and friends?
(As Puerto Ricans, they are probably accustomed to racial prejudice and unfair treatment.)

Why does she like the grocery store so much?
(She likes being trusted with money and walking to the store by herself. She also likes wandering the aisles looking at the products for sale. She says that she learned English by reading the labels on the products in the store.)

Why do you think this doll is important to her?
(The doll is important to her because she has admired it for so long.)

How does she feel about the man in the butcher's apron?
(She feels confused by his words because she knows that she is not dirty. She has done nothing but touch the doll. She says that his yelling was the first time that she ever considered the effect of skin color on human relations.)

Vocabulary

1 stature
2 naively
3 *la gringa*
4 covet
5 repertoire
6 A
7 A
8 B
9 A
10 B

III. Gather Your Thoughts

AUTHOR'S VIEW OF HERSELF: ugly after the chicken pox, invisible, independent, innocent, humiliated, different from her friends

conscious of skin color

OTHERS' VIEW OF THE AUTHOR: tall, short, white, American, colored, foreign, dirty, thief

Assessment

1 C 6 B
2 C 7 B
3 D 8 A
4 A 9 D
5 D 10 D

CHILD OF THE AMERICAS

III. Gather Your Thoughts

(Students' answers will vary.)

1. Detail: ("a flashing knife blade of crystal, my tool, my craft") **Sense:** (sight or touch)

2. Detail: ("ripples from my tongue") **Sense:** (hearing or sight)

3. Detail: ("flying gestures of my hands") **Sense:** (touch or sight)

Vocabulary

1 mangoes
2 passion
3 ripples
4 ghettos
5 Spanglish
6 C
7 E
8 A
9 G
10 B
11 D
12 F
13 J
14 H
15 I

Assessment

1 C 6 A
2 D 7 A
3 A 8 C
4 D 9 B
5 D 10 A

THE WAR ARRIVES
III. Gather Your Thoughts

Annie:
Annie thinks Hitler is a bad man whom the English and French will eliminate. She doesn't like to hear reports of the war on the radio because they scare her. She wants her parents to be happy and pleasant to each other.

Mother:
Mother doesn't want to leave Holland and start a new life in America. She often gets headaches as a result of stress. She feels they will be as safe in Winterswijk as they would in America.

Father:
Father wants to go to America, where Hitler can't harm them. He builds the house in Winterswijk because Mother won't agree to go to America. He listens to the radio and thinks about where the Germans are in relation to his family.

Vocabulary

1 stay
2 able
3 yes
4 very angry
5 hard to understand
6 place to go in
7 conducted
8 very small
9 protest
10 drop of liquid from the eye

Assessment

1	B	6	A
2	B	7	D
3	A	8	C
4	B	9	C
5	A	10	D

DISASTER AT SEA
II. Read

(Students' answers will vary.)

1. Kennedy and Lowrey are officers on two boats that miss a nearby ship battle.

2. Kennedy doesn't know what kind of confrontation has occurred, but he knows that there are enemy ships nearby.

3. A Japanese destroyer called the Amagari comes steaming in towards Kennedy's boat.

4. Kennedy wants to fire a torpedo at the Japanese ship, rather than turn away.

5. Kennedy's boat won't turn and he's unable to get it into the proper firing position.

6. The Japanese destroyer crashes into the boat and splits it in two pieces. Gasoline burns and the boat begins to sink.

7. Some engineers and personnel on the boat are trapped by the flames and rising water.

8. Kennedy's section of the boat is still afloat because it has watertight compartments.

9. Kennedy is afraid the flames may damage the floating section of the hull, so he orders the men to abandon ship. When the flames go the other way, the men reboard.

Vocabulary

1 huge warships
2 going to
3 close
4 brave
5 split in half
6 circumnavigate
7 navy
8 navigate
9 navigation
10 naval

Assessment

1	B	6	A
2	A	7	D
3	C	8	D
4	A	9	B
5	C	10	B

SUPER-DUPER-COLD SATURDAYS

III. Gather Your Thoughts

A. DESCRIBE A SETTING

SOUND	SIGHT	FEELING	TASTE	TOUCH
"furnace was banging and sounding like it was about to blow up," the sound from the TV, the sounds of the family talking	"your breath kind of hung in the air like a hunk of smoke and you could walk along and look exactly like a train blowing out big, fat, white puffs of smoke.", the image of the family sitting huddled together under the blankets on the couch	"so cold that if you were stupid enough to go outside, your eyes would automatically blink a thousand times all by themselves, probably so the juice inside of them wouldn't freeze up," "about a zillion degrees below zero," "cold automatically made us want to get together and huddle up"	"if you spit, the slob would be an ice cube before it hit the ground," the way he describes the cold air you can almost taste how cold it would be to breath it	"Byron . . . didn't think it was "cool" to touch anybody or let anybody touch him, even if it meant he froze to death," "felt like Jack Frost had moved in with us"

Vocabulary

1 cushion
2 thermostat
3 generate
4 automatically
5 respectable
6 forecaster
7 forehead
8 foresee
9 foreman
10 foreshadowing

Assessment

1	B	6	B
2	A	7	C
3	A	8	D
4	D	9	B
5	D	10	A

NEW KIDS

I. Before You Read

3. "I knew that God had finally gotten sick of me being teased and picked on all the time."
2. "I got on the bus and took the seat right behind the driver."
1. "The worst part about being teased was riding the school bus on those mornings when Byron and Buphead decided they were going to skip school."
4. "Whenever someone new started coming to Clark, most of the kids took some time to see what he was like."
5. "The bus was real quiet. We'd never seen the driver get this mad before."

II. Read

(Students' answers will vary.)

Why does Poindexter, the narrator, hate riding the bus?

(He is different from the other kids who ride the bus, and he isn't friends with them. They tease him on the bus and sometimes even fight with him.)

In what way is this new boy Poindexter's "personal saver"?

(The boys will now tease the new boy because of his different accent and raggedy clothes. They won't have reason to tease Poindexter anymore.)

What causes the bus driver to fly into such a rage?

(The boys are mean to the new kids, and Larry Dunn throws an apple core at them. The bus driver says that they should be nice to the new boys because they have manners and respect and because they haven't done anything mean to anyone else.)

Vocabulary

1 troublemakers
2 greeting them
3 yes
4 no
5 criticizing
6 sign + al
7 defi + ant
8 factu + al
9 pleas + ant
10 person + al

Assessment

1	C	6	C
2	B	7	B
3	C	8	D
4	A	9	C
5	D	10	A

Index

PE signals a pupil's edition page number.

TG signals a teacher's edition page number.